Good
Eating

The Christian Practice of Everyday Life

David S. Cunningham
and William T. Cavanaugh, series editors

This series seeks to present specifically Christian perspectives on some of the most prevalent contemporary practices of everyday life. It is intended for a broad audience—including clergy, interested laypeople, and students. The books in this series are motivated by the conviction that, in the contemporary context, Christians must actively demonstrate that their allegiance to the God of Jesus Christ always takes priority over secular structures that compete for our loyalty—including the state, the market, race, class, gender, and other functional idolatries. The books in this series will examine these competing allegiances as they play themselves out in particular day-to-day practices, and will provide concrete descriptions of how the Christian faith might play a more formative role in our everyday lives.

The Christian Practice of Everyday Life series is an initiative of The Ekklesia Project, an ecumenical gathering of pastors, theologians, and lay leaders committed to helping the church recall its status as the distinctive, real-world community dedicated to the priorities and practices of Jesus Christ and to the inbreaking Kingdom of God. (For more information on The Ekklesia Project, see <www.ekklesiaproject.org>.)

Good
Eating

STEPHEN H. WEBB

Brazos Press
A DIVISION OF
Baker Book House Co

Published by Brazos Press
a division of Baker Book House Company
P.O. Box 6287, Grand Rapids, MI 49516-6287

Printed in the United States of America

Library of Congress Cataloging-in-Publication Data

Webb, Stephen H., 1961–
    Good eating / Stephen H. Webb.
        p.   cm. — (The Christian practice of everyday life)
    Includes bibliographical references and index.
    ISBN 1-58743-015-0 (pbk.)
    1. Food—Religious aspects—Christianity. 2. Animal welfare—Religious
aspects—Christianity. I. Title. II. Series.

BR115.N87 W43 2001
241'.693—dc21   2001035449

Unless otherwise noted, all Scripture is taken from the New Revised Standard Version of the Bible (NRSV), copyright 1989 by the Division of Christian Education of the National Council of the Churches of Christ in the USA. Used by permission.

Scripture marked as (NEB) is taken from *The New English Bible.* Copyright © 1961, 1970, 1989 by The Delegates of Oxford University Press and The Syndics of the Cambridge University Press. Reprinted by permission.

For current information about all releases from Brazos Press, visit our web site:
http://www.brazospress.com

For Andy Laue
Brother in Christ
who remembers those Englewood potlucks
and introduced me to Ralph's Cuban cuisine
and for three couples with whom I have shared
many heavenly meals
Joyce and Aron
Jane and Matt
Lisa and Dave

———

"Meanwhile, the disciples were urging him, 'Rabbi, eat something.' But he said to them, 'I have food to eat that you do not know about.'"

John 4:31–2

Contents

Acknowledgments

■ Jim Poyser, with his usual flair of whimsy and wisdom, first encouraged me to write this book. Andrew Linzey and J. R. Hyland provided much personal inspiration and sound guidance. I have especially fond memories of a wonderful vegetarian meal with Andrew while visiting him in Oxford, and I am particularly thankful for J. R.'s work in cultivating this theological frontier with a brave and persistent devotion to the Christian tradition. Bill Placher and Jim Spiegel read this book with a dedication that only close friends can muster. John Wilson gave me a chance to write about this topic for a new audience, which helped shape my prose. Dan Fisher was the first to read and write about this book while it was in manuscript form, and his enthusiasm gave me some much needed energy to finish it. Frank Burch Brown taught me to be more sensitive to the sublime and wild side of nature, while Michael Brown gave me some aid on New Testament issues. Brenda Charrier has translated some of my ideas into a mission project for the dogs of San Luis, Mexico. I continue to be uplifted by her remarkable passion for those animals who most need our help. I need to give special credit to Nathan Braun for his hard work in founding and directing the Christian Vegetarian Association (ChristianVeg.com). This lively organization (which I chair) is an international and ecumenical ministry, and I have been helped by some email exchanges with its members, especially Albert Fecko and Keith Akers. I am grateful to Alan M. Beck, director of the Center for the Human-Animal Bond at the School of Veterinary Medicine at Purdue University, for an invitation to try out my theological ideas on a scientific audience. Gary

Dorrien, professor of religious studies at Kalamazoo College, gave me the opportunity to sharpen my thinking about animals and heaven in that college's beautiful Stetson Chapel. Gary's warm hospitality and stimulating conversation—at a difficult moment in his life—were inspiring. I especially need to thank the Wabash College students in my theological ethics classes over the years, who have responded to my theology of pets with vigorous and sympathetic debate. By the clarity of their reservations, they have taught me how to write about this topic for a curious but skeptical audience. Rodney Clapp has been the most wonderful editor, a close and encouraging reader who brings a generous and focused vision to publishing. I could not have asked for a better person to deliver my book to the world.

I need to offer special thanks to David Cunningham, who has faithfully reviewed all of my books. In a critique of an earlier work of mine on animals, he persuaded me to venture out in new directions. Fortunately, he read this book—with remarkable care, editing it as if it were his own—before it was published, so that I could benefit from his ideas before I put mine into print. I am in his debt in many fundamental ways. Diane Timmerman, as always, was my last reader, saving me from many awkward moments. Although Charis and Barek are too young to read this book, I wrote it thinking about their future, hoping that when they are old enough to read it, all the arguments here will seem obvious to the point of being mundane.

Introduction
A Potluck Story

■ Churches have always used food to welcome guests and build community, which is why nearly every church in America has a kitchen. Some of the new megachurches even have food courts, but in older churches, the kitchen is often located discretely in the basement. When I was very young, before there were fast food restaurants on every corner, eating at church was about the only time we ate outside the home. There were two worlds at church, the somber service in the sanctuary and, directly beneath it, the lighthearted chatter of the fellowship hall. I probably remember more about what went on after the service than during it. We could not wait for the potluck dinners, where we would try to guess who brought what and hope that old Mrs. So-and-So remembered to make our favorite dessert. The dinners were an emblem of both bounty and restraint: You had to work your way through the gelatin salads, scalloped potatoes, and green bean casseroles before you got to the cakes and pies. At that point there was always the dilemma of whether to balance your dessert on top of your burgeoning mound of food, which made you look like a complete glutton, or come back for it later, when the good stuff might be gone. Walking down that long row of white-papered tables still represents for me what church is all about: an invitation to fill our hunger, both spiritual and physical, with a community that is grateful for God's good gifts. Food brought us together—in the modest consumption of bread and grape juice upstairs and the abundant feast of fried chicken

11

and meatloaf downstairs—even though we did not think much about what we ate or what food meant.

Nowadays the potlucks I go to have a more exotic fare, and people love to talk about what they eat. When I graduated from my Hoosier, white bread diet, which defined a square meal as anything with meat and potatoes in the center, to a more environmentally friendly cuisine, I had to learn how to defend my food choices. The truth is that I was a vegetarian for years before I was able to articulate how Christianity supported my diet. I had an intuitive feeling that eating less meat was a part of my journey in following Christ, but I did not know how to put those two things together. My church had taught me to look at a lot of things through the lens of the Bible, but food was not one of them.

That all changed several years ago when, at a gathering at the home of some friends, I stood next to an acquaintance who noticed that I was not putting any meat on my plate. She asked if I was a vegetarian. I replied in the affirmative, and we made our way to some chairs. When she asked me why, I felt a flutter of nervous energy in my stomach and heard myself begin to stammer. I started to say, "Well, you know, the usual reasons," but then I got up the courage to tell the truth: "Because I am a Christian." I could just hear her thinking: As if it were not enough that I was making her feel guilty for eating meat, I had to bring religion into the picture!

Actually, she looked surprised and curious, hesitating about whether to ask me to say more, and I started to rehearse in my head some way to briefly explain how I think food is a part of faith. I did not want to convert her to a meatless diet, because I did not think that vegetarianism was a way of obtaining salvation. I put my faith in God to save the world, not some dietary revolution. Nevertheless, I believed that God so loved the world that I should too, which meant, among other things, changing the way I eat. How could I explain my position to her in such a casual situation? I was almost relieved when she turned the conversation to another topic.

That encounter motivated me to do my homework in order to be ready to give a testimony to my faith in God's peaceful plan for all of creation. Now I look forward to being asked about my diet, because that is an opportunity to talk about the Bible in ways that surprise even the most dedicated Christians. The more I studied the Bible and early church theologians on the issue of food, diet, and animals, the more convinced I became that *Christian* vegetarianism is something completely different from the animal rights movement. This book is my answer—more than briefly put, I confess—to that acquaintance who wanted me to give a reason for what I eat.

The first aim of this book is to set the record straight on the biblical view of animals and Christianity's crucial contributions to the animal rights movement. The animal rights movement has monopolized debates about animals and vegetarianism, often by dismissing Judaism and Christianity as the religions responsible for our poor treatment of animals today. Moreover, it tends to portray vegetarianism as an all-or-nothing affair. Animal rights advocates thus uphold vegetarianism as an absolute moral law, which can strike many people as not only unreasonable but also impossible. Can we really eat in such a way that no animals are ever harmed by us? Doesn't this lead to a quest for moral purity that inevitably results in self-righteousness?

Biblical vegetarianism is a clear alternative to the utopian rigor of the animal rights movement. Since Christians believe that perfection cannot be achieved here and now, Christian vegetarianism will not be a legalistic and absolutist practice. Instead, it will be a way, gradually and humbly, of looking forward to God's restoration of creation, the fulfillment of God's promise to complete history by returning the whole world to God's original intentions. This diet of hope can be one way of witnessing to the good news of Jesus Christ. I thus want to persuade animal rightists that Christianity is more original and provocative about animals than they might suppose, and I want to persuade Christians to give their own tradition a chance to transform their attitudes about the importance of vegetarianism and animal welfare.

A second aim of this book is to sort out what the biblical notion of stewardship means in our relationship to animals. Rather than following the animal rights movement in erasing all boundaries between humans and animals, I think that the responsibility for animals can emerge from a recognition of the uniqueness of human beings and our God-given role in the world. What does it mean that we are to exercise our authority over the animals in ways that are in harmony with God's own love for creation? Rethinking the role of animals in Christian theology involves the reformation of nearly every Christian doctrine, from start to finish. Thus, creation (chapter 3), biblical authority (chapter 2), Christology (chapters 4 and 6), ecclesiology (chapter 10), and eschatology (throughout) are all revisited and revised here from the perspective of God's own ongoing compassion for all living creatures. Most provocatively, I analyze the decline of our imagination of heaven and ask what it would mean to revitalize that essential Christian belief by putting animals back where they belong, in the everlasting arms of God (chapter 7).

The third aim of this book is to present the first modern systematic theology of diet (I say modern because the topic of diet was dealt with in very systematic terms by many early theologians). This book is systematic in the sense that it makes a variety of logical connections among biblical narrative, theological themes, and church doctrine as they relate to food. It is not a comprehensive theology of diet because, although I deal with the topic of food in general and explicate the morality of eating, my focus on vegetarianism means that I do not treat every culinary topic.

There are so many dietary plans and so much advice about eating that one more hardly seems needed. Nonetheless, the Bible and early Christian theologians had a lot to say about food, especially the moral warrants for restricting one's diet. People are hungry for a spiritual foundation for their eating habits, just as they are desperate for concrete spiritual practices that can put their faith into action. There is a lot of recent interest, for example, in the topic of fasting, a practice with a long history in Christianity. Rarely is it acknowledged, however, that fasting, for early Christians, almost always meant going without meat, rather than going without food altogether. The time is ripe, then, for a theological vision of food that would draw together the biblical emphasis on caring for animals, the early church's admonishments about fasting and frugality, and modern concerns with eating a more compassionate as well as a more healthy diet.

The fourth and final aim of this book is to contribute to a variety of fascinating historical questions concerning diet, food, and animals. The question of whether Jesus was a vegetarian, for example, is controversial and complex, and I lay out the related issues in a comprehensive manner (chapter 5). This involves discussing an obscure group of Jewish Christians called the Ebionites; delving into the diet of James the Just, the brother of Jesus; analyzing evidence about the diet of John the Baptist and the Essenes; and coming to terms with the attitude that the Apostle Paul took toward food. Throughout the book I also deal with other issues that have long interested historians, like the origin and role of animal sacrifices in the ancient world (chapter 4); the Bible's ambiguous attitude toward meat-eating; the role of fish in ancient diet and the puzzle of why fish were often eaten by groups that otherwise ate no meat; the question of why so many Gnostic and heretical groups were attracted to vegetarianism; and the mystery of why vegetarianism gradually became marginalized in the church after so much interest in the topic by the church fathers (chapters 8 and 9).

The first chapter is a general statement of my goals and ideas, while the second chapter distinguishes my position from the animal rights movement. The rest of the chapters are both constructive and investigative, building on my defense of a distinctively Christian vegetarianism while weighing the historical evidence for a biblical theology of diet. The last chapter discusses in detail what the diet of Christian vegetarianism entails, and it offers advice about how Christians can be vegetarians without becoming self-righteous or contributing to further schism in the church.

Finally, I have saved for an appendix my detailed survey and criticisms of the various ethical models that theologians draw from in their deliberations about animals and diet. The appendix will be of special interest to those who want to know more about the methodological presuppositions of my position, as well as the reasons why I rely on a narrative approach to the Bible (as opposed to environmentalism, ecofeminism, process theology, and natural law ethics). The appendix also draws on the work of Reinhold Niebuhr to defend my view of Christian vegetarianism as a hopeful but not utopian movement. The theoretical nature of this material made me put it in an appendix, but those interested in such things might want to read it after chapter 2 and before my narrative rereading of Scripture.

The Unexamined Meal Is Not Worth Eating

■ When I was growing up, a meal was defined as much by the presence of meat as by a prayer. Anything else was just a snack. At school, we grudgingly ate fish on Fridays to accommodate the Catholic kids, but every other lunch was centered on "real" meat. When they tried to use a little soy to stretch the hamburger, we rebelled. At home, the most solemn meals were graced with the biggest and best cuts of meat and thus demanded the longest prayers, so that we had to be especially patient for Sunday dinners to begin. At church, even the vegetable casseroles had to be seasoned with ham. Today, when I attend church potlucks, I am more sensitive to the overwhelming predominance of meat. In fact, when I am invited to dinner with my non-Christian friends I am much more likely to be served a vegetarian option than when I dine with my Christian friends. In a time when people are cutting back on their meat-eating for all sorts of reasons, many Christians seem to be oblivious to meat alternatives and to the motivations for eating less meat.

Vegetarianism, which is usually associated with the animal rights movement, is growing in popularity in this country, but it is being fed by resources and energies that lie far outside of Christian communities. Especially among young people, vegetarianism has become almost a rite of passage. And for lots of people it has become a very concrete way to express a fundamental dissatisfaction with how our society treats animals. Everyone seems to be talking about animals these days—everyone, that is, except churchgoing Christians.

The problem is that the animal rights movement is a very secular affair. When it is connected to religion it is usually associated with New Age spirituality and neopagan themes. Perhaps that is why Christians are seldom interested in addressing the issues raised by this movement. Nevertheless, these issues will not just go away, which is why Christians need the confidence to contribute to debates about the ethical treatment of animals from the perspective of the traditional themes of Christian faith.

Parents especially must be prepared to deal with some hard questions. What do you say when your child loses a pet and asks you if her dog or cat will go to heaven? Or, more likely today given the faddishness of vegetarianism, what do you say when your teenager suddenly asks you why you eat meat? Most of us have a beloved pet, but must we love all animals? Is that practical, or even possible? Does even God do that? And if we do try to love all animals, does that mean we can never eat any of them?

Indeed, what should the church say when communities face controversial problems pertaining to the overpopulation of deer in state parks, the regulation of hunting, the treatment of animals in circuses and zoos, and the use of animals in scientific experiments in laboratories and schools? Is the Bible relevant for such modern, complex issues?

■ Learning to Eat

Christian vegetarianism is based on an old saying with a slight twist: The unexamined meal is not worth eating. When we pray before meals, we ask God's blessing not only for ourselves but for the food that we eat, that it may strengthen and nourish us. Christian vegetarians suggest that if we pray over our food, then our food should be a reflection of God's intentions for the world. What we eat should say something about the kind of God we worship. Our diet should be holy if we want all aspects of our lives to reflect God's grace. If we say grace over our meals, then we should have grace in our meals, which raises the question of the ethical implications of a diet based on animal flesh.

The act of eating and sharing food is one of the most fundamental gestures of what it means to be human. Every society and every family has rules about what, when, where, and how to eat. People are inevitably choosy about what food they will put in their mouths because eating, after all, is a very intimate act. We learn what foods we like and dislike at a very early age, so that food preferences are among our earliest and longest lasting traits. Diets can become so habitual that we have a hard time imagining eating in any other way than the one to which we are accustomed. We live a stressful and hurried lifestyle, so a regular, predictable, and even monotonous diet can be comforting, and such diets in North America almost always center around meat, more specifically, the ubiquitous hamburger. Our diet, then, can seem perfectly natural to us. Even when we learn to try new foods, certain dishes will always be comforting to us due to the associations with memories they raise. But trying new foods can also be a rite of passage into the broader world, a way of showing our independence from familiar customs and family ties.

Unfortunately, today we do not often think of eating as a ritual because we frequently eat in a rush, on the go, in search of food that will be as fast as we are. Journalist Eric Schlosser has documented how 90 percent of the American food buget is spent on processed food, which is subjected to so many canning, freezing, and dehydrating techniques that its flavor is mostly destroyed. As a result, a vast industry has arisen to add flavor, both artificial and natural, back into our food, so that we can have the simulated experience of eating a wholesome diet. Our noses can be tricked, but reality cannot be so easily manufactured. Our rushed diet reflects cultural ideals and social standards that are anything but wholesome. When I was growing up, dinner table rituals were unquestioned, but today many families do not reserve a special time and place to eat at all. We live like we eat. We see our bodies as machines, and we treat food as fuel. We do not want to think about what we eat because we do not have the time. We do not ask where our meat comes from and what the conditions are at the slaughterhouses for workers and animals alike, just as we do not ask where our shoes were made or how our purchases affect the environment.

Yet food is morally charged in our culture, and every meal is a moral battle between our conflicting desires for pleasure and health. We live in what has been called "Diet America," where we are obsessed with calculating the fat and calorie count of every bite we take. Dieting, in fact, is too frequently only the flip side to our celebration of gluttony in all-you-can-eat restaurants and the pervasive abundance of junk food, so that dieters anxiously oscillate between overeating and undereating. The people who most pay the price for our unhealthy attitudes toward food are generally women, who are repeatedly told to reduce, reduce, reduce! Thinness has become a symbol of self-control and power. Women are supposed to take up as little space as possible. Tragically, anorexia is often the result.

■ A Holy Diet

The manic pursuit of a perfect diet has obvious parallels with religious fanaticism. Writers like John Money and Gerald Carson have shown how diet is a kind of secular religion, a fact most vividly illustrated in the nineteenth century when various food reforms, including products like whole grain bread and cornflakes, were the direct result of religious revival. Sylvester Graham and John Harvey Kellogg, for example, advocated spartan diets—void of all stimulants, including meat—in order to control the craving for alcohol and to discipline sexual urges. They thought they could transform human nature by regulating what people eat—a revolutionary view that was parodied in the wonderfully comic novel, *The Road to Wellville,* by T. Coraghessan Boyle.

After the fervent experimentation of the nineteenth century, most of the twentieth saw little change in America's meat-oriented diet, but lately Americans seem eager to connect diet to spirituality again. Paul Theroux presents a comic portrait of this trend in his brilliant novel, *Millroy the Magician.* Millroy is a mix of con man, connoisseur, and charismatic prophet who gains fame and fortune by promoting a diet based strictly on the Bible. There is only one fat person in the Bible, he claims (King Eglon in Judges 3:17), and ancient biblical characters like Methuselah lived for hundreds of years for a reason. They ate the right foods. Millroy insists that Jesus was a vegetarian, and he dreams of commissioning a new translation of the Bible that would enshrine his vegetarian reading of scripture. On the principle that eating right is a form of worship, Millroy starts a restaurant where the plates have messages like, "I will lead you into a land of milk and honey" and "Ye cannot drink the cup of the Lord and the cup of devils." He serves Daniel Lentils, Jacob Pottage, and Ezekiel Bread, and cooks with cucumbers, leeks, melons, garlic, figs, olives, grain, and pulses (legumes).

The Book of Daniel provides the inspiration for Millroy's experiments, since Daniel describes what can only be called the first clinical study of nutrition. During the Babylonian captivity, Daniel and his friends were summoned to serve in the king's palace. There they were given government food rations consisting of fatty meat and wine. Instead of being grateful, however, Daniel was worried about breaking the Jewish dietary laws. Daniel needed to come up with a diet that would keep him from being defiled by this pagan food. His solution was simple. He proposed that he and his friends consume nothing but vegetables and water for ten days, at which point they could be compared to those servants who ate the heavier fare. At the end of the test, Daniel and company were in such better condition that they were allowed to continue with their strict diet. Vegetarianism preserved both their religious observances and their health.

For Millroy, the whole Bible is one long experiment with diet, a heavenly cookbook, beginning with the appetites of Adam and Eve and continuing with the Old Testament food regulations. He calls Leviticus, for example, nothing more than a shopping list. There is something to this view, because the Bible was written at a time when most people spent their lives battling hunger, so it is full of instructions about food. The danger, of course, is that Millroy begins looking in the Bible for what he wants to find there, using it as a casebook to support his arguments. Consequently, his theology becomes increasingly narrow. He is more interested in scatology than eschatology, which leads him to organize The Church That Keeps You Regular. His position is no better than those who argue that God approves of filet mignon because a fatted calf was prepared for the prodigal son. The increasingly angry responses to Millroy and his own moral faults make for fun reading, but the fact that a leading novelist could mine more about diet from the Bible than any contemporary theologian should provide much food for thought.

■ Fasting Versus Fast Food

Theroux's novel shows that the mixture of diet and religion can be inspiring and explosive. In fact, what Theroux imagined in a humorous way is now taking place in all seriousness across the country. A recent bestseller, *The Bible Cure,* gleans from the Bible God's nutritional laws, promising to help you lengthen your life, avoid infectious diseases, and build a stronger immune system if you follow biblical dietary principles. The implication is that you can lose weight and gain eternal life at the same time.

Most Christians, however, do not consult the Bible before making dinner, but they do desire a better integration of religion and lifestyle issues. This has led many churches to sponsor workshops on weight loss, connecting Bible study with eating habits in search of a "Godly weigh." Such programs suggest that the problem is not in the food we eat but in the spiritual desolation that drives us toward destructive diets. The idea is that the more you look to God for answers, the less you will look to food to fill up your emptiness. The popular text for these workshops comes from John 4:34: "Jesus said to them, 'My food is to do the will of him who sent me and to complete his work.'" The goal is to become "slim for Him" or to have "more of Jesus and less of me." Christians should not only have the benefits of salvation but also the appearances of health and happiness that come from a righteous lifestyle.

The work of historian R. Marie Griffith shows how many of these faith-based diet programs end up affirming secular rather than religious ideals. Being thin is a sign of social approval and self-worth today, but being a Christian is a matter of pleasing God, not satisfying secular standards of sex appeal. God desires not thin bodies but people who are dedicated to ushering in God's kingdom. We should base our diets on obedience to God, not social trends and fads. Eating less is important if we are gluttons who turn to food like an idol that falsely promises to make us happy. But substituting the idolatry of thinness for the idolatry of gluttony is hardly much of an improvement. Instead, we should focus not just on how much we eat but also on what we eat. North Americans not only overeat, but they also eat much more meat than the rest of the world. Can our good eating be for a greater good than the satisfaction of our fickle appetites? Is there such a thing as not only a healthy diet but also a holy diet?

For much of Christian history, the expression of piety and the practice of spirituality were bound up with food. Giving up certain food items, usually meat and alcohol, was one of the fundamental manifestations of living a life of sacrifice and thus imitating the sacrifice of Jesus Christ. Such sacrifices were essential both for self-discipline and for creating a more just society. Giving away food, which usually meant limiting one's own diet, was, in the ancient world, the primary means of practicing charity. In societies with scarce resources, eating less was one of the only ways to assure that more people could eat at all.

Although we have an apparent abundance of food today, much of the world's population still struggles to find enough to eat, and such problems will only increase as the world's population continues to grow. Even America is not immune to such worries. Patrick McCormick notes the irony of the fact that, "While fifty million Americans are currently dieting to lose weight, nearly half that many are collecting food stamps and/or standing in line at the local food pantry" (p. 45). Christians need to learn, then, how their personal practices of fasting can be linked to a broader vision of what is good for the earth as well as how the earth's resources can be more justly distributed. One very practical way of making that link is to give up eating meat.

Of course, persuading children to clean their plates and eat a good diet is surely hard enough without worrying about trying to find substitutes for the meat on their plates. Indeed, meat is at the center of the American diet. A meat-based diet has become an American right and a sacred repast, an inherent part of our cultural identity. Even atheists, so goes the joke, believe that God grants humanity the right to eat meat. When Europeans first came to North America, they saw it as a land of bounty. In Europe, meat-eating was limited for the lower classes, and hunting belonged to the wealthy and privileged. America, however, had plenty of game to hunt and plenty of room to raise farm animals. The expansive frontier thus promised that meat could be eaten three times a day!

Recently, however, scholars have begun to question these claims about pioneer life. As historian Michael Bellesiles has documented, guns were not nearly as prevalent or dependable prior to the Civil War as many Americans think. Historical questions aside, however, the frontier that once promised unlimited expansion is now full of people, and most Americans recognize that the bounty of our country is not infinite. Nevertheless, eating meat—and lots of it—remains a part of the definition of what it means to be an American.

Another one of our enduring national myths is that the English Pilgrims who landed at Plymouth Harbor feasted on turkey. In actuality, they had to depend on beans and corn from the Native Americans to make it through their first year, and in 1621, when the Pilgrims and Indians celebrated a harvest festival together, they would have feasted on corn mush, nuts, fruits, popcorn, bread, pumpkin, and squash, with some deer meat and game birds on the side. They were grateful to God just to be alive, but today their vegetable-laden harvest feast has been transformed into a meat-centered tradition. Thanksgiving today seems to be more about our gratitude for the stuffed turkey than for the variety and abundance of food options God has given us.

Thanksgiving serves as a national myth about the salvific power of meat, but there are also regional variations of this ideology. Religious studies professor Wade Clark Roof, for example, has examined the symbolic resonance of pork barbecues in Southern culture, where the rural radio stations still broadcast "hogs and hymns"—noontime reports on local stock prices mixed with gospel music. The barbecue functions as an analogue for the Eucharist in Southern Christianity. It is a sacrificial ritual that has the power to evoke memory, establish a distinctive identity, and draw together family and church into one fellowship.

There is power in the blood of meat, a deep craving for red and juicy flesh that can blind meat lovers to the consequences of their diet. Tragically, the overconsumption of meat is tremendously costly to the environment, since livestock agriculture results in more soil erosion, excessive use of water, and deforestation than plant agriculture. Seventy percent of all the grain in the United

States goes to feeding herds of livestock. It takes up to sixteen pounds of grain to produce a pound of beef. In fact, the world's cattle alone consume a quantity of food equal to the caloric needs of 8.7 billion people—more than the entire human population on earth. Such an inefficient use of resources explains why President Truman, on October 5, 1947, asked the American people to forego meat on two days a week in order to save precious grain for distribution to starving Europeans. Livestock agriculture is also costly to us. About nine thousand people die every year from food poisoning, and the USDA estimates that 70 percent of all food-borne illnesses are caused by infected meat and poultry. Moreover, livestock now produce one hundred and thirty times as much waste in America as people do, which threatens to taint the drinking water in many communities.

But the real cost is paid by the animals themselves. Only by raising animals with great efficiency in factory-like farms, and thus with no regard for their natural habits, can Americans eat meat in such great quantities. On an average day in America, one hundred and thirty thousand cattle, seven thousand calves, three hundred and sixty thousand pigs, and twenty-four million chickens are killed. To meet those production goals, farmers keep hens in battery cages where they are so cramped they cannot spread their wings, confine calves to veal crates where they are unable to turn around, and immobilize pigs during pregnancy in sow stalls. Cows are kept pregnant and full of hormone injections to satisfy our demand for milk. To keep these animals alive in such bedlam, they are filled with antibiotics and drugs as well as growth stimulants. Only by raising animals in ways that are clearly contrary to the life that God intended for them can animal flesh be sold so cheaply and in such great supply.

The international scene looks no better. Traditionally, other countries have not relied on meat to the extent that America does. With rising economic standards around the world, however, non-Westerners increasingly want to eat like Americans eat, a trend that represents a major shift in global agricultural priorities. Resources are being diverted from producing crops for direct consumption to harvesting grain for pigs and chickens, frequently with disastrous results. Yet even as the West exports its diet, new ideas about food are changing American eating habits. The soya plant is the most widely eaten plant in the world, and it is used as the primary source of protein by much of the world's population. Until recently, people outside Asia have shown little interest in this plant. From the fifteenth century on, according to food historian Maguelonne Toussaint-Samat, Western traders knew about it, but they were largely indifferent to it, even in times of famine (pp. 51–6). In the last several decades, however, it has become an important crop in the United States. In fact, I can look out my window to a field that grows corn and soybeans on alternate years. The soybean plant is good at replenishing soil that has been impoverished by crops that need more nutrients, and soya can be made into a variety of useful foods and products. It provides, in balanced proportions, many of the components needed to sustain life: complete proteins, fats, carbohydrates, vitamins, and mineral salts.

I have found that it is easy to persuade people about the healthiness of vegetarianism, but it is much harder to convince them to change their lives. The Bible itself is very realistic about the potential for most people to make sudden changes in their dietary habits. Look, for example, at the story of the Israelites eating manna (a vegetarian diet) and yet longing for the fleshpots of Egypt. Dramatic change will come only when the church begins to take God's plan for the end of the world seriously and individuals come to see that vegetarianism is not a fad but the evidence of a total transformation—a conversion away from the values of this world and toward the world as God originally created it and will one day create it anew. Christianity, after all, is about radical conversion, not self-improvement. A biblical vegetarianism would not be based on improving your diet in order to lose weight or look better. Instead, it would be a product of a radical change in how we look at the world and how we read the Bible.

■ Biblical Food for Thought

So what does the Bible say about animals and diet? The biblical story begins and ends with a peaceful creation, but in between, God explicitly permits meat-eating after the flood, Jesus eats fish, and Paul criticizes vegetarian Christians for being weak and superstitious (Romans 14–15). Can there by a consistent biblical position on this issue?

Certainly no Christian theologian can argue that the Bible absolutely condemns all meat-eating. However, there is a good case to be made that vegetarianism is a valid and valuable way of anticipating the kingdom of God by practicing what God most intends for the world. It is a sign of our trust in God's intentions for the world and our hope in God's plan for the world's ultimate redemption. Christian vegetarians want to press the issue of whether the way animals are raised today in factory farms, with little room to move and no opportunity to smell the earth, is how God wants creation to sing God's praises.

Unfortunately, our familiarity with the Bible often keeps us from seeing what the Bible really says. We can think we know a biblical story, but our vague memories and impressions should not be a substitute for looking at sacred Scripture from a fresh perspective.

The biblical narrative is about people who are all too human, full of sin and greed, and dependent on the mercies of God. Their stories are framed by an account of peaceful beginnings in Genesis and the restoration of the world in a new creation in Revelation. In between is the decisive manifestation of God in the life of Jesus Christ, the second Adam who comes to begin the restoration of the world to God's original purposes. As I will show in chapter 3, those original purposes did not include meat-eating, yet after the flood God did allow Noah and his descendants to eat meat, just as he later let the Israelites conduct their worship services around animal sacrifices.

The Hebrew prophets, however, often criticized these animal sacrifices, and when they talked about the end times when God's purposes would no longer be thwarted by human sin, they portrayed the world in the same harmonious terms that describe the paradise of Eden in Genesis. It seems clear to me, then, that God allows for meat-eating as something far below the ideals that God originally conceived for humankind. A carnivorous diet is a concession to human sin, not a model for what God always wanted from humanity.

There is an analogy for this in our own lives. Parents often let their children do things that are less than what is best for them. Parents let children watch too much television and eat more junk food than is good for them. All parents know that they have to pick their battles with their kids by ordering priorities and setting realistic goals. Parents know that it takes years for children to internalize and fully understand what the family standards are. Maturation is a process, and what children teach parents most is the virtue of patience.

God too is patient, like a loving parent who does not expect too much too soon. The question is whether the time has come for us to begin living up to God's expectations concerning diet. People in the ancient world did not have plentiful sources of non-animal protein. They were dependent on animals in order to get enough protein in their diet. Even today, there are millions of people in poorer countries who do not have a sufficient number of protein alternatives to animal flesh, even though they eat meat rarely. But those of us who live in industrialized countries do have such alternatives, so we can now expect more of ourselves than what was possible hundreds of years ago.

Even with scarce food resources, early Christians regularly associated holiness with vegetarianism. The early church often encouraged Christians to abstain from eating meat as an appropriate way of remembering that Jesus came to die on the cross in order to end and abolish the animal sacrifices of the temple. Early Christians were also worried, however, about distinguishing themselves from their Jewish rivals, so they frequently feared that requiring vegetarianism for Christians would look too much like continuing the Jewish (kosher) food laws. Christians did not want vegetarianism to become a new law, a legalism of the sort that they had rejected when they parted from Judaism.

Moreover, vegetarianism was also often connected to pagan movements and Christian heresies, like Gnosticism, in the ancient world. So as the church grew, developing a specifically Christian theology of vegetarianism became a less practical possibility. As I will argue in the next chapter, vegetarianism today is still frequently connected to Gnostic and pagan spirituality, so it is understandable that many Christians continue to see vegetarianism as a diet that is incompatible with Christian faith.

In the Middle Ages, theologians taught that animals have no souls, and for many Christians that settled the issue of how to treat animals. Today, however, we live in a culture that is increasingly acknowledging the value and integrity of animals. When a police dog was shot while protecting his master in California recently, he was given a traditional police officer's burial, and a monument to the dog outside the police station reminds all of the officers of their dependence on dogs for protection. This dog is valued and remembered by the police community in ways that make us ask how God values and remembers him. The church needs to take a stand on the value of animals that will help people come to terms with the significant role animals actually play in their lives.

■ Saints and Stories

Our society loves to talk about animals, and stories about how animals have demonstrated the virtues of loyalty, sacrifice, and love abound. These stories represent a return to the kinds of stories that Christians used to associate with saints. Many Christian saints were known for their compassion toward animals.

One of my favorite stories about saints and animals concerns St. Ciaran, one of the first monks to live in Ireland in order to convert the Irish to the Christian faith (see Waddell, pp. 91–95). St. Ciaran's first convert was, according to tradition, a fierce boar, who was made tame by God and subsequently cut down the twigs and grass for the saint's little hut. Later, other animals, including a fox, a badger, a wolf, and a deer, came and stayed with St. Ciaran, obeying him as if he were the abbot and they were his monks. The saint made the animals take a vow to follow a vegetarian diet, so that they could live in peace and harmony. The fox, however, was shrewd and cunning, and one day he stole the saint's shoes and carried them off to the forest to eat them. The saint sent the badger to bring back the fox, and the saint chastised him, saying that if he had a longing to eat flesh, he should have asked God to make it from the roots of trees. Otherwise, he should abstain from flesh, so that everyone could live sociably with the others. The fox repented, and the animals thereafter lived happily with the saint, tame and familiar.

Obviously the saint's shoes must have been made out of leather, if they tempted the fox to abandon his vegetarianism! So St. Ciaran was not a purist when it came to the use of animal products. Clearly, the point of the story is not that saints should never depend upon animals in any way. Nor is the point that animals should be converted to vegetarianism—only God can change their natures—although obviously that is a prerequisite for a more peaceful nature. The point is that saints perceive possibilities for peace that most of us ignore. Saints are on the front line of our interaction with animals, pointing us in the direction of God's surprising grace. Unfortunately, most Christians today have little interest in saints, in part because they think of them as otherworldly and life-denying figures. These stories show that saints did not flee the world. Instead, they tried to change it. They could not have been more involved with God's creation. Their attempts to exercise reasonable authority over nature while refraining from abusing or exploiting animals should make them more relevant today than ever before.

Stories like this probably emerged not only from folk beliefs about the power of holy men to tame wild animals but also from the actual practices of mystics, sages, and monks who lived in the wild and learned to get along with animals in peaceful ways. What is fundamental is that Christians loved to tell stories about saints who brought the message of God's love even to the furthest reaches of the wilderness. Holy men, in the early Christian imagination, brought peace to the whole world, demonstrating that the gospel message of peace has no limits. Vegetarianism is the fruit of a passion for a totally harmonious world, a society that would be all-inclusive.

The closer you are to God, these stories suggest, the closer you will also be to the animals. Indeed, one of the criteria for sainthood seems to be the compassionate treatment of animals. If one is participating in God's kingdom, then he or she will be ushering in the kingdom for animals as well as people. A saint is someone who takes God's love to seemingly impossible heights, pushing the boundaries of who or what is lovable.

We are all called to be saints. We may not be able to accomplish heroic deeds by living among dangerous beasts and bringing peace to nature. Nevertheless, we can begin in small ways to serve the gospel by changing our diet and working toward a more compassionate treatment of animals in all areas of our society.

Before we try to change the world, however, we should listen to what the Bible says about animals. In *Of the Farm*, a beautiful novel about the value of land and the old way of raising and living with farm animals, John Updike has his main character enter a small town church where he hears a sermon preached about animals:

> Are not the dumb creatures of the earth in very truth our companions? Does not some glint of God's original intention shine out from the eyes of the dog, the horse, the heifer even as she is slaughtered? Has not Man, in creating civilization, looked to animals not only as beasts of burden and sustenance but for inspiration, as in the flight of the birds and the majesty of lions? Has not, in honesty, an eternal pact been honored and kept? And is it so strange that Adam's first piece of work was to name his mute helpers? Is not language an act of husbandry, a fencing-in of fields? (pp. 150–1).

This passage raises a lot of questions, and I will address them in the coming chapters by taking seriously the biblical language about the origin and destiny of animals. It is a moving passage, full of ideas that I have never heard preached in a church. Perhaps it takes a writer with the imagination of John Updike to put such words in the mouth of a preacher behind a pulpit.

To be a Christian vegetarian is to see the world as it could be, the way God intended it, not as it now is, full of pain and strife. Christian vegetarianism, then, is one small step on the road to the new kingdom of God. It need not be meant as a sign of moral purity or a new political movement to split and divide the churches. It is not a new religion, nor is it a new path of salvation that excludes meat-eaters as irredeemably condemned. It is a very concrete way of practicing a life of hope, a hope that respects differences and boundaries even as it radiates outward with the encompassing rhythms of God's grace. Christian vegetarianism should not make anybody feel guilty. It is a joyful diet, a diet for the new millennium, a diet that finds the love of God in every meal. Eating without inflicting pain on animals can be an expression of God's own love for the whole world, as well as God's intention to restore the world to its original peace and harmony. What better way to give witness to one's deepest hopes than to practice this less cruel diet of the future, a diet that uses fewer resources and is less demanding on our planet. Such a diet provides hope that all can be fed from the abundance of God's gifts to us, and that none need go hungry in a just and righteous world.

2

A Biblical Alternative to the Animal Rights Movement

■ Classical thinkers often wrote about animals and some, like Pythagoras, advocated vegetarianism. He based his dietary preferences on the idea of the transmigration of souls, an influential belief that is still prevalent in much modern-day vegetarian literature. Pythagoras's reputation for teaching compassion and self-restraint can be measured by the fact that a meatless diet was often called a Pythagorean diet until the 1840s, when the term *vegetarianism* was coined. The hesitancy of some members of the early Christian church to embrace vegetarianism can be explained in part due to the long shadow that Pythagoras cast over the issue of how to think about animals.

The organized animal rights movement did not begin until the early nineteenth century in England. Most of the earliest animal advocates in England and North America were Christians who were also worried about the treatment of children, the injustice of slavery, and the working conditions of the poor. The founder of the Society for the Prevention of Cruelty to Animals (as it was called before it became "Royal"), which began in 1824, was an Anglican priest, Arthur Broome, and its second full-time secretary was Lewis Gompertz, a Jewish philosopher who wrote an important early work on animals and ethics. Even earlier, in 1776, Humphrey Primatt wrote *The Duty of Mercy and the Sin of Cruelty,* which is arguably the first systematic theology concerning our responsibilities to animals. Many of the arguments made on behalf of animals were grounded in the language of sympathy and compassion rather than rights, as illustrated by Anna Sewell's *Black Beauty,* which has been called the *Uncle Tom's Cabin* of the horse. The American Society for the Prevention of Cruelty to Animals was founded in 1866, on the heels of the Emancipation Proclamation and the passing of the thirteenth amendment abolishing slavery. The movement for the humane treatment of animals was led by moral pioneers who were involved in a variety of social issues. They saw the compassionate treatment of animals as one among many different ways they could try to spread the gospel message of the love of God.

In its modern guise, however, the animal rights movement is often hostile to religion and single-minded in its focus on animals. The modern animal rights movement is a radicalization of the welfare movement that was begun by Christians. Peter Singer's book *Animal Liberation,* which more than any other work can be called the founding document of the modern animal rights movement, intentionally imitates the rhetoric of the various liberation movements that came out of the 1960s. Singer defends the calculative method of utilitarianism—acting in such a way that the good is maximized and harm is minimized—to defend animal welfare, but most animal activists prefer to employ the stronger language of rights.

The idea of animals having rights echoes other liberation movements in the modern world, and by extending human rights to animals, the strongest possible language is used to guarantee the individual integrity of all animals. Consequently, the secular language of rights has largely displaced the supposedly weaker Christian language of compassion and stewardship. If the animal rights movement has any connection to religion at all today, it is more likely to use Eastern religions to support the Pythagorean belief in the transmigration of souls than to rely on anything from Christian tradition or the Bible.

The earliest stage of the animal welfare movement resulted in the establishment of humane societies that were mostly concerned with the treatment of domesticated animals. Today the animal rights movement is more concerned with liberating all of nature from human control and with displacing the role of humanity in the world by rejecting the uniqueness of human rationality. Singer, for example, popularized the term *speciesist* to denote anyone who allows the interests of the human species to override the interests of any nonhuman animal species. He depicts the human use of animals as a tyranny that demands revolutionary action.

Among such writers, the Bible, which teaches that humans are uniquely created in the image of God, is blamed for encouraging an attitude of human superiority over nature. As Singer categorically and inaccurately states, "It is beyond dispute that mainstream Christianity, for its first 1,800 years, put non-human animals outside its sphere of concern" (p. 3). As with any zealous social movement, animal rights advocates must look for a scapegoat to explain why they remain in the minority, and Christianity is the most convenient target. The Bible, the critics claim, does not value the wildness and independence of animals but instead places them under the authority of humanity and, ultimately, God. Animal rights advocates, by contrast, want to liberate animals from human control and influence.

Much of the most severe abuse of animals in modern Western society is, of course, a direct result of the industrial revolution and the pressures of capitalism to cut costs in the production of meat—factors that have little or nothing to do with the Bible. However, the description of the Bible by its critics is not completely off the mark, because the Bible does place humans at the center of the world and the Bible does give humanity authority over nature.

I will argue that the Christian view of nature is superior to the animal rights view because we cannot escape the authority that makes us responsible for the natural world. Whether we like it or not, population growth has forced us to take all of nature under our management, and no animals are unaffected by human intervention into nature. Nonetheless, this does not mean that people of faith can do with nature whatever they want. One of the central themes of the Bible is the question of what constitutes proper authority, and so we must read the Bible carefully to see what kind of dominion God grants us.

When the animal rights movement is not scapegoating Christianity for every abused animal, it is turning to bad theology for a supporting framework. Many advocates for animals are committed to pantheism, which identifies God with the natural world and thus views animals as sacred. It is almost as if this approach thinks that we cannot learn to treat animals with respect unless we see them as manifestations of the divine. They must have souls that are identical to our own, as Pythagoras believed, if we are to acknowledge their worth and integrity. Only by promoting them to that status will we be motivated to cease exploiting them for our own benefit.

In much pantheistic literature, animals are portrayed as our teachers. What is natural is good, these books assume, so we have much to learn from animals. Listening to them is one way of recovering our true selves. The stories from Susan Chernak McElroy's popular book, *Animals as Teachers and Healers,* are poignant: by watching how her boyfriend treats her two horses; a woman decides to leave an abusive relationship; the friendship of a dog saves a man from alcoholism; a cat suddenly leaps out of the arms of a woman, who chases her and thus avoids being hit by an oncoming car. There are many stories about animals who appear after the death of a loved one, acting in such ways as to convince the grieving that they embody the spirit of the deceased. In these anecdotes, animals serve as guardian angels, talismans, and spiritual guides. Such stories function as urban legends, helping those who have little contact with nature to escape from their problems by imagining a world in which everything is upside-down—where the animals are wise and we humans their lowly followers. It is true that animals have much to teach us about the range and depth of God's love. Unfortunately, however, this romantic view of nature leaves little room for the uniqueness of human rationality and responsibility.

Throughout this book, I will contrast this pantheistic foundation for animal rights with a biblical alternative. The pantheism of animal rights has its own story to tell about who we are and how we should value animals, and it is a story that borrows from, but seriously distorts, the biblical narrative. In the pantheistic version of primordial history, the fall occurs not when people turn their backs on God but when people decide to exploit and dominate nature. Paradise, according to this theology, is not a world where community flourishes under the benevolent authority of God. On the contrary, if all life is divine and equal, then no hierarchy can be justified. Pantheism identifies authority with a principle of natural vitality, shared by all, which is defined in nebulous terms as a sacred life force. A pantheistic paradise thus promises a freedom from all constraints only by denying the basic differences between classes of entities. Translated into politics, the result would be a libertarian world run amok, where the sole purpose of the government is to guarantee every entity's (including animals and even natural objects like trees) right to pursue its own bliss.

On the issue of animals, bad theology often drives out good theology, in part because the church has kept silent for too long about the biblical resources for an answer to the pantheism implicit in much animal rights literature. Americans love their pets and are very hungry for a religious framework for thinking about animals, but Christian theologians have been slow to respond to this need. Even the nineteenth-century Christians who urged a better treatment of animals were often seen as eccentrics, and their ideas were not supported by church officials and theologians. Every Christian should be ready to give testimony to the value of animals, their value not just to us, but more importantly, their value to the God who created them. In fact, I want to suggest that theological reflection on animals leads inexorably to the very heart of Christian faith.

Putting animals on the agenda displaces humans from the center of theology and thus opens a space for the return of God to the pinnacle of all our concerns. This shift does not have to be anti-human, but it can help us to escape the Promethean humanism that has infected even the most orthodox theologies of the modern period. To say that God's love extends beyond human beings is not to diminish God's love for us, nor to deny the special moral role we play in the world. But to say that God loves *only* us is surely to betray our limited imaginations and the self-interest that governs even the most theocentric theological models. Thus, putting animals on the agenda can, among other things, serve to save theology from the distortions of human pride.

▪ A Biblical Theology of Animals in a Nutshell

Throughout this book I will argue that the Bible is radical in its views on the treatment of animals. Against the pagan religions of the past and against the New Age revivals of paganism today, the Bible does not treat animals as messengers of the gods. Animals do not carry secret messages for us, they are not divine, and they do not determine the fate of humanity or the world. Although we can learn from them, we are not to worship animals or to treat them as a part of divinity. They are simply not that important in the Bible. The Bible also does not treat animals as equal to humans. Humans clearly are superior to animals not only in intelligence but also in their divinely given place in the cosmos. The biblical world is an ordered world, and humans have the most important role to play in that order.

Nevertheless, humans are not given absolute power over animals in the Bible. Instead, humans are given certain basic responsibilities toward animals, because animals too are loved by God and have a special role to play in God's good creation. The Bible treats animals as others who are really different from us and yet similar enough to merit kindness and to be included in God's plan for the world. Humans are God's representatives on earth, put here for a variety of purposes, one of which is to mediate God's original purposes and intentions to animals.

Of course, God's plan for the animals, like God's plan for us, has been savagely compromised by what theologians call the fall. Christian theology teaches that nature, whether human or animal, is not what it was meant to be. This means that Christians cannot look at nature as something that is completely good in its present state. The world is good because God created it, but much that happens within the world, including within the animal world, is far from good. This is why nature needs human intervention, not in terms of exploitation and abuse for economic and personal gain but in terms of management and care, in order to become a reflection of God's original intentions. Humans cannot save the world, but we can be good stewards of God's many gifts. Animals in the wild thus should not be romanticized, as if animals were meant to be separated from humans and to be fighting each other. Moreover, Christians cannot derive their ethics from observing nature or studying ecology and biology. Biology is not destiny; God is.

A Christian ethic of nature and animals is derived from an active recollection of God's plan, a plan that is now blurred by a world full of violence. Christians live in anticipation of the day when God will consummate God's intentions for the whole world, including but not limited to us. The work that results from this life of hope is not a burden but a joy. Such an ethic is not utopian, even though it believes in a future of peace and harmony, because Christians understand that God works in mysterious ways and that human effort will accomplish nothing unless it is a grateful response to the grace that God gives us.

Simply put, there are three components to this biblical theology of animals. First, animals are not equal to humans or to God; nevertheless, animals do have their own integrity and dignity as a part of God's good creation. Second, humans do have a God-given power over the animals, but that power is meant to be administered responsibly and in accordance with God's intentions. Third, the world, including the violence of the animal kingdom, is not what it was meant to be; fortunately, God is working toward and will one day restore the world to its original state of peace and harmony.

■ Why the Bible's Vision of Animals Can Be Hard to Understand

Although I have presented a concise and straightforward statement of a biblical theology of animals, the fact that the Bible both affirms and contradicts some of the usual attitudes people have about animals makes it susceptible to misinterpretation. The Bible presents a deceptively simple view of animals that must be interpreted with much care in order to avoid the common mistakes that both Christians and critics of Christianity have made in arguing about what Christianity says about animals. For example, even a quick reading of the Bible will suggest that the Bible does not value animals as much as humans. If one approaches this fact with a negative prejudice against the Bible, the biblical realism about animals can be easily turned into a charge against Christianity. However, from the biblical point of view, it is simply irrefutable that humans have a more complex relationship with each other and with God than animals do. Humans have a level of freedom and rationality that allows them to exercise great responsibility over their actions, and thus they play a more important role in the world than animals do.

One could also conclude from the Bible that humans need not worry about their power over animals. Many critics and defenders of Christianity alike argue that the Bible lets humans do whatever they want with animals. Strangely enough, I have heard atheists appeal to the Bible as a justification for their carnivorous diets. I will show throughout this book, however, that God has other plans for the animals and that the biblical permission of meat-eating is a begrudging concession to human sin, not a free pass to do whatever we want to animals. The authority of humans over nature is never absolute in the Bible. Indeed, that power is seriously circumscribed in the Old Testament (the Hebrew Bible), and the notion of what kind of power humans should exercise is radically reenvisioned in the New Testament by the example of Jesus Christ.

Finally, a reader of the Bible could err either on the side of utopianism, optimistically working toward a world free of violence toward animals, or cynicism, pessimistically waiting for God to change the world without human participation or cooperation. Either reading of the Bible would be one-sided. The doctrine of providence does suggest that God's rule over history is absolute, not partial, but God's ultimate authority does not mean that we are to do nothing but wait for God to act. We are called, as Christians, to follow God's lead by responding to God's grace and actively pursuing holiness here and now. We are called to take the gospel message to the whole world, so that we might mediate to animals something of that grace that Jesus mediates to us. The church is the body of Jesus Christ on earth, the concrete place that witnesses to the ways in which God assumes the world's suffering as God's own.

The Bible, then, can be easily misunderstood on the topic of animals, not only by outsiders but also by insiders, that is, Christians themselves. From a sociological point of view, the situation of the Christian churches is itself a major reason why it is very hard today to develop and give voice to a biblical theology of animals. The church is too frequently divided between liberals and conservatives who bring political agendas to the reading of Scripture. Religious liberals might be open to thinking about our obligations toward animals, but they tend to adopt the arguments of animal rights advocates and add little if anything distinctively Christian to those arguments. Religious conservatives are tired of hearing Christianity blamed for antianimal attitudes. They also react against the very obvious ways in which our culture condones moral relativism in theory and moral promiscuity in practice. They fear that granting animals moral attention will only add another loud and strident voice to the chaotic chorus of special interest groups pleading for recognition. They suspect that the animal rights agenda is one aspect of a broader movement that has as its goal the dismantling of traditional religious beliefs and practices.

Religious conservatives often want to defend the absolute nature of human power over animals as an understandable reaction to what they see as attempts by animal rights advocates to lower human value to the level of the animal world. To them, animal rights represents an antihuman relativism, threatening to plunge traditional values into moral chaos.

A theology of animals grounded in biblical integrity thus seems to be not only a theoretical impossibility but a practical irrelevancy. Even if it could be articulated, who would believe it? Can liberals find in the Bible alone a unique position on animals that would ground their desire to be relevant to the world? And can conservatives find in the Bible a pattern or logic that challenges a practice like meat-eating that is so embedded in the modern church that many Christians take it to be a sacred right, if not a divine duty? It is my wager that a biblical theology can surprise both liberals and conservatives, who agree only on this, that the Bible has nothing positive to say about animals. Liberals turn their backs on this interpretation of the Bible, while conservatives embrace it—but what if both groups are wrong? What if the Bible is much more subtle and profound on the issue of animals than the simple slogans of both conservatives and liberals would lead one to think? Even more, what if the biblical message on animals is more radical, challenging, and plausible than the rhetoric of the animal rights movement, so that Christians can take a public position on animal issues that is at once relevant to current debates and a witness to the integrity and creativity of Christian faith?

◼ What Is So Christian about Vegetarianism?

The internal divisions in the church make vegetarianism appear to be a faddish phenomenon that liberals might adopt for secular reasons but that conservatives avoid because it has no relation to the Bible. I want to defend a Christian vegetarianism that embraces a non-meat-eating diet for strictly theological reasons. This does not mean that I think that vegetarianism should be a test of faith. A Christian is a vegetarian not out of some new form of moral legalism that would require everyone to give up meat in order to merit God's grace. Such rigor leads to self-righteousness, which is contrary to the central Christian belief in human sinfulness and God's graciousness.

I often wonder how many Christians are turned off by vegetarians who take a holier-than-thou attitude with their meat-eating friends. Vegetarians sometimes seem more interested in their own moral purity than in animals or in being friends with those who disagree with them. There is a vegetarian fundamentalism that is every bit as rigid and severe as biblical fundamentalism, though vegetarian fundamentalists would never admit that they mirror the one group they most vociferously reject. Talking to a vegetarian can be a polarizing experience for many people, especially when the vegetarian turns the conversation into a debate by trying to score cheap points.

My first close friend who was a vegetarian made me feel so guilty about my meaty diet that it took me years to take vegetarianism seriously. He was someone who was always looking for a new kind of spirituality to practice, and when he became a vegetarian he thought he had found the solution to his life's problems. When my wife and I lived in his apartment for a month while he was overseas, he made us promise not to bring meat into his kitchen. Looking back at that attitude, I can understand it better now. The pursuit of holiness involves habitual practices and strict rules that heighten and clarify one's closeness to God; asking others to respect those rules is not necessarily an exercise in barren legalism. At the time, however, it felt like he was trying to impose his beliefs on us. By bringing meat onto his premises, we would pollute his kitchen and defile its purity. He was concerned not so much with converting us to his beliefs as with protecting his world from us. It seemed to us that he had become a neophyte in a new religion, a cult that divided the world into the saved and the damned, and we certainly were not part of the vegetarian elect.

We had to find our own way to a more spiritual diet, and for us that had to be through, not around, the Christian faith. To embrace vegetarianism, we first had to figure out what we did not believe about the animal rights movement. Christians should not be vegetarians because they think that animals are the same as us or because they think that humans have no authority over the animals. Christians do not need to try to prove that animals are just as smart as us in order to make an appeal that they be treated with compassion. Animals are subordinate to humans, and as long as that relationship is based on a responsible exercise of authority, it is legitimate from a biblical perspective. Thus, some Christians who may be reluctant to embrace fully the demands of a vegetarian diet may still want to eat free-range meat only, meat that comes from animals who have been raised with an amount of freedom commensurate with their natures.

Indeed, according to a biblically-based theology, Christians have no moral obligation to abstain from all meat by-products, which is what distinguishes vegetarians from vegans. Christians who choose to use diet as a part of their witness often will be ovo-lacto vegetarians. They will include eggs and dairy products in their diets because it is not inherently wrong to rely on the service of animals. Nevertheless, when such relationships become so one-sided that dairy cows and egg-laying chickens are not treated with any respect whatsoever, Christians too will consider veganism—or at least soy milk and free-range eggs—as a protest against the obvious perversions of God's natural order.

A vegetarian diet is one concrete way for Christians to experience and practice God's grace. When I am asked why I am a vegetarian, I take that as an opportunity to give an account of my faith. Eating is thus an occasion for witness and ministry. I do not avoid meat in order to feel superior to others. Nor do I avoid meat in order to ease my scrupulous conscience. I also do not want to lay down a burdensome guilt trip on my many friends who do eat meat. I avoid meat because I await God's total and redeeming power, and even now I want to identify with the direction of God's providential march through history.

Diet can be one way that Christians take a stand for God and God's peaceable kingdom. For many centuries Christians were known as people who did not eat meat on Fridays, a tradition that continued into the modern period as a badge of honor for Roman Catholics. What would it mean if Christians today were known as people who did not eat meat at all? What would it say to the world about our willingness to put grace into practice and to witness to our own faith in God's love and our hope in God's ability to restore the world to God's loving intentions?

■ The Cultural Shaping of Vegetarianism

It is possible that even the most articulate voice of Christian vegetarianism might get lost in our culture, because vegetarianism has become a symbol that means everything *but* Christian faith. In other words, there are basic features of our culture that prohibit a biblical vegetarianism from taking shape. Many religious people are discouraged from thinking about vegetarianism because of the way vegetarianism is presented in our culture. Although Christian monks and saints were frequently vegetarian in the history of the church, the media today rarely portrays vegetarianism as a religious decision that puts into practice traditional Christian doctrines concerning creation, providence, Christology, and eschatology. There are no vegetarian vows that would make this life-changing decision a public part of one's spiritual journey. Instead, vegetarianism is seen as a private lifestyle issue that reflects the rage for fitness, a political statement that dramatizes social policy needs, or a spiritual journey that takes one away from traditional beliefs and practices. It is portrayed as an alternative to, rather than a deepening of, traditional Christian faith.

Simply put, it is hard to imagine or practice a Christian vegetarianism because vegetarianism has become a symbol of cultural currents that are frequently inimical to traditional Christianity. How has this happened? Why is vegetarianism so immediately linked with social trends and cultural institutions that seem alien to most Christians? To answer that question, we need to sketch some of the fundamental features of our current cultural situation. Then we can see what vegetarianism has become, in order to try to imagine what it could be if it were relocated as a part of traditional Christian belief and practice.

One way to understand the world we live in is to say that we value the expression of personality over the development of character. Personality and character need to be carefully distinguished as terms that imply a set of assumptions and values that are largely at odds with each other. Personality is a form of style, something we can design or fashion and thus change to fit the needs of the moment. Robert Bellah has noted in *Habits of the Heart* that Americans have always valued self-reliance. However, our consumeristic culture goes even further. What Bellah calls expressive individualism turns what were once normative commitments (like family, job, religion) into alternative strategies of self-fulfillment. Sacred commitments become useful attachments in our increasingly disposable society, where we throw away anything that does not satisfy an immediate need.

Character consists of habits of thought and action that are developed over many years and are revealed in times of crisis and challenge. Character displays the long-term commitments that enable us to sustain relationships and loyalties across the changing circumstances of life. What does it mean to have character in an age that celebrates cosmetic surgery as the answer to self-doubt? If even our bodies are merely a means of self-expression— instruments that can be redesigned to meet social expectations— what remains constant long enough to count as a virtue? How can we develop habits of mind that lead us to do the right thing even when our appetites point us in the wrong direction?

Perhaps we do not stay put long enough in our quickly changing world to develop character anymore. The term *personality* better fits our optimistic sense that we can remake ourselves to fit any situation and that we are judged not by who we are but by how we present ourselves. To be personable is to be likable, while the development of character might be offensive if we take a strong stand on an issue or demonstrate that we have beliefs we are not willing to compromise.

The highest form of personality is to become a celebrity, someone who begins by being adored for entertaining us and ends by being famous no matter what they do. According to the thesis of Neal Gabler's recent book, *Life the Movie: How Entertainment has*

Conquered Reality, we live in a world where life itself has become a medium of performance and fun. Gabler calls this world the Republic of Entertainment. If something is not entertaining, then it is not real. It is not just that life has the dramatic qualities of a movie, so that we often feel like we are playing roles that somebody else has written for us. Gabler argues, more radically, that in a culture saturated with the media, advertisements, and television, life itself has become a kind of art or drama. Everything we do, from politics to the marketplace, has to be packaged as entertainment. Entertainment is no longer a special break from the everyday. Indeed, reality TV is not something radically new but the culmination of the idea that everyone has an obligation to entertain everyone else.

Even religion is not exempt from these pressures and influences. Celebrities have replaced heroes and saints (people who were remembered for doing things for others, rather than just being the object of endless fascination). Churches have responded by absorbing many of the lessons of Hollywood, selling the gospel as an easy answer to life's questions or as a maudlin melodrama that can recharge your emotional batteries. The churches that are growing most quickly are those that most resemble a movie theater with comfortable seating, lots of visuals, short and humorous sermons, and upbeat music. As theologian Michael Budde has argued, the church is tempted to become another Magic Kingdom instead of striving after the kingdom of God.

Religion has been transformed in the Republic of Entertainment. Under this new regime, religion is all about giving expression to one's personality, not developing the kind of character that comes with a patient and gradual immersion in the same rituals and beliefs year after year. Theologians like John Hick support such trends by arguing that all religions are basically the same. The function of religion is not to make truth claims but to lead people to a richer life by satisfying their spiritual needs. Religions facilitate the need we all feel to be connected to the divine and to each other. It does not matter what you believe, as long as you believe in something. As Dwight Eisenhower is reported to have said, "Our government makes no sense unless it is founded in a deeply felt religious faith— and I don't care what it is."

Less subtle New Age theologies simply suggest that religion should lead people to richer lives—period. In other words, you don't have to believe in anything as long as you believe in yourself. We are encouraged to help ourselves to the great smorgasbord of various religions, sampling them to see which one fits our own needs best. Religion is the spice that enhances the quality of life. With the right amount, it guarantees the success of even the hardest of life's courses. As a result, religious traditions that demand a long initiation into a complex set of beliefs and practices are seen as not cost-beneficial. We want our religious investments to pay a quick and easy dividend.

All of these cultural forces shape the ways in which vegetarianism is practiced and presented in our society. The result is a variety of vegetarian and animal rights groups, many of which seem totally at odds with traditional Christian beliefs and practices. What follows is a typology of vegetarianism today, a list of basic types of vegetarianism that does not necessarily correspond to specific groups and organizations, but is meant to show how vegetarianism is typically practiced and presented in a culture that emphasizes personality, entertainment, and religious eclecticism. The prevalence of these types goes a long way toward explaining why Christians have not been active participants in the animal rights movement. The five types are: expressive, healthy-minded, Gnostic, New Age, and political vegetarianism.

◼ Five Types of Non-Christian Vegetarianism

The first type of non-Christian vegetarianism is, to borrow a phrase from Robert Bellah, an "expressive" vegetarianism. For this group, being a vegetarian is an expression of a lifestyle choice. Although the vegetarian movement frequently has been associated with bohemian values and countercultural lifestyles, the emphasis on health and longevity in the 1980s led to a mainstreaming of vegetarianism, so that now, even much of the middle class gives lip-service to a veggie diet and disdains "red" meat. Social commentator David Brooks has argued that there is a new ruling class in America, which he calls Bobos, whose main achievement is precisely this synthesis of bohemian and bourgeois values. Bobos are both trendy and practical, looking for lifestyle options that are socially relevant and yet personally advantageous. Vegetarianism is their perfect fad because it is a badge of distinction that demonstrates environmental concern as well as a disciplined and healthy style of life. It is a way of being on the cutting edge while still making sure that you are doing what is best for yourself.

Corporations and the media have not been slow in responding to this new lifestyle option. Vegetarianism is fashionable because it mixes consumer goods (vegetarian food, cookbooks, health products) with ethical concern, and celebrities are quick to promote vegetarianism as a way of promoting themselves. What could be better than a diet that not only helps you to lose weight and live longer but also expresses your compassion for animals and your ecoconscious mistrust of multinational corporations and huge factory farms? Vegetarian magazines make vegetarian food as tasteful and attractive as possible, as if to say that the ethical choice in diet is also the choice that can bring you the most pleasure. Vegetarianism thus does not require self-sacrifice. It is not a moral decision at all. Instead, it is at once wholesome and hedonistic. The market sells vegetarianism as a look, a way for people to express their individuality while also appearing to be socially concerned and politically engaged.

Unfortunately, vegetarianism as an alternative lifestyle will not persuade many people to radically transform their diets. Eating vegetarian food because it makes you feel good about yourself is a weak motivation when convenience, desire, or social pressure tempts you to eat meat. Expressive vegetarians do not shape their diets according to the traditions and beliefs of a specific religious tradition precisely because they define themselves in opposition to all institutions, which they perceive as infringements on their freedom. By its very definition such a lifestyle must be hip and countercultural. It appeals to the young who are in search of a new identity during the transitions of adolescence. Its power comes from the fact that people who choose it perceive themselves as acting in ways that are out of the ordinary and against the status quo. When vegetarianism becomes just another lifestyle, however, it will be subject to the same fate as all fashion trends. Without a theological foundation and an institution like the church for support, revolutionary dietary practices become prey to every kind of fanciful belief and thus risk being swept away by the fickle winds of social change.

For the second type of vegetarians, diet is merely a tool for self-improvement, not a way of life. These vegetarians are, to borrow a term from William James, the great psychologist of religion, healthy-minded. The healthy-minded are people who feel like everything is fine with their lives, as opposed to the sick-souled, those who need religion as an aid to personal crisis and despair. The healthy-minded have no complaints against life; they just want more of it. They use vegetarianism as a prudent means to prolong their lives. It is, after all, commonly accepted scientific wisdom that it is the safest diet one can practice.

Seen from another perspective, however, this type does have a thoroughly religious outlook on diet. The healthy-minded vegetarian treats the body as a sacred object and has transferred belief in an afterlife into the hope for longevity in this life. Medicine replaces the church and doctors are substitutes for ministers and priests as individuals pursue health as an end in itself, the ultimate value in a world void of any transcendent purpose.

People cling to the inflated promises of revolutionary diets because they have no other way of making sense of suffering, disease, and death. They want to postpone the inevitable and prolong the transient by enjoying life to the fullest. This type of vegetarianism is one aspect of the cult of the body that so pervades our culture. It is one more way to sculpt or mold the body to conform with some unrealistic ideal.

Healthy-minded vegetarianism promises abundant life to those willing to brave the strenuous labor of an enlightened diet. Whereas fasting in the tradition of the Christian church was a means of self-reflection and an encouragement to serve others, today a self-denying diet is too often really a means of enhancing the self in a narcissistic way. A little bit of self-discipline in terms of limiting meat consumption results in a more durable and desirable body. Christians, who are told to treat their bodies as holy temples (1 Corinthians 6:19), can have some sympathy for this view, but Christianity ultimately places the body in the service of something higher, which is traditionally called the soul. A belief in the perfectibility of the body, and thus an enthusiastic passion for trying to slow down the inevitable decay of the body, will only result in false hopes and misplaced confidence.

The third type of vegetarianism is more explicitly religious, and unlike the expressivists and healthy-minded, the Gnostic vegetarians are purists when it comes to what they will eat. Gnosticism was a religious movement during the first few centuries of the common era that Christians considered to be heretical. The word *gnostic* comes from the Greek word for knowledge. Gnostics thought that they could find salvation through secret knowledge about the cosmos. They developed elaborate myths to explain how humans are souls stranded on earth in alien bodies and how we need to overcome our embodiment by freeing ourselves in preparation for a return journey back to God. Gnostics are anti-institutional, antidogmatic, and antiauthoritarian. The material world is not important or ultimately real; enlightenment must come from within, not without. Gnostics are also elitists. Only some humans are able to obtain special knowledge of God, because only a few are brave enough to employ the spiritual tools of magic and the occult that traditional Christians reject.

One reason I have picked up this term for a certain kind of vegetarianism is that many Gnostics themselves were vegetarians. Gnostics did not reject meat-eating out of compassion for animals, however. They were concerned about keeping their souls clear from the taint of mixing with animal souls. They also wanted to deny their bodies in order to make them less burdensome on their souls. Today, Gnostic (or better, neo-Gnostic) vegetarians are not so concerned with their souls, but they are concerned about not polluting their bodies with animal matter. This type of vegetarian practices a rigorous diet of self-control in order to free the body from anything that would be unnatural or unhealthy. The world is a radically polluted place, neo-Gnostics believe, and they must separate themselves from all the unhealthy practices that could corrupt them. Neo-Gnostic vegetarianism is about finding your true self by regulating your contact with the world, just as the ancient Gnostics wanted to save themselves by turning their backs to the world through secret knowledge and ascetic discipline. Like their ancient precursors, neo-Gnostics believe that suffering comes about through ignorance, not sin, so an enlightened diet can bring salvation.

Christians cannot sympathize with neo-Gnostic vegetarians today any more than they could agree with the ancient Gnostics who battled the early church. Christianity does not reject the world. The world is a good place, created out of love, and God affirmed that goodness by becoming incarnate in the person of

Jesus Christ. Yet Christians are called to set themselves apart from the ways of the world when the path of Jesus departs from the path of the godless and unfaithful. Christians should not eat just like everyone else. Instead, they should have a diet that reflects their beliefs about and their hope in the coming kingdom of God.

One of the tasks of a Christian theology of diet is to affirm the goodness and abundance of the earth's resources while also exercising responsibility and compassion in the way we harvest those resources. And that must be done without falling into a Gnostic quest for purity, which stems from an anxiety about a world radically at odds with human life. The world is here for us, Christianity teaches, so that we do not need to flee it out of a sense of radical alienation. As conservative Christians often emphasize, God gave us the world for our benefit. Nonetheless, we are also here for the world as representatives of God's original intentions, so that we are not permitted to exploit the world by treating it as a mere means to our own needs and desires. The world and the animals are a gift, but all gifts should be cherished according to the wishes of the giver.

Similar to the Gnostic variety of vegetarianism is what I call New Age vegetarianism. For this fourth type, vegetarianism is a symbol for the unity of all religions. To be religious is to believe in a peaceful and harmonious world of which we are but one small part. Humans do not stand apart from the world but instead are a part of the world. It is a dogma of New Age circles that all true religions teach the same basic beliefs about nature, the divine, and humanity. New Agers support this tenet with a litany of key terms—karma, ahimsa (nonviolence), and reincarnation—that count as evidence for the priority of the belief in the oneness of all reality. This ancient intuition, they allege, was eclipsed by the rise of monotheistic religions, beginning with Judaism.

New Age vegetarians thus accept a theology of pantheism—the idea that God is immanent, a part of all that is, rather than transcendent, standing apart and above us as a holy being whom we must worship from a respectful distance. They argue that people will begin to treat animals compassionately only if they recognize them as equal parts of the mosaic that comprises the world. They advocate learning how to think like a mountain, rather than trying to figure out the point of view of the One who created the mountains.

49

Salvation for humans, New Agers argue, comes with a return to nature. That humans exploit nature and abuse animals is evidence of an estrangement from nature that must be reconciled. Nature is not the enemy of humanity. Instead, humans become most fully themselves when they recognize that the rhythms and patterns of nature are our true home. We should relinquish the power and control we have over nature by treating the world as a friend to be loved, not an enemy to be conquered. Western religions have betrayed this original vision of harmony by portraying humans as masters of the world. This Western view of humans is rooted in the monotheistic portrait of God as a ruler from the skies who stands over and against humans, just as humans are able to stand over and against nature.

New Age vegetarians are thus steeped in an uncritical mixture of Eastern religions and usually have little sympathy for Western religious traditions. This need to find heroes and villains in humanity's treatment of nature has especially led to a romanticization of Native Americans as environmentalists ahead of their time (see the contrary evidence in Krech). Vegetarianism becomes another stop on the itinerary of spiritual tourists who also practice chanting, yoga, astrology, vision quests, and other alternative religious rituals. Vegetarianism becomes for the New Agers a criterion for distinguishing between what counts for true or authentic religiosity and what is false or inauthentic. Jainism, for example, gets high marks due to the extremity of its affirmation of all life. So does Taoism, with its romantic conception of nature as the mysterious force that cannot be conceptualized or understood. All religions can be tried and sampled as long as they conform to vegetarian tastes. This search for the nonviolent root of all religions, however, often ends up with the creation of an entirely new religion based on a vegetarian creed. Animal advocate Rynn Berry illustrates this tendency when he talks about the elements that comprise a vegetarian religion—elements that are drawn from several Eastern religious traditions. Only those religions that support vegetarianism are true, and the only truth of religion is vegetarianism.

Certainly the New Age emphasis on befriending nature is admirable, but from the perspective of traditional Christianity, it does not provide any ethical foundation for a more favorable treatment of animals. How can humans be expected to care for animals when human reality is reduced to the level of nature itself? That is, New Age religion refuses to acknowledge the very real power and authority humans have in the world. By collapsing God into the world and reducing human authority over the world, they risk not only divinizing the world but also drawing their ethics from nature itself. As everyone knows, nature is full of violence and strife, so that nature as it is can hardly offer a moral basis for thinking about our obligation to animals. As French philosopher Luc Ferry has demonstrated, European romantic movements that have insisted on a duty to nature that precedes our duty to each other—an ideology known as "deep ecology"— have often led to antihumanistic and totalitarian political consequences.

If New Age thinkers are open to Christianity, it is only when they argue, against all the available evidence, that Jesus was a vegetarian who was influenced by Eastern philosophy. Indeed, they often suggest that all great religious mystics and saints have been vegetarians. This highly speculative portrait of Jesus is prevalent and popular in writings about vegetarianism. Thus Jesus lies at the center of debates about vegetarianism, which makes it all the more important for Christians to take a strong stand on what Jesus did and did not teach about animals. By creating Jesus in their own image, New Age vegetarians demonstrate that they are more interested in constructing a new religion than in discovering what the various religious traditions actually teach about animals and diet.

Christians are right, then, to suspect that vegetarianism can itself become a new religion, with its own stories, doctrines, and practices. It is a religion that is, in the end, more concerned about finding answers within the self than turning the self toward God. Taoism is a case in point. The Taoist mystics practiced vegetarianism as a way of increasing vital energy and prolonging life. Vegetarianism was all about liberating and enhancing one's inner spirit. Eating meat is bad for your spiritual state; it is a form of spiritual pollution. Even the connection of vegetarianism to the transmigration of the soul places the emphasis on one's own salvation, not compassion toward the suffering of animals. People who believe in reincarnation avoid doing harm to animals in order not to end up becoming an animal, which implies that being an animal is not a very worthy state. Moreover, reincarnation means that bodies are dispensable—that no creature is unique—since every life con-

tinues as it changes shape and form. Why take any individual creature seriously if it will end up being something else? Why worry
about animals when they are inhabited by souls working out their
salvation by undergoing punishment and discipline? Rather than
leading to a respect for individual animals, reincarnation sub-
merges individuals in an endless stream of ongoing transformations, chained by a strict law of causation to a destiny that cannot
be altered or denied.

All of these types of vegetarianism—expressive, healthy-minded,
Gnostic, and New Age—are influenced by the individualism of
American culture. They all say that vegetarianism is not only something you choose but also something that is intensely personal. It
has to do with self-discovery and self-growth. New Agers illustrate
this emphasis on the self and not the other when they argue that
religions should be judged not on the basis of their truth but on
the basis of their usefulness, and religious beliefs are useful to the
extent that they lead to personal happiness. Christian theology, by
contrast, is guided by the insight that the pursuit of happiness will
only lead to misery unless humans are open to a power that is
greater than themselves, a power that is demanding as well as
uplifting.

When vegetarianism is not an aspect of expressive individualism or the private quest for perfect health, it becomes part of a
utopian political agenda. This is the fifth and final category in my
typology, the approach that I call political vegetarianism. The main
purpose of members of this group is to promote social change, and
they often use all of the elements of the world of entertainment to
achieve that goal. They see vegetarianism as both the most direct
means to and the most potent symbol of a radical social revolution that would call into question not only diet but also the unique
role of humanity in the world. They see meat-eating not as a symptom of sin, for example, gluttony, but rather as a symptom of sexism, man's domination over both nature and women. Thus, liberating animals from humans will, at the same time, liberate women
from male control and authority.

To stretch the point a little bit, political vegetarians are not too
dissimilar from communists in America in the twenties and thir-
ties. They have a plan for the world, and you are on the side of
either the oppressive carnivores or the liberated vegetarians. The

proof that you are with them is your willingness to forego the pleasures of meat-eating. They look at meat-eating as a dominant ideology that must be totally defeated, and thus they wage a diet war, battling the hot meals of cooked animal flesh with the cold meals of raw vegetables. Their plan for the world involves a belief that only massive governmental intervention can save the animals from us. Only by a huge legislative effort that would extend human rights to animals can the animals ever have a chance for freedom and dignity.

Religious and political conservatives see this as a bureaucratic nightmare, as well as an attack on human dignity. They are correct to see this movement as, at best, utopian. How could animals have rights? Would that include all animals, or only the higher animals? How could those rights be enforced? How do we know when the interests of an animal have been violated? Who gets to speak for the animals, since they cannot tell us what their own interests are? What about situations when animal rights clash with human rights? The frequently unasked questions about this agenda could go on and on.

Christians, no matter how sympathetic they are to the notion that animals do have some kind of rights, are not utopians. Utopianism is both a product and a failure of the Christian tradition because it tells only half of the Christian story. It holds out hope for a better world, but it ignores the sinful condition of humanity as well as the fallen nature of the world. It imagines that if only the laws were changed, then human attitudes would also change. It also contends that one standard or measure of equality can be applied across the board to all individuals, whether human animals or other animals. In the next and final section of this chapter, I will look more closely at the notion of animal rights, spelling out why Christians need a biblical theology as the basis for their beliefs about animals, not the legislation of rights.

■ The Problem with Giving Rights to Animals

Throughout this book I will use the label "the animal rights movement" as if there were only one movement concerned with animals. In actuality, there are many different kinds of people and organizations that try to help animals, and some of them prefer terms like animal welfare, humane society, animal compassion, or animal liberation. All of these terms emphasize different aspects of the animal rights movement. Some emphasize pets, others laboratory animals, still others, wild animals and endangered species. Some work on legislation having to do with farm animals, others work against the fur industry and hunting practices. Some groups are more radical than others, but most groups do believe, as a matter of public policy, in the notion of animal rights. That is what, by and large, holds them together and makes for a coherent movement, even given all of the diversity of goals and methods.

Although expressive and healthy-minded vegetarians are not overly concerned with politics and social change, they probably do give their assent, if push comes to shove, to the proposition that animals are deserving of rights. Vegetarianism and animal rights are so closely tied together in the media and in popular understandings that they are nearly synonymous. Nevertheless, they can be separated, which is what I intend to do when I argue for a biblical theology of compassion for animals that is not equivalent to the notion of rights. Christian theology should not play the role of being the chaplain to the animal rights movement, giving moral advice or adding a pious sheen to political activism. Instead, as theologian Rodney Clapp argues, the church should marshall all of its resources to develop an alternative to secular discourses like the language of rights, one that reflects the particularities, even the peculiarities, of the Christian faith.

Why not just say that biblical theology also lends support to the notion that animals have rights? To recall my earlier discussion about contemporary culture, we live in a world with very little moral consensus. We no longer share enough religious tradition to agree about the moral shape of life and the obligations and duties that make life worth living. America has always been a culture that emphasizes freedom and individualism. It is hard, beginning with those two terms, *freedom* and *individualism,* to get to some shared sense of morality that would be good for the nation as a whole. "You do your thing and I'll do mine" is what we hear all the time. Morality only steps in to say that when you do your thing, don't bother me, and I won't bother you either. Morality is thus taken to mean leaving each other alone. As long as you do not hurt somebody else, you are free to follow your own path.

Without any agreement about what is good, true, and beautiful, the only morality we can have is procedural, not substantive. That is, we can only agree about how to adjudicate our differences, since we cannot agree about any ultimate norms or absolutes to guide our conduct. Our moral discourse is reduced, therefore, to a legislative process that assigns us rights and punishes us for violating each other's rights. Unfortunately, this process can degenerate into a popularity contest where rights are determined by the political strengths of special interest groups. As a result of partisan power plays, people lose faith in the possibility of a morality-based politics, and consequently the judicial process quickly replaces the legislative. That is, we turn to the courts to figure out how to assign and defend rights, so that the legal system, not the schools or the churches or the politicians, end up determining what morality is. The courts, however, are better at establishing the rules of how to fairly resolve a dispute than the ideals that should inspire and govern human behavior.

The whole language of rights, then, emerges from a social situation of mistrust and opposition. The best we can do is to agree on a minimal set of standards for our common life and a set of rules that establish the boundaries of fairness in resolving disputes. We cannot agree about what kind of life is the best kind of life to lead, nor can we agree about what the purpose of life is or why living in community is so important. To return to my earlier discussion about the triumph of personality, we seem unable to establish and support those institutions that would encourage and promote the virtues that enable the development of character. We can only decide how to draw lines around each and every individual so that freedom is maximized and people can defend themselves when those lines are crossed. Litigation is not a last resort but the *only* resort for a society that has no notion of civility, responsibility, and moral character. Without a shared moral tradition to make sense of the various ways we depend on each other and therefore must share each other's burdens, we are left with an attitude of entitlement, so that everybody deserves everything and there is no limit to individual freedom.

If applied to the complex world of animals, the legislation of rights would inevitably end in massive litigation, resentment, and confusion. To take but one example, animals do not know that they have rights, and they cannot defend those rights in a court of law. But who has the right to speak for the animals? That question must be answered before animals are given rights, but if animals have rights, then we do not have the right to speak in their place. Even if we can imagine animals permitting us to be proxies in their place, what about multiple claims on the animals? Under whose jurisdiction do they fall? Who owns them? And if we own them, how can we say that they have rights? Ironically and tragically, giving animals rights could only result in giving humans even more power over the animals, because humans would be the ones determining what those rights are and how they should be enforced. If the battle over human rights has ended in an explosion of lawsuits on every conceivable matter, the more ambiguous and complex case of animal rights could only end up perplexing and burdening the courts even more so.

No system of laws could ever fully protect the rights of animals. Animals are vulnerable precisely because we have so much power over them. Humans are born equal in dignity and worth, so it makes some sense to talk about human rights; but animals are not born equal to us or to each other. The only rights they have are the rights that we are willing to give to them. But why should we give them rights? And, since they certainly could never have all of the rights humans have (animals do not need the right to vote, for example!), which rights would we give them? Won't we give them only the rights that do not inconvenience us? Realistically speaking, then, we have to rely on human compassion and care in our relationship with animals rather than an unenforceable legal code. Thus, on practical grounds alone, love is the more fundamental gesture than rights.

The argument about the fundamental priority of compassion over rights can be made in more strictly philosophical terms. In the world of humans alone, rights do not work unless people are willing and able to forgive each other for the wrongs that inevitably occur in society. No legal system can resolve every dispute. Indeed, a democracy depends on its people voluntarily limiting their rights to freedom and individuality; otherwise, chaos would ensue. Moreover, the legal system itself works only because we are willing to accept its authority. When a court rules against us, we must have the virtue that enables us to let go of the past and to make amends with our enemies if we are to live in a society ruled by law. These religious elements of forgiveness and faith are all the more true with regard to animals. No number of laws will ever protect all the animals, so we must pray for patience and compassion rather than pass yet more laws. On this side of the eschaton, the world will never be free from cruelty to animals, so the only alternative to locking up nearly everyone will be an attitude of forgiveness.

In sum, only if we choose to treat animals with compassion will it be possible to assign animals certain rights that can be protected by the courts. Philosophically put, if we are the ones who give rights to animals, then the act of giving precedes the acquisition of rights. We will only give rights to animals if we act out of a love and compassion for them, so it is more important to work toward reforming those institutions that teach the virtue of compassion than to put one's faith in the judicial system of laws and rights.

An animal rights activist might agree that there seem to be insuperable problems to granting animals legal rights, but the activist might still insist that animals, just like humans, do have basic moral rights. At this point the Christian church needs to articulate a better alternative to the language of rights. Defending each others' rights might be the most that a pluralistic and democratic culture can accomplish in the moral realm, and it might be an admirable goal for a secular culture without any moral absolutes, but it is not enough for the Christian church. Christianity does not espouse individualism and freedom as the highest values. The point of existence for a Christian is to be in community, with God and with others. As a Christian, my life is not my own. Instead, it belongs first to God, and then to the community and tradition that teaches me that gratitude to God is the first principle of morality. The importance of gratitude is that it suggests that life is not a private possession but an expression of God's good favor, a gift to be shared and not kept. I find myself not by protecting my rights but by giving myself to others.

The language of love, then, takes precedence over the language of rights. The person who loves will take chances and risk connections that defy the lonely individualism that permeates American culture. Perfect love, in fact, claims no rights of its own (1 Corinthians 13:5). Few people, of course, can learn to live a life of love so fully and completely. That is why we need institutions that cultivate and sustain the everyday practices that turn the special virtues of compassion and care into the ordinary habits of good character. We also need moral models, which is why Christians look up to saints and revere their memory. Moral perfection is a transcendent ideal, yet a life of compassion is the goal for all Christians. Such a life is made possible when we respond to God's grace with a gratitude that is sufficient to overturn the self-centeredness that lies at the heart of a society obsessed with rights.

All those interested in animals need to ask, then, where such love can come from. How can we learn to love animals? What would motivate such love? And all Christians likewise need to ask about the scope of Christian love. If God gave God's Son to die on the cross because God so loved the world, why do we think that God loves only us, and not the whole world?

Rights are utopian and legalistic. They lead only to more disputes and conflict, not to moral consensus and social peace. When people read slogans in vegetarian literature stating that "a rat is a pig is a dog is a boy," or "meat is murder," the animal rights movement looses public credibility. Hearts need to change more than the law, and people need to be realistic about their goals for animals. We need to read the Bible again, almost as if for the first time, for inspiration about how to develop a theological ethic that will give people the motivation and courage to transform their lives and, in that process, become kinder toward the animals. A biblical ethic of animals will promise hope, but it will also teach a much needed caution and patience on this difficult issue.

3

The Once
and Future Peace

■ I once led an adult Sunday school class on one of my pet topics, the Bible and vegetarianism, and the minister was taken aback when I pointed out that Adam and Eve were vegetarians. He insisted that I must be mistaken. Maybe I should have been surprised by his reaction, but I was not. Why is it that most Christians, including many clergy, do not know what the Bible has to say about animals? Why is it that the Bible's vision of an original and eventual vegetarian world is almost completely absent in the church today?

■ A Different Time

Many ancient religions imagined an original time when everything was perfect, a time that was much better than the present. The ancient Greek poet Hesiod, for example, in his *Works and Days,* portrayed a Golden Age when the first race of humans lived like the gods. They did not have to work and they did not grow old.

Food was bountiful, there for the taking. When Hesiod looked at his contemporaries and thought about the current age, the Iron Age, he saw a world that was full of suffering, hardship, and war. Life had become a struggle, so that people now killed for their food. A carnivorous diet was one indication of the declining fortunes of the human race.

Religions often teach that people used to be much happier and better off than they are now. Mircea Eliade, the great historian of religion, has argued that primordial religious traditions are inherently nostalgic about returning to such mythic beginnings. The point of archaic religions is to recreate ritually the origin of the cosmos and thus to escape the relentless march of history. Time is the enemy because history is terrifying: through time things change, decay, and vanish. Time brings destruction and death, but time can be vanquished by returning to the eternal past, which is ever the same.

One way that ancient mythology expresses a longing for a more innocent time is through stories about people who were raised by animals in a natural state, completely separated from society. *The Epic of Gilgamesh,* a heroic poem written in the Middle East around 2000 B.C.E., offers us the example of Enkidu, a wild man who is at one with the animals, eating a vegetarian diet of grass, until he is initiated into the human world by Shamhat, the temple girl, and by Gilgamesh, who takes him along on a violent adventure to prove their valor. The point of story is that the hard task of becoming human involves giving up the instincts of the animal world in order to join with a woman and fight like a man. When Enkidu returns momentarily to his fellow beasts, the animals no longer recognize him, and he can no longer keep up with them because he has grown soft.

Christianity, by contrast, is an historical religion, a trait it inherited from Judaism. This means that it takes time seriously as a creation of God that humans cannot obliterate or negate. Significantly, there is little nostalgia in the Bible for the initial paradise of Eden. The garden is gone and there is no turning back. Being a Christian does not mean trying to recover a bygone era. Instead, the Garden of Eden functions as a forward-looking story, not a sentimental myth about how things used to be better than they are now. The story of the Garden of Eden shows us God's original intentions for the world, intentions that God is working toward by moving through history, not by bypassing time altogether. Time thus has a direction and goal. The rhythm of the Christian experience of time is structured more by anticipation than remorse. The Garden of Eden cannot be recaptured, but it does function as a clue for what God is doing now, where God is going, and what will happen at the end of time.

The Eden story, then, is not about a time when human consciousness was completely submerged in the natural world. Although Adam is created on the same day as the land animals, he is not portrayed as exactly like them. And while Eve is given to him as a companion in one version of the story, Adam is not reluctant to separate himself from the animals or anxious to return to them. And even though Adam and Eve are expelled from the garden, Adam does not need to go on a grueling journey in order to prove himself as a man. The message of Genesis is that the world is originally ordered as a peaceful kingdom, where humans and animals both know their place, although their respective places are quite different.

The peacefulness of the Garden of Eden story is even more striking when compared to other creation stories of the ancient world. In the Babylonian creation epic, the *Enuma Elish,* the origin of all things lies in violence, not peace. Apsu and Tiamat are the founding gods, and they are jealous of the younger gods. Apsu sets out to kill them, but he is killed first before he can act. Tiamat, in a rage, tries to seek revenge, and only Marduk can stop her. The price of his victory is that he will rule over all the other gods. Marduk then creates the world out of the remains of Tiamat's body. The message of the myth is that chaos can only be ordered through a struggle that involves the violent imposition of a hierarchical rule.

Some scholars have argued that Yahweh is not as different from Marduk as theologians have wanted to maintain. After all, in some biblical passages Yahweh wrestles with sea monsters and struggles to create order out of chaos (see Psalm 74:13–14 and Isaiah 51:9–10). The idea that God creates out of nothing is a later interpretation of Genesis. The first reference to the idea that the creation in Genesis is *ex nihilo* is in 2 Maccabees 7:28. Nevertheless, the creation of the world as portrayed in Genesis does not involve any bloody sacrifice. Many ancient creation stories begin with the discovery of fire (which was essential for cooking meat), but there is no mention of fire in the Garden of Eden. There is no meat-eating in Eden not just because there is no cooking, but because God has given everything necessary for humans to flourish. The Bible begins, then, with peace and abundance: the most fundamental truth about God and God's relationship to the world, including us, is that God is peaceful, and God's way of working in the world is through the gift of blessing.

■ The First Vegetarians

Most critics of Christianity point to the Genesis story as the root of all of Christianity's problems. It justifies, these critics argue, the human exploitation of the earth. In contrast to Eastern religions and ancient traditions like those practiced by Native Americans, it sets humans apart from the world and thus treats nature as something to be used and not revered. Is this true?

What is unique about the Genesis creation story is that the world is both ordered and peaceful. Today we tend to think of freedom and peace as incompatible with authority and hierarchy. We can be free only where there is no intruding body of rules and regulations that we must follow. The Bible does not know this peculiarly modern conflict. In the Bible, true peace and freedom follow from, and only from, God's benevolent ordering of the world. To live outside of that order is to experience a violent chaos, not a liberating anarchy. God orders the world, however, not just so humans can benefit from it. The order of the world is for the benefit of the world as a whole. God's authority does not sanction every kind of human greed and ambition. Instead, the divine order commends a radical way of life that is in harmony with the entire cosmos.

The most fundamental sign of God's peaceful order is the description of Eden as a world without violence, so that nothing is killed in order to be eaten. In Genesis 1:29, we read, "God said, 'See, I have given you every plant yielding seed that is upon the face of all the earth, and every tree with seed in its fruit; you shall have them for food.'" Moreover, the very next verse makes it clear that animals too are to eat a vegetarian diet: "And to every beast of the earth, and to every bird of the air, and to everything that has the breath of life, I have given every green plant for food." What is most remarkable about these commandments is that they come *after* God has granted humans dominion over the animals. Obviously the kind of dominion God had in mind for us did not include killing and eating animals. As the great twentieth-century theologian Karl Barth has written, "Creation means peace—peace between the Creator and creatures, and peace among creatures themselves" (1958, p. 209). At the beginning of creation there is no sin, and thus there is no need for any life to be sacrificed for another.

Much has been made in biblical interpretation about the idea that humanity alone was created in the image of God. The idea of the image of God has frequently been interpreted as rationality or speech, both thought to be unique to humanity alone. Some infer from this the erroneous conclusion that humans alone are valued by God. To counter this conclusion, animal rights advocates sometimes argue that animals too can think and communicate. However, there is no indication in the Bible that the image of God has anything to do with rationality. More likely, it has to do with our *relationality.* Humans stand in a special relationship to God and to the other animals. Humans are called to stand above (but not against) nature in order to fulfill their special role in God's plan. The question is, what is that role?

A consensus in scholarship is emerging that the image of God means that humans are supposed to reflect and put into practice God's holiness. Humans are to be God's stewards of the good creation. What power we have has been delegated to us, and we should never act according to our own interests alone. Stewards in the ancient world were house slaves—those servants who were responsible for the management of the master's possessions. Even more than being servants, Christians believe that we are the children of God, heirs to all of God's blessings. This does not mean, however, that we can do whatever we want with God's creation. We are to exercise authority over the world in a way that would be pleasing to God.

For Christians, the concept of divine power and authority is most clearly defined and illustrated in the self-sacrificial life of Jesus Christ. But even in the first few pages of Genesis we can see what kind of authority God wants us to exercise. God sees all the works of God's hands and pronounces them good. Humans are a *primus inter pares* (first among equals) in relation to the animals, carrying out a commission that is not of our own making. As Karl Barth has written, "Man is not their Creator; hence he cannot be their

absolute lord, a second God" (1958, p. 187). The divinely commis-
sioned power that we have over the world, then, is not the power
to destroy. Instead, we are meant to celebrate, enjoy, and take care
of what God has made.

Perhaps the key passage in Genesis concerning human stewardship of animals is the story of Adam naming the animals:

> Then the Lord God said, "It is not good that the man should be alone;
> I will make him a helper as his partner." So out of the ground the
> Lord God formed every animal of the field and every bird of the air,
> and brought them to the man to see what he would call them; and
> whatever the man called every living creature, that was its name.
> The man gave names to all cattle, and to the birds of the air, and to
> every animal of the field; but for the man there was not found a
> helper as his partner (2:18–20).

It is not clear from this story whether Adam's naming of the animals was more akin to what we would call species, or whether he
named them individually. What is clear is that Adam named the
animals as the first act of husbandry in the exercise of humane
authority. Notice that when Adam names the animals, he is without any other companionship (this is before the creation of Eve),
and so this story is about both the importance and the limitations
of human-animal friendship. Some rabbinic commentators suggest
that this story shows that the animals were the first companions
of man. This is hardly an absurd thought, because the Judean
farmer would have spent a lot of time with his animals. We forget
today just how intimately humans and animals shared their lives
in the ancient world.

Sometimes people today read this story as an example of human
power over the animals, but the act of naming in the Bible ordinarily suggests a close and caring relationship. Today, as in the
ancient world, we only name those to whom we are closely related
and responsible. In the Bible, identity and destiny are often connected to one's name, because family ties and one's rootedness
in the past are so crucial. Name changes, for example, are symbolic of a change in one's life, such as a new relationship with God.
In Judaism, the naming of a baby boy at a circumcision ceremony
is a sacred event. Naming is never associated in the Bible with
control and domination. That Adam named the animals is evidence

of how much affection and responsibility he felt toward them. Animals are not meant to be a substitute for human companionship, but there is no denying that we have a powerful bond with animals, as represented by our ability to name them. Today, for example, we typically only eat animals that we have not named, and those animals that are a part of our household are given human names. In Eden, Adam named all the animals because all were a part of God's good creation and none were treated like meat.

There are other examples in Genesis of a close and caring relationship between humans and animals. Land animals are made on the same day as humans, which demonstrates their similarity to humanity; but they are also pronounced good independently of humans, which shows that they too are a focus of God's providential care. As biblical scholar Richard H. Lowery has pointed out, blessing (*barak* in Hebrew) refers to an affirmation of the intrinsic value of the other (p. 90). Karl Barth concurs: "A thing is blessed when it is authorized and empowered, with a definite promise of success, for one particular action as distinct from another which is also a possibility" (1958, p. 170). The blessing that God gives to humans in Genesis 1:28, to be fruitful and multiply, is the same blessing that God gives the animals—the power of fertility and reproduction. Because of that fertility and abundance, we are in the position to benefit from creation, but we are to accept God's generosity with the proper display of gratitude. Gratitude means receiving a gift in the spirit in which it was given, and thus not abusing something that was not originally ours to keep.

There is language about dominion in Genesis, and some scholars argue that it is meant to remind the Israelites that they are not to idolize or worship the earth. Nothing in the world is as important as God. Moreover, if the creation account became important to the Israelites during the exile, as many scholars contend, then the emphasis on subduing the land was probably meant to encourage the Israelites to return to their land, which was rightfully theirs. But it is significant that humanity is not authorized to treat the land in any way that would contradict God's own intentions for the world. The message of the story is that the Israelites can use the land as long as they do not violate the original harmony of paradise.

Perhaps what is most remarkable about the Old Testament is what it does not say about animals. Animals are not, as they are in

65

much New Age literature, magical creatures, full of symbolic or real power. Indeed, compared to other literature from the ancient world, the Bible demythologizes the world of animals. Animals are neither divine nor demonic. They do not magically interfere with human affairs. In a word, the Bible is realistic about animals, not romantic or superstitious. Part of that realism is accepting the similarities of human and animal life. When Genesis uses the phrase "all flesh" (*kol basar*), for example (Genesis 6:12, 13, 9:11, 17), the Bible joins humans and animals together in a basic kinship that recognizes their common origin in God's generous creativity.

Of course, what Christians call "the fall" changed everything. One of the chief symbols of the fall is the disharmony that resulted between humans and animals, as represented by the enmity between the woman and the serpent. After their expulsion from the garden, Adam and Eve had to work hard for their food because God cursed the ground and it became full of thorns and thistle. Getting enough to eat became a daily chore, and humans had to depend increasingly on animals for clothing and food. Abel thus brought a sheep from his flock as an offering to God. Vegetarianism, however, was still the diet of the day. Thus God reiterates to Adam, "You shall eat the plants of the field" (Genesis 3:18). Even in a world of sin, God still expects Adam to follow a peaceful diet. Sin, then, is no excuse for the lust for animal flesh.

■ The Question of the Coats of Skin

After the fall, clothing was needed. In Genesis 3:21, God makes coats (tunics or garments) of skin for Adam and Eve, an incident that is often used against defenders of animals by suggesting that God's action legitimates hunting. This passage, though, can be interpreted in different ways. Origen, the great Alexandrian theologian who lived from about 185 to about 254, evidently thought that Adam and Eve were originally like the angels, that is, they were without bodies, so that only after the fall did they become embodied, their souls wrapped in flesh. The fall thus consists of a second creation, where the spiritual world becomes mired in matter. The full image of God can be restored to humanity only when bodies are cast off and human souls in all their bareness are reunited with God. Skin is thus made necessary by sin, but salvation will unite us with God in a way that will make our bodies obsolete.

Orthodox theologians rejected Origen's account of this passage because it belittled the very flesh in which Jesus Christ became incarnate. Some theologians, however, did partially follow Origen by interpreting these tunics to mean the animal nature of humanity. Humans now became corporeal in a more distinct way, they argued, encumbered by the ways of the flesh. The body is now subjected to pain, disease, hunger, and all kinds of unruly desires. Adam and Eve had skin before the fall, but after the fall their flesh became a burden to them. They felt their flesh as a weight that made them mortal and as a means for every kind of temptation, and this punishment is symbolized by the story of God making coats of skin.

The more common interpretation is to see this as a sign of the beginning of enmity between humans and animals. Humans now will hunt animals and use their skin for clothing. The text, however, does not say this. It is God, not Adam and Eve, who obtains the garment of skin, and there is no hunting at this point in the narrative. Does that mean that this story is about a change in God's attitude toward non-human animals? Does God now slaughter some animals in order to provide clothing for humans? Earlier, in Genesis 3:7, Adam and Eve became aware of their nakedness and "sewed fig leaves together" for loincloths. Were Adam and Eve more sensitive about using animals for clothing than God? Some commentators note that the coats could have come from the skin of a creature who was found dead. Such literalism, however, is probably inappropriate for the symbolic nature of this story. The author of Genesis wanted to demonstrate how God provides us with what we need, even at our lowest point. He did this by drawing from the customs of his culture in order to fill out the details of his portrait of God's blessings. Those customs would have included using animal skins for clothing.

The fact is that coats of skin does not necessarily mean animal skins. The Bible is full of metaphors, and this could very well be an expression meaning nothing more than clothing as a second skin (see, for example, Job 10:11). God gave humans protective wear that functioned as another layer of skin because they needed it, having been expelled from Eden and into a harsh and unfriendly environment. They needed to develop, as we would say today, a "thicker skin" in order to survive. God gave Adam and Eve tunics to remind them of their sin and their shame—as well as to shield them from their vulnerability to the severe weather of a fallen world. "Mostly by default," theologian J. R. Hyland laments, "scholars have allowed the unsubstantiated, popular interpretation of the event to prevail. They have allowed this because they, like most people, think animals are expendable" (1998, p. 14). To read this passage in the light of God's compassion for all living beings is to realize that there is no need to jump to the conclusion that God was the first hunter and killer of animals. As Hyland argues, to attribute to God the cruelty that characterizes human nature is nothing short of blasphemy.

◼ Noah, the Flood, and God's Promise for the Animals

The fall was not a one time event. Defying God's expectations, things continued to get worse, until the deterioration of the situation climaxed with Noah and the flood, one of the most engaging and memorable stories in all of biblical literature. The story is too good for only one culture to have told, and in fact, this story was widely disseminated in the ancient world. Scholars used to think that it originated in Mesopotamia, in what is now Iraq, where torrential rain and the melting of the snow in the spring could lead to the flooding of the Tigris and the Euphrates. The Babylonians passed their story onto the Canaanites, Greeks, and Romans. A more recent theory suggests another source. About seven thousand years ago the Mediterranean Sea broke through a land channel to flood what was then a smaller freshwater lake. A cataclysmic event thus suddenly put a vast amount of land underwater, creating the Black Sea. Whatever its origins, the flood story spread so widely because it was a dramatic way of talking about the relationship between God and the world while taking into account the moral decline and depravity that ancient people lamented as much as we do today.

Interestingly, in the Mesopotamian version of the story, the destruction is a result of the impatience and jealousy of the gods. The gods themselves bring disorder to the world by fighting among themselves and with humans. The biblical God, Yahweh, on the other hand, acts as a righteous judge who is outraged by the widespread violation of the divine will. The biblical God does not compete with humans, but Yahweh is disappointed that humanity cannot live up to the original ideals of Eden.

Most scholars now think that the Hebrew version of the story was probably written sometime between 550 and 450 B.C.E., during the period of the Babylonian exile, when Nebuchadnezzar occupied Jerusalem, Solomon's Temple was destroyed, and the Davidic monarchy ruined. The world of the Hebrews had fallen apart, and this story spoke to that collapse of order. The flood represented the chaos of the Babylonian invasion, and Noah and his family symbolized the hope that a small remnant of righteous Israelites could survive the turmoil.

The details of this biblical story are important, although most people today know it only in its barest outline. Ten generations after Adam, humans had become very wicked. According to the New Testament, part of that wickedness had to do with what humans were eating (Luke 17:27). Indeed, both Jewish and Christian commentaries on this text often connect human sin with unrestrained gluttony and ruthless feasting on animals. The depravity, however, was not limited to the human species. Animals too became corrupt in their ways (Genesis 6:12). What this means precisely we do not know, but ancient authors speculated that animals and humans alike were behaving in all sorts of promiscuous and deviant ways. It seems that animals had become carnivorous, fighting each other, and humans were imitating them in their thirst for blood.

Clearly, God had expectations for humans and animals alike that were not being met. God was able to find only one righteous man, and God instructed him to build a wooden ark. He took his family into the ark, as well as a pair of every kind of bird, mammal, and reptile. The flood God sent destroyed all flesh, demonstrating that God held the animals accountable for their behavior no less than the humans.

The Noah story is really a second creation story. God wants to start all over when God becomes disgusted with the way the world has developed, and so God sends the flood. Animals and humans had violated the order of the world, so that the earth itself was defiled and needed to be ritually purged and cleansed (Simkins, p. 202). Things were so bad that only through destruction could the world be recreated.

In the postdiluvian era God wants to start things off in the right way, so God promises never again to cause such a cataclysm. To inaugurate this new world, God establishes a covenant with Noah and his descendants. This covenant provides a foundation for all other covenants in the Bible. Indeed, Jewish tradition interprets this covenant as an obligation on all of humanity, since it is prior to the more specific Mosaic covenant that God makes with Israel at Sinai. The sign of this covenant is the rainbow, which is given as a means of reminding God about the divine promise. "When the bow is in the clouds, I will see it and remember the everlasting covenant between God and every living creature of all flesh that is on the earth" (9:16). Since hanging up a bow signifies a warrior's retirement from battle, the rainbow was an appropriate symbol for God's decision to no longer wage war against creation.

Not only does the Noachian covenant apply to all people, but it also applies to all animals. It is literally universal, since it encompasses the whole world. In fact, God clearly states that God will never again destroy every living creature (Genesis 8:21). This promise is repeated again in 9:8–11, where God clearly includes animals in the divine promise of peace. The story emphasizes the fact that God's promise includes the animals so repeatedly that one can only wonder why it is so often overlooked. To this new Adam, Noah, and to all creatures, God also repeats the command to be fruitful and to multiply, a command originally given to Adam and Eve and the animals in the garden.

God also acknowledges that the animals will fear humans, which seems more like a mournful description of a world still fallen than a benefit given to humanity. God seems resigned to the fallen state of nature. "For your own lifeblood I will surely require a reckoning: from every animal I will require it and from human beings, each one for the blood of another, I will require a reckoning for human life" (9:5). Here God treats animals as responsible partners in the covenant who can be punished for the act of homicide. Humans, however, with their greater level of responsibility, are to be held especially accountable for their acts of violence. God is trying to deal with the human thirst for violence and blood by subjecting the taking of life to the rule of law, because God realizes that the flood has changed very little about human nature. Rather than threatening complete destruction, God has devised a way to control human behavior. Humans may impose the death penalty as the ultimate sanction against the reckless disregard for life.

The death penalty was not the only thing that changed after the flood. While in the ark, Noah and his family were vegetarians. Only after they had saved the animals did God grant them permission to eat meat (9:3). This is the first time that God allows this practice in the book of Genesis. Such killing, however, is not unregulated. Meat-eating is allowed only when the animals have been properly killed, thus beginning the Old Testament's insistence on ritual sacrifice as a necessary prerequisite to meat-eating. At the heart of this ritual killing is the command that humans are not to consume the blood in the animals (9:4).

Ancient Jewish and Christian commentators have long puzzled over this very late permission for meat-eating in the Bible. Some see it as an emergency measure, since the flood would have destroyed most vegetation. Others suggest that God has lowered the divine standard of morality, accepting the fact that humans could not live up to the ideals of Eden. Yet others suggest that Noah, by his very act of stewardship, had won permission to eat the very animals he had saved.

Most scholars today argue that there are two different narrative traditions that have been brought together in this story, what they call the Yahwist and priestly sources. The Yahwist is the earlier source, and it does not include the permission to eat meat. The priestly source, which was written from the perspective of the later temple sacrifices, does include this permission, and many scholars see this as an attempt to legitimate the temple rituals.

Regardless of the historical composition of the text, the story is clear. Human dominion over the earth needs to be regulated. The spilling of blood must be ritualized and limited.

In fact, God's acceptance of meat-eating should be seen in the context of God's reluctant approval of the death penalty to stem the human tide of violence. God allowed both kinds of killing in order to keep a bad situation from getting worse. Both practices were an attempt to make humans more sensitive to and less eager for the spilling of blood.

The ban on consuming blood made sense in the ancient world because people believed that life resides in the blood, and Scripture taught that the life of animals belonged to God alone. After

Noah, then, a tradition began of draining animals of their blood and soaking meat to extract the blood, a tradition that Orthodox Jews continue to this day in their kosher laws and that Christians also followed for centuries (for evidence of this, see, for example, Eusebius, *Ecclesiastical History,* 5.1.25–6 in Schaff, p. 214).

What should be clear from the story is that this permission to eat meat is neither a divine commandment ("Thou shalt eat meat!") nor a permanent moral law ("Meat-eating is forever and everywhere acceptable"). Instead, God's change of heart about meat-eating is clearly portrayed as a concession to human sinfulness and to the hardness of our hearts. The divine ideal has not changed; God's claims on us are eternal. But how God works through history to achieve those ideals involves a lot of detours. The permission to eat meat is an example of how God deals with us as we are, not the way we should be. Furthermore, the fact that God does not allow the consumption of blood demonstrates how God was trying to restrict and constrain meat-eating, just as God sanctioned capital punishment as a means of deterring murder. God did not want humans to satisfy their thirst for blood through violence or diet.

The closest parallel to this kind of divine concession can be found in 1 Samuel 8, where the people of Israel demand a king. God is not happy with their request, because the desire for a king is tantamount to a rejection of God, who should be a sufficient King for the people. Samuel tries to warn the people about the dangers of kings—their burdensome taxes, vicious armies, and indiscriminate power. The people, however, insist, and so God, against God's better judgment, finally relents and lets Samuel appoint a king. God knew what was best for God's people, but God also is realistic about moral progress and human development. The lesson here is that, for better or worse, we are God's agents in history, so God chooses to work with us to achieve the divine aim.

Jewish tradition honors Noah's compassion for the animals by granting him the honorary title of a *zaddik,* that is, "one who practices charity." In the Christian tradition it was long popular to interpret the story of Noah's ark allegorically. Many early Christians believed they lived in the end times, when fire would soon destroy the earth. Noah was seen as a precursor of John the Baptist, warning everyone of the coming end (although in the biblical story Noah does not preach). Other early Christian writers even saw

Noah as a prototype of Jesus Christ. His emergence from the ark was seen as a parallel to Jesus' resurrection from the tomb. Some even suggested that the wood of the ark prefigures the cross, the flood represents the baptismal waters (just as the flood destroyed all flesh, the waters of baptism destroy the penitent's fleshly desires), and the ark itself symbolizes the church, because both the ark and the church save those who hold fast to God. These allegorical readings of the story are instructive, but they should not distract us from a more literal reading of its moral message. It is unlikely that God calls us to save all the animals; that was Noah's special mission. But we can at least try not to destroy the animals in wanton ways, just as God promised both humans and animals not to destroy them again. After all, this story is a graphic illustration of the fact that we, humans and animals, are all in the same boat.

■ The Mosaic Covenant and Humanity's Obligation to the Animals

The promises God made to Noah were meant for all people and all of creation. God made more specific promises to, and had higher standards for, his chosen people, the Israelites. The covenant between God and the Israelites is an attempt to restore the fallen world to God's original intentions. The Mosaic covenant spells out humanity's duties toward the world—obligations based on the shared origin and destiny of all created life. The central tenet of the covenant is the honor given to a day of rest, the Sabbath, which was a weekly reminder that the world is a good place and that God created the world for delight, enjoyment, and peace. Significantly, the Sabbath regulations were meant to apply to animals as well as humans. The fourth commandment, for example, forbids all work on the Sabbath, including the work of cattle (Exodus 20:10). Jewish law allows for exceptions to this, especially when a human or animal life is at stake. Exodus 23:10–11 requires the Hebrews to let the land lie fallow in the seventh year, so that the poor may use it. What they leave behind is for the wild animals, so that humans even have a responsibility for them. The point is that the seventh day, the seventh year, and the Jubilee (the fiftieth year) were set aside to encourage the Israelites to correct their relationships with each other and with the animal world. The New Testament uses the theme of the Sabbath when Jesus announces the coming of a new kingdom, where righteousness will be restored.

The Mosaic covenant with Israel is full of commandments concerning the treatment of animals. An ox and an ass are not to be yoked together, since the differences between the two would put a strain on the weaker of the pair (Deuteronomy 22:10). Mother cattle are not to be slaughtered on the same day as their young, which would cause added anxiety to the mother (Leviticus 22:28). Israelites were obligated to help another person's donkey that had fallen under too heavy a load (Exodus 23:4–5; Deuteronomy 22:1–4). From rules such as this the rabbis derived the concept of *tsaar baalei hayyim,* which means doing nothing that will contribute to the pain of living creatures. The Old Testament thus recognizes that we have specific duties and obligations to animals, based on their status as being created, sustained, and loved by the same God who made us.

Perhaps these duties are best illustrated not in the rules of the covenant but in the stories that the Hebrews liked to tell about animals. One of the most poignant is the story the prophet Nathan told to King David in order to rebuke him. It concerns a poor man's pet lamb. "It used to eat of his meager fare, and drink from his cup, and lie on his bosom, and it was like a daughter to him" (2 Samuel 12:3). The lamb is stolen and slaughtered by a rich man, which prompted David to reply, "As the Lord lives, the man who has done this deserves to die; he shall restore [that is, pay for] the lamb fourfold, because he did this thing, and because he had no pity" (12:5–6). Sheep were very important to the Israelites, and they were often treated like pets. In fact, the rabbis tell the story that it was only after Moses tracked down a runaway lamb and, finding it exhausted, carried it back to the flock, that God chose him to lead the people. God said to Moses, "Thou hast compassion with a flock belonging to a man of flesh and blood [the flock belonged to Jethro, his father-in-law]! As thou livest, thou shall pasture Israel, My flock" (Ginzberg, vol. 2, p. 301). The Israelites were like sheep to God, and God wanted their leader to have all the qualities of a good shepherd. This is one of the origins of the idea that those closest to God should also be closest to the animals.

■ Manna in the Wilderness

The great event in God's relationship with the Israelites is their liberation from Egypt. After fleeing Egypt, the Hebrews wandered in the wilderness for forty years, awaiting permission to enter the promised land. During their journey they were given manna to eat, a vegetarian bread that looked like coriander seed, according to Numbers 11:7. This bread is the ultimate symbol of the abundance of God's blessing. Nobody had to struggle to eat because no matter how much the Israelites gathered, everybody had enough (Exodus 16:17–18). Some of them, however, grew tired of this monotonous diet, and they longed for the fleshpots of Egypt. "If only we had meat to eat!" some exclaimed (Numbers 11:4). They even complained about their lack of strength on this diet, a rationale meat-eaters to this day offer when pressed about their diet. Now we know that muscles are built through exercise and protein that can come from a variety of sources, but this superstition persists.

In response to such gluttony, God angrily relented and gave them enough quail to eat for a month. The abundance of quail is God's ironic comment on their rejection of the abundance of manna. God gave them so much quail that they should eat, God said, "until it comes out of your nostrils and becomes loathsome to you" (11:20). Later, God strikes the ungrateful people with a plague, so that they had to bury "the people who had the craving" (11:34). The place where they were buried is called the graves of greed. Gluttony was the inevitable human response to God's request for a simple vegetarian diet.

The moral of the story is clear. Although God gives us plenty to eat so that we do not need to kill animals, gluttony is a persistent and pernicious symptom of human sin. God is willing to accommodate our carnivorous diet, but not without a price. Our excessive meat-eating will be its own punishment, something we are increasingly seeing as more and more people die of heart disease and other maladies due, in part, to a meat-concentrated diet. Indeed, the trivialization of the sin of gluttony is surely one of the reasons why Christians, according to a 1998 Purdue University study, are typically more overweight than other Americans (Mead, p. 50).

■ The Peaceful Message of the Prophets

The Israelites did not always obey the covenant, and so God inspired the prophets to bring them back in line. We often imagine the Hebrew prophets as preachers of doom and gloom, pronouncing judgment on Israel when God's chosen people strayed from the path of righteousness. This is only half the story of the prophets. The other half is that they continue and strengthen the Genesis emphasis on an original peace and blessing. When Deuteronomy 8:7–10 describes the ideal diet for the Hebrews, meat is excluded, and this vegetarian theme is picked up by the prophets. Indeed, we should see the promises and the judgments of the prophets as two sides to the same message. The people will prosper only if the land and the animals are treated well. When the last day comes, God will restore the whole earth to God's original blessing.

The prophets often connect the Mosaic covenant to the treatment of the land and animals. To fulfill the covenant meant to care for nature; to violate the covenant moved the Israelites closer and closer to both political and ecological disaster (see Deuteronomy 7:12–15). The righteous person is one who is right with even the wild animals: "At destruction and famine you shall laugh, and shall not fear the wild animals of the earth. For you shall be in league with the stones of the field, and the wild animals shall be at peace with you" (Job 5:22–23). The Israelites could maintain a right relationship with God only if they acted in a righteous manner toward the land and the animals.

Just as God made the world, God can allow it to become unmade if humanity neglects God's intentions. Hosea, when he criticized the people for their lack of faithfulness, concluded, "Therefore the land mourns, and all who live in it languish; together with the wild animals and the birds of the air, even the fish of the sea are perishing" (4:3). God delivers an ecological warning about the consequences of sin through Zephaniah: "I will sweep away humans and animals; I will sweep away the birds of the air and the fish of the sea" (1:3). Indeed, when Joel imagines the last days, he pictures most vividly the destruction of animals: "How the animals groan! The herds of cattle wander about because there is no pasture for them; even the flocks of sheep are dazed" (1:18). This theme is continued by the apostle Paul when he notes how the whole universe is frustrated and awaiting God's total redemption (Romans 8:19–22). The condition of animals is an indicator of God's displeasure with human behavior as well as the mystery of the unfolding of God's providential plan for the world.

When the prophets foretell the coming of the kingdom of God and the setting right of the world, they portray the restoration of harmony between people and animals. In an echo of the Noachian covenant, Hosea looks forward to the day when God will make "a covenant on behalf of Israel with the wild beasts, the birds of the air, and the things that creep on the earth, and I will break bow and sword and weapon of war and sweep them off the earth, so that all living creatures may lie down without fear" (2:18, NEB). Animals can only lie down without fear if vegetation takes the place of meat. As God proclaims through Amos, "I will restore the fortunes of my people Israel, and they shall rebuild the ruined cities and inhabit them; they shall plant vineyards and drink their wine, and they shall make gardens and eat their fruit" (9:14). And when God speaks to the Israelites in exile in Babylon, God tells them, "Build houses and live in them; plant gardens and eat what they produce" (Jeremiah 29:5). Isaiah continues the garden image, promising that, "The Lord will comfort Zion; he will comfort all her waste places, and will make her wilderness like Eden, her desert like the garden of the Lord" (51:3). Ezekiel also imagines a day when the wild animals will be banished from the earth, people will live in harmony with nature, and vegetation and fruit will be more than enough to eat (34:25–29).

A garden is a place where wild animals must be kept at bay, thus it is not the perfect image for the biblical vision of human-animal harmony. The prophets, however, imagined a garden where even the wild animals would be tame, so that none need be excluded. This is most famously stated in Isaiah 11:6–9:

> The wolf shall live with the lamb, the leopard shall lie down with the kid, the calf and the lion and the fatling together, and a little child shall lead them. The cow and the bear shall graze, their young shall lie down together; and the lion shall eat straw like the ox. The nursing child shall play over the hole of the asp, and the weaned child shall put its hand on the adder's den. They will not hurt or destroy on all my holy mountain; for the earth will be full of the knowledge of the Lord as the waters cover the sea.

Christians, of course, have long read this passage as an anticipation of Jesus Christ. If Adam and Eve were the first vegetarians,
then the destiny of all living creatures is to become the final vegetarians, and Christians believe that Jesus Christ, as the second
Adam, will lead the way. Perhaps this is why Jesus went into the
wilderness to be with the wild animals (Mark 1:12–13) and the early
disciples handled and tamed snakes as a sign of their holiness
(Mark 16:18, Luke 10:19, Psalms 91:13). The power of God restores
nature to a peaceful order.

■ Does God Treat All Animals Like Pets?

Is it possible that all animals began as pets and that all animals
will one day return to that blessed state? Will the end be like the
beginning? Will animals and people someday live peacefully
together, in an ordered community, so that our domestication of
some animals anticipates in a fundamental way the fate and destiny of all animals?

We live in a fallen world, where the animals have turned against
us and each other as much as we have turned against them, so we
cannot base our moral decisions on what is presently the case. We
must look to the past to see God's original intentions for the world
and to the future to see where God is directing the world. But God's
grace also sustains us in the present, and it extends to those domesticated animals that so intimately share our lives and draw us into
relationships of obligation and mutual responsibility.

Every approach to the ethical issue of animals has a picture of what
kind of animal is the paradigmatic animal. Environmentalists value
wild animals above domesticated animals because wild animals represent freedom and spontaneity. Environmentalists and animal rights
activists alike see human power over nature in largely negative terms,
so it is natural that they idealize those animals who are not under
human control. Consequently, they often see domesticated animals
as nothing more than the product of human manipulation and greed.
They are degenerate versions of their wild cousins. In practical terms,
this prioritization of animal types determines what issues an animal
rights group will be most interested in. Thus, for many environmental groups, it is more important to work for the protection of wild
species than the welfare of domesticated animals.

These groups do not consider that the most recent genetic research demonstrates that domestication is a process as old as humanity itself, and that some animals have benefited from this process. The dog, for example, voluntarily gave up its life in the wild to join the circle of human companionship, adding its skills to those necessary for human survival. The dog used its social skills of adaptation to take advantage of our need for companionship. In return, the dog is treated like an honorary member of the human family. As animal behaviorist Konrad Lorenz has written, "The fidelity of a dog is a precious gift demanding no less binding moral responsibilities than the friendship of a human being. The bond with a true dog is as lasting as the ties of this earth can ever be" (p. 139). It seems appropriate, then, that, according to rabbinic Midrash, the sign that God gave Cain to protect him from the consequences of his murder was a dog, who accompanied him as he wandered the earth (Ginzberg, vol. 1, p. 112).

Farm animals too are brought under human care and out of the wild, even though they must work for their food and shelter. At their best, these relationships provide for a mutual benefit. Both humans and animals enter into a kind of covenant, where animals will be treated well precisely because they are so important to human existence. Only in modern times, with the rise of industrialized agriculture, has this contract been widely discarded.

It is my argument that the Bible presents a picture of animals that privileges the role of domesticated animals, especially pets, as the paradigm of what all animals once were and what they all will become again. The first-century Jewish philosopher Philo, for example, longed for the day when all wild animals would become tame, growing "gentle in emulation of the docility and affection for the master [humankind], like little Maltese lapdogs who fawn with their tails, which they cheerfully wag" (Winston, p. 295). Pets are a kind of parable about the potential for mutual transformation when humans encounter that which is so utterly different and yet so similar to themselves.

The fullness of humanity includes the exercise of a proper authority over the animals. As Irenaeus taught, "It is right that when the creation is restored, all the animals should obey and be in subjection to man, and revert to the food originally given by God (for they have been originally subjected in obedience to Adam), that is, the production of the earth" (Roberts, vol. 1, p. 563). Community stands at the beginning and end of history, shaped by God's own communal life in the Trinity, and that community is all-encompassing. The human-animal relationship, then, is natural. Of course, that relationship is as full of abuse and manipulation as any other human endeavor. Nevertheless, we are meant to keep the company of animals, who are a gift from God to ease our loneliness by drawing us out of the human circle and into an experience of otherness that is so surprising as to be utterly sublime.

One of my favorite passages in the Bible is Psalm 104:25–26. In celebrating the sea as the great creation of God, the Psalmist sings, "Here is the great immeasurable sea, in which move creatures beyond number. Here ships sail to and fro, here is Leviathan whom thou hast made thy plaything" (NEB). God plays with the sea monsters. This is not meant merely to show the power of God, although it certainly does demonstrate that. God can toy with a wild sea monster who, for us, symbolizes the unruly and chaotic sea. It is also meant to show God's mercy, God's tender lovingkindness. Even the most powerful monster is tenderly cared for by God. Even the leviathan is one of God's pets! According to the Babylonian Talmud, God spends the last part of every day playing with the leviathan (Neusner, p. 221). It is a deeply moving picture of God as one who, like us, wants companionship in the form of pets. God, then, takes pleasure in God's creation. No animal is meant to be turned against the order of the world. All animals, even the most wild, are really tame and mild when considered in relationship to God.

Tamed animals are thus the original form of all animals. Domesticating animals is not a matter of imposing some alien human influence on that which is wild and free. Instead, it is a matter of bringing the wild back into an ordered relationship. Obviously we cannot and should not try to domesticate all of the animals of the world. But we must take responsibility for all of the animals, because whether we like it or not we are becoming the managers of the wild as the human population continues to grow and the wilderness continues to shrink. The idea of animals being subordinated to humans, in a relationship of mutual trust and benefit, is not only the origin but also the destiny of the animal kingdom.

There are several practical implications of the fact that the Bible views human-animal relationships as natural and, at least potentially, mutually beneficial. First, we should not pretend that we can put big chunks of nature out of human reach. Whether we like it or not, we have been granted enormous responsibility over nature, and thus all animals, in a way, are our pets. We have the power to influence animals throughout the world, so that we must take responsibility for them. Even when we reintroduce wolves into a specified area, we give them tags and names and track their movements. Inexorably, we are moving in the direction of ever closer relations between humans and animals. God's intention for the world is for all creatures to exist in relationship with each other, not in isolation or in competition.

Second, we should not take our moral principles from the wild. Nature is sublime, and it reminds us of how small we are in the cosmos. Nature can be a symbol of God's infinity and omnipotence. However, nature is fallen, and untamed nature cannot be the source of our deepest spiritual needs. We can save what we can from nature, but we cannot save ourselves by trying to find consolation in a nature stripped of all bloodshed.

Third, zoos are often a target of criticism and attack by animal rights activists; but zoos, when well run, can be a reminder of the intimate bond between humans and animals and our obligations to protect endangered species. The best zoos can be modern-day arks, saving animals from the inevitable expansion of the human population, and thus they should be supported for this service.

Fourth, we should devote as much of our efforts as we possibly can to domesticated animals, to the terrible overpopulation of dogs and cats and the wretched conditions in which most farm animals live, as well as the brutal ways in which they are frequently killed. These are the animals that have entered into a covenant with us, only to be betrayed by greed and neglect. If pets are in many ways the paradigmatic animal, the living example of the harmony toward which God is working in history, then our treatment of all animals should follow what I call the Dog Rule of animal compassion: Never do unto any other animal what you would not want done to your own dog. To treat the entire animal world as an extension of God's grace would result in dramatic transformations of every aspect of our behavior, not least of which would be what we choose to eat.

4

Did God Want Animal Sacrifices?

■ The writers of Genesis reflect what must have been a troublesome tension in the theology of the Israelites. They relied on animals for food, clothing, tents, wineskins, tools, and protection (see Borowski). Given their dependence on animals, how else but through revelation could they have had a vision of a vegetarian paradise that would one day become the norm for the whole world? The Israelites also relied on the ritual killing of animals to worship God. Indeed, the Bible confirms archeological evidence that animal sacrifices are almost as old as civilization itself. The Bible traces them back to Abel, Abraham, and Noah, before the rules for how to perform them were given to Moses. Yet it is clear that Yahweh, the Hebrew God who transcends the world and has no competitors, did not need to be fed or appeased like the pagan gods. Why, then, the long tradition of animal sacrifices? Did God need bloodshed to be God? Does God undergo a change of heart from the days of Eden to the time of Noah and Moses?

To answer these questions, we need to put animal sacrifices in a broad context in order to distinguish Hebrew from pagan rituals. Animal sacrifices are often all grouped into the same category and dismissed as barbaric and primitive, even though the way we treat animals now is hardly any better. True, we talk about making sacrifices all the time today, but the reality of sacrifice in the ancient world was totally different. Today, making a sacrifice means putting moral effort into something that does not come naturally. We give up some selfish pleasure in order to do the right thing. In the ancient world, it was animals that were given up in order to satisfy the gods and to create a law-abiding community. Nonanimal food could be used in sacrifices, but it was animals that held the highest place of honor at the altar. Most temples had dining areas so that the feast could be an integral part of the ceremony, and meat could also be taken home or sold on the markets. If fast food restaurants and meat are inseparable today, so that when you think of one you think of the other, in the ancient world the same could be said of temples and meat. Quite frequently in the ancient world people would not have eaten meat in any other context than a ritual sacrifice.

The dramatic slaying of an animal, with all the right words and gestures, was the highest form of religious worship. What could be more exciting? People gathered around the fire and the priestly leaders of the tribe chanted the ancient hymns, drowning out the cries of the animal as everyone eagerly anticipated the feast that would follow. Such rituals functioned to unite the group and to pass on the sacred stories. They also served to establish hierarchical and gender rankings by making the priests, an all-male caste, crucial for the maintenance of cosmic order. Sacrifices were thus political as much as they were religious. Consequently, rejecting animal sacrifices in the ancient world was tantamount to treason. To eat food other than the cuisine of sacrifice, meat and wine, put you outside the law, literally making you an outlaw. Why was the shedding of animal blood so crucial for social solidarity, and how could that be so pleasing to God?

■ Saved by the Blood

Scholars love to speculate as to why animal sacrifice was the universal ritual of all ancient religions. On the face of it, it is not clear why killing animals should become such a fundamental aspect of the most primordial religious traditions. Some scholars think these rituals began as a way of negotiating the first steps humans took to distance themselves from the animal world. Humans and animals are, after all, very much alike. If humans were going to treat each other differently from the way they treated animals, they needed to establish a clear line separating humans from animals so that humans could eat them and not each other. They needed a way of saying that the killing of animals was justified, even necessary, and that such killing was very different from the taking of a human life.

Just try to imagine the first hunters who took an animal's life. They must have been unnerved by the experience of it, the terror of the chase and the bloody climax of the animal's death. Classicist Walter Burkert has hypothesized that the ritualized slaughter of animals began in such anxious experiences. After all, primitive societies could exist only by making the spilling of blood taboo, and yet in the hunt, men gathered together to do precisely that. Hunting an animal must have seemed disquietingly similar to hunting other people, so the killing of animals had to be set apart from the ordinarily prohibited spilling of blood. Animal killing had to be conducted according to strict rules in order to control the violence that could erupt with the spilling (and consuming) of blood.

One fascinating theory about sacrifices is that they were a way of making the animal sacred and thus justifying the eating of meat. Sacrifices turn a violent activity into a holy one. The spirit of the animal returns to sacred earth through the spilling of blood, which demonstrates that all living beings are connected together and belong to each other. Thus, the revelry of the feast is a way of putting into practice the theology of pantheism, where there are no absolute boundaries and the spirit of life spills from one life form into another.

Ancient peoples who thought of animals as being divine took care in killing animals. They wanted to appease the spirit that had made its home in that animal. The animal victim was to be treated with reverence and even thanked for offering its life to the hunters. Some Native American tribes, for example, would place something to eat by the mouth of a slain deer in order to feed its spirit as it passed onto the next life (see Harrod).

Ironically, many New Age vegetarians assume that thinking about animals as god-like will insure that no one will eat them, but in the ancient world just the opposite was the case. Ancient cultures believed that animals were a part of the divine, and for precisely that reason they were eaten—in order to partake of divine energy and substance. Turning animals into gods is thus no guarantee that people will avoid eating meat. The Christian position, which treats animals as distinctive beings who are less than humanity and yet more than mere matter, is both a more realistic and a more affirming way of looking at animals.

Some scholars today are not so sympathetic to ancient religious practices. They suggest that sacrificial ritual is an elaborate scheme of blame-shifting. The animal that is sacrificed is portrayed as a willing volunteer, eager to undergo the sacrificial ordeal. The priests who do the killing are thus cleansed of any guilt by the excuse that they are doing the will of the gods and that the animal is a willing participant. Indeed, it is the gods who are really to be blamed, because they want the smell of the meat more than the humans. Thus, a bit of the flesh is thrown into the fire and blood spilled on the ground as a way of placating the appetite of the gods, who demand to be fed. The gods are satisfied with the smell of the roasting meat, but not the humans. The rest of the meat can be eaten because it is left over from the primary purpose of the feast, which is to keep the gods happy. This seems to be the theology behind the sacrifices of the ancient Greeks, for whom every meat meal began with a sacrifice. Homer's *Odyssey,* for example, is replete with sacrifices to the gods and the sharing of meat.

■ A Delicate Compromise

As primordial religions developed, animal sacrifice became the centerpiece of all communication with the divine. In pagan cultures, such sacrifices were a way of telling the future, appeasing the wrath of the gods, persuading the gods to act in a certain way, and even feeding the gods. Animal sacrifices were all about manipulation and control: people were afraid of the gods, and they wanted to do their best to please them. They thought that the smell of burnt flesh, wafting toward the heavens, would influence the gods to grant their wishes.

It is thus highly significant that, for Israel, animal sacrifices do none of these things. Israel no doubt adopted the practice of killing and eating animals as a religious ritual from its neighbors. We know through archeological evidence that animal sacrifices in Canaan long predate the time when Israel entered that land. For Israel, however, sacrifice is all about atonement and reconciliation, not bribery and appeasement. The sacrifices are not an attempt to predict or manipulate the divine will. They are made necessary by human sin, but they also emerge from human gratitude for all that God has provided. God accepts Israel's choice of using animal sacrifices as a form of prayer, but changes that ritual into a totally new system of religious worship. God does not take delight in the death of the animal. The point of the offering is not to inflict violence on a lowly creature but to treat all of God's creation with due respect, even in the midst of offering that life to God.

The history of animal sacrifices in Israel is long and complex. Early in the history of Israel there were many altars in various local shrines, so that every meat meal could begin with a ritual sacrifice. Gradually, however, the sacrifices were centralized in the Jerusalem temple, built by Solomon around 950 B.C.E. King Josiah forbade all sacrifices outside of this temple in 622 B.C.E. (recorded in 2 Kings 22–23). This edict made pilgrimages to Jerusalem an inherent part of the sacrifices. This consolidation also rendered the other shrines obsolete. The office of the priesthood, comprised of a hereditary class of ritual experts, became increasingly important.

After Josiah's reform it was necessary to develop the distinction between sacrificial and less ritualized forms of animal slaughter. This distinction is absent in the book of Leviticus. Indeed, Leviticus 17, written out of a priestly tradition, requires all animals to be brought to the tabernacle for sacrifice and forbids the killing of domestic animals apart from sacrifice. The consequence of violating this rule was tantamount to committing murder. But Deuteronomy tries to mitigate this priestly power. "Yet whenever you desire you may slaughter and eat meat within any of your towns, according to the blessing that the Lord God has given you" (Deuteronomy 12:15). Ritual slaughter, however, continued to be the model for the killing of all animals, an ideal to be followed as much as possible.

Animals were not the only offering made at the temple, of course, but nearly a quarter of the laws in the Torah—150 out of 613—do deal with animal sacrifice. The level of detail that Jewish law devotes to the killing of animals demonstrates how seriously they took the shedding of any blood. In nearly all animal sacrifices the owner would lay his hands on the animal before giving the animal over to the priests, an intimate gesture of identification and substitution. Generally speaking, the fat from the animal was burnt on the altar, parts of the animal were set aside for the priests, and the rest was returned to the person who brought it. The sobriety of the sacrifice, in addition to the burning of the fat and the draining of the blood, made the Israelite ritual quite different from the wanton celebrations of their pagan neighbors. Animals can sense the minds of humans, so a calm and solemn ceremony would have subdued and reassured them.

The rules governing the slaughter of animals include the distinction between clean and unclean animals (Leviticus 11–15). This distinction is part of the holiness code, which emphasizes the separation of Israel from its neighbors. There have been many debates about the precise meaning of these categories, but their consequences are clear. With only a few animals being recognized as clean, the meat-eating of the Israelites was severely restricted. Philo, the first century Jewish philosopher, argued that pork and scaleless water creatures were forbidden in order to restrain gluttony, precisely because they were so delicious. He also speculated that wild and carnivorous animals were forbidden to keep humans themselves from turning into beasts. Maimonides, the great medieval Jewish philosopher, agreed. The dietary code vastly limited the number of species that could serve as food, thus encouraging the reverence for life.

The sacrificial system came to an end with the destruction of the second temple in 70 C.E. The Jewish community now faced a momentous decision. If animals can no longer be properly sacrificed, can they be eaten at all? Jewish tradition, of course, did have rules for the proper slaughter of animals outside of the temple precinct, but some Jews took the end of the temple to imply the end of animal sacrifice altogether. This helps explain why the Passover meal, which originally included lamb, eventually excluded meat in recognition of the end of the sacrificial system.

To this day, in memory of the temple, orthodox Jews spend nine days every summer going without meat, culminating with the observance of Tisha Be'Av, the major fast day commemorating the destruction of both Jewish temples.

The end of the temple also meant the banishment of the Jews from Jerusalem and their scattering throughout the Roman Empire, a terrible disaster. In response to this, we know that some Jews became vegetarians because they could no longer enjoy eating meat while mourning the loss of their holiest place. The Babylonian Talmud, in the *Baba Batra* tractate (60b), records a debate among the rabbis about whether Jews should eat meat after the destruction of the second temple (see Bokser, pp. 196–7). Even if this debate was more literary than historical, it demonstrates the close connection between meat-eating and the temple. According to the Talmud, several important rabbis thought that eating meat without the sacrificial rituals of the temple was not permissible. Other rabbis thought that this put too heavy a burden on the people. Most of the rabbis were primarily concerned with the survival of the Jewish people, so they rejected dietary practices that they thought would have made that survival more difficult. Nevertheless, vegetarianism was carefully considered as an option all Jews should embrace.

The Jews mourned the loss of the temple, and rabbinical texts continued to discuss, with great attention to detail, the animal sacrifices. Nonetheless, in later Jewish writings, the temple became more heavenly than earthly, something the Jews hoped would be restored by an act of God. This trend in thinking about the temple as ideal actually began after the destruction of the first temple, and it only increased after the failed uprising against Rome. Interestingly, the ideal temple that was to descend from heaven is often portrayed without the animal sacrifices. "Given the prominence of Temple imagery in the Hebrew Bible, it seems odd that sacrifice, the main business of the earthly Temple, seldom appears in Jewish accounts of the heavenly one. Only late texts such as 3 Baruch (first century B.C.E.) and the Christian Book of Revelation refer to sacrifice in heaven, and then only as the offering of good works" (Russell, p. 31). In both Christianity and Judaism, the temple is increasingly identified with the whole people of God, and the language of sacrifice is equated with charity, prayer, penitence, and obedience.

In the diaspora, where Jews lived far removed from the temple rituals, the rabbis refined an oral tradition on animal killing and consumption that was eventually codified in the Talmud. These dietary laws, call *kashrut,* continued the humane emphasis of the temple practices. The temple priests were replaced by a ritual slaughterer, the *shochet,* who followed the slaughter rules known as *shechita.* These strict rules include specifications about the sharpness of the knife and the placement of the cut, all intended to minimize pain to the animal and to make death as quick as possible. The *shochet* is expected to be a morally righteous man with a blameless character, which is further evidence of how seriously Jewish tradition takes the death of an animal. Today, when slaughterhouse jobs are so poorly paid and the workers there are frequently injured, contributing to a high turnover, the Jewish tradition stands out as the most systematic attempt to reconcile the killing of animals with a good and gracious God.

The animal sacrifices of the Old Testament, as well as the development of that tradition into the kosher laws of rabbinic Judaism, are clearly a compromise between the strict vegetarianism expected of Adam and the unrestrained gluttony that preceded the great flood. It is a compromise that broke down for Christianity when Christians, led by the Apostle Paul, decided to spread the good news without requiring obedience to the Torah. Nowhere are relations between Christians and Jews more strained than in Christian interpretations of the Jewish rituals and laws concerning food and diet. If Christians could understand the Jewish food laws as an attempt to make their diets holy by bringing them into partial alignment with the original intentions of God, then Christianity could go a long way in removing the anti-Semitic stereotype of Judaism as a legalistic and moralistic religion (see Berman).

■ Story of Rabbi Judah the Prince

Although today we think of the whole system of animal sacrifices as barbaric and primitive, from the Jewish perspective animal sacrifices could coexist quite well with an emphasis on compassion for animals. In dealing with an ancient Jewish ritual that many Christians find difficult to understand, it is important, therefore, to remember that in many ways the Jewish tradition shows more concern about animals than Christianity. In fact, the rabbinic tradition is full of stories about the fundamental importance of treating animals well. Most of these stories are to be found in the *aggadah* portions of rabbinic writings, the legends and stories that are distinct from the *halakhah,* the legal discussions of the rabbis. Some of the *aggadah* consists of elaborations of the Bible, filling in blanks or explaining obscure details of biblical stories. But there is also a vast amount of *aggadah* that refers to Jewish sages who lived in the period after the Hebrew scriptures were written. This material can be found in two main sources: the Talmud, which records and codifies the rabbinical discussions covering the period from 200 B.C.E. until 500 C.E., and the collections of Midrash that serve as expositions of books of the Bible.

One of my favorite stories from rabbinic lore concerns Rabbi Judah the Prince. One day, while walking to his study, he saw a calf being led to the slaughterhouse (see Pearl, p. 94). The calf ran to the rabbi and hid under his coat, trying to escape his fate. The rabbi sent the animal back to his owner, saying, "Go, since this is what you were created for." Immediately, the heavens decreed, "Because Judah showed no compassion to the dumb animal, therefore let him be afflicted with painful illness." Thereafter the rabbi suffered for several years from a debilitating illness.

One day during his illness, Rabbi Judah's maid was cleaning the house. She found some tiny mice and began sweeping them into the yard. The rabbi noticed what she was doing and cautioned her, "Leave them alone, for our Bible teaches that 'His tender mercies are over all His works' (Psalm 145:9)." After that, a new decree was issued from heaven: "Because Rabbi Judah showed compassion let his pains leave him," and the rabbi was cured.

Rabbi Judah was a direct descendant of Hillel, the famous first-century sage, and he lived in the end of the second and the beginning of the third century. He was known for his wisdom and scholarship. In fact, he compiled and edited the Mishnah, the body of Jewish oral law. Many stories are told about him. It is interesting that he is not only credited with kindness to animals but also portrayed as having to learn that virtue. Even the greatest scholar of his time, according to the tale, must be humbled before he learns to appreciate the world of animals. In the Hebrew language, this virtue of kindness toward animals is known as *Tzaar Baali Hayyim,* which literally means "not causing pain to any living creature." The Psalm that Rabbi Judah quotes uses the Hebrew word *rahamim,* which is usually translated as compassion. The root *rehem* means "womb" and thus connotes a connection that is as intimate and profound as the attachment of a mother for her unborn child. In the harsh climate of the Middle East, where living conditions pushed people to the limit, we find a striking and emphatic declaration that animals deserve our most intimate compassion.

■ The Second Thoughts of the Prophets

The sacrificial rules enabled the Jews to eat meat with a fairly clean conscience, but the tension between the original vegetarian message of Genesis and the killing of animals remained. This tension had to snap at some point, and it was brought to the breaking point by the prophets. True, God does command the sacrifices (Exodus 12:1–7), but the prophets portray God as displeased with them. Amos proclaims that God prefers justice and righteousness over festivals and sacrifices (Amos 5:21–24). Isaiah goes so far as to call the sacrifices a "human commandment" (29:13). This apparent contradiction in the Bible demands explanation.

God permitted the sacrifices at a certain stage in the development of Israel. After the flood, Noah was allowed to kill animals, and that killing was systematized by Moses. God tolerated the sacrifices as a way of controlling and restricting the all-too-human lust for animal flesh. But the killing of animals had become rote—a habit of greed, not piety.

The temple rituals teach that sacrificing animals is acceptable to God only if the killing is done with the right heart. If the killing is done thoughtlessly or as an empty formula that had to be mindlessly repeated, then the sacrifice became something very close to murder. This is made clear in Isaiah: "Whoever slaughters an ox is like one who kills a human being; whoever sacrifices a lamb, like one who breaks a dog's neck" (66:3). Rote formalism is quite close to mere brutality. Karl Barth shows how this lesson still holds true today when he remarks that the killing of animals is "at least very similar to homicide" (1961, p. 352). Only humility, compassion, gratitude, and self-restraint mark the difference.

The system, then, was not working. Consequently, Hosea states, "Though they offer choice sacrifices, though they eat flesh, the Lord does not accept them. Now he will remember their iniquity, and punish their sins; they shall return to Egypt" (8:13). People were just eating meat for the pleasure of it. They were going through the motions of the sacrifices without thinking about what they were doing. The form counted more than the attitude, which meant that the animals were being treated as a mere means to a selfish purpose rather than as living beings whose lives should only be taken with fear and trembling.

The prophets clearly state that God was getting sick about what the people were doing. Some of the prophets wanted reform, so that the sacrifices would be practiced with the humility and discipline of the old days. Others thought that things had gone so far that there was only one choice left, which was to do away with the sacrifices altogether. As Jeremiah proclaims, "Shed no innocent blood in this place" (7:6 NEB). Habakkuk went so far as to suggest that human violence against animals will be turned back against humans: "For the violence done to Lebanon will overwhelm you; the destruction of the animals will terrify you—because of human bloodshed and violence to the earth, to cities and to all who live in them" (2:17). These were the kinds of debates that provide the background for Jesus' own entrance into the temple.

Most importantly, the prophets were concerned about building a just society in Israel, and they argued that the sacrifices should lead to the compassionate treatment of the poor, sick, and elderly. Notice how Ezekiel uses the language of sacrificed animals to criticize the elitism that was always a temptation for the priesthood:

Ah, you shepherds of Israel who have been feeding yourselves! Should not shepherds feed the sheep? You eat the fat, you clothe yourselves with the wool, you slaughter the fatlings; but you do not feed the sheep. You have not strengthened the weak, you have not healed the sick, you have not bound up the injured, you have not brought back the strayed, you have not sought the lost, but with force and harshness you have ruled them. So they were scattered, because there was no shepherd; and scattered, they became food for all the wild animals (34:2–5).

Just as a shepherd cares for his sheep, God expects rulers to care for their people. Ezekiel says that God eventually will "rescue my sheep from their mouths, so that they may not be food for them" (34:10). This is a powerful image of how political injustice parallels the gluttony of a carnivorous appetite. The poor of any society are often treated like animals, victims of the unlimited desires of the rich. Likewise, justice begins with everyday practices, like what one eats. Caring for animals, then, is not irrelevant to the goal of social reform for the poor.

◼ Jesus and the Temple

Jesus himself read and studied the prophets. Indeed, he was a prophet, and his teachings should be placed in that context of justice and compassion. For example, he twice quotes from Hosea 6:6, "I desire mercy, not sacrifice" (Matthew 9:13, 12:7). The event that most connects him to the prophets—the so-called cleansing of the temple—is also one of the primary events that led to his death. When he entered the temple and caused a disturbance, the authorities took notice and his fate was sealed. This is one of the most famous scenes in the Gospels, and it is also the most fundamental piece of evidence concerning Jesus' attitude toward animals.

In scholarly circles there is much debate about what attitude Jesus took toward the temple. Some scholars speculate that the writers of the Gospels had a more negative attitude toward the temple than Jesus. After all, the Gospels were probably written by Christians with little knowledge of what went on in the temple. They were also written for communities that were trying to distance themselves from the Jews, who were their competitors for converts. Moreover, much Christian theology developed after the destruction of the temple, which Christians took as a sign of God's judgment against the Jews for rejecting Jesus as the Messiah. So it has become common for critics to argue that the Gospels exaggerate the differences between Jesus and his contemporaries, in spite of the fact that the first century saw many intense rivalries among Jewish groups based on politics and theology.

The Gospels certainly remember Jesus as fundamentally opposed to the temple. He predicted its destruction (Mark 13:1–2), and his accusers at his trial testified that he threatened to destroy it himself (Mark 14:58). Moreover, during his crucifixion he was taunted as one who threatened to destroy the temple. These incidents hardly would have become such a central part of the memory of Jesus if he had not fundamentally opposed at least some temple rituals.

Admittedly, the evidence on this point from the Gospels can be unclear and inconsistent. Jesus attended the temple and encouraged his followers to do likewise, but he is never shown participating in an animal sacrifice. After healing a leper, Jesus told him to go to a priest and make the proper sacrifice (Mark 1:40–45), but this could have been Jesus' way of showing how irrelevant the sacrifice was when compared to his own healing power. The recommended sacrifice in this story seems like an afterthought. It also might have been Jesus' attempt to show his respect for the priestly customs, so that he would not fall out of favor with that powerful class until the time came for his dramatic entry into the temple.

The important point is that Jesus never required a sacrifice as a means for obtaining forgiveness or becoming righteous. His very mission to the outcasts of Israel challenged the priority of the temple rituals, as the passage from Ezekiel demonstrates. By going directly to the poor with his message about the mercy of God, he was literally taking food out of the mouths of the priests. The power of the priests depended not only on the tax that all Jews paid but also on the many sacrifices that the people brought to the temple. Jesus, by proclaiming the unlimited love of God, was on a course that was bound to conflict with the ruling powers of Jerusalem.

In any event, the earliest Christians seem to have continued a tradition of Jesus' teachings about the temple, as demonstrated by Stephen's aggressive and blunt criticisms of temple ritual (Acts 7:46–50). Some scholars infer from Acts 2:46 that the early Christians sacrificed at the temple, but the passage does not say that they engaged in temple worship. When the faithful are in the temple, they are preaching about Jesus and conducting healings in his name, thus building a movement that had no need of the temple sacrifices. They met in the temple courtyard, by the colonnade known as Solomon's Portico on the side of the court of the Gentiles, because that was the most convenient and important public meeting place in Jerusalem (Acts 3:1–11; 5:12–16).

Arguably, then, the cleansing of the temple is the key to under-standing the very heart of what Jesus taught. Historians like Bruce Chilton, N. T. Wright, and Richard A. Horsley argue that this inci-dent was a crucial symbolic expression of what Jesus preached. There are many different theories about what Jesus was doing on that day. He chose to visit the temple on Passover, which was a national holiday. Jerusalem was full of crowds of people wanting to eat lamb sacrificed at the temple. Jesus certainly did not expect to destroy the temple with his own hands. Instead, he was doing what is now called political theater—staging a provocative event in order to draw attention and make a point. He overturned tables and drove out those who sold animals (Mark 11:15–18, Matthew 21:12–13, Luke 19:45–46, John 2:13–22). The usual explanation for his actions is that he was angry at the money-changers for cheat-ing the people and turning the temple into a "den of robbers" (Mark 11:17). However, pilgrims to the temple could not be expected to bring their sacrificial doves from home. They brought various cur-rencies with them, so they had to change their money to a reliable coinage in order to pay for the sacrifices and the temple tax. Sac-rificing animals always creates a thriving business—as much in those days as it does today.

Instead of focusing on the money-changers, I think we should focus on the animals. It is hard for us today—when animal sacri-fice is so rare and most temples in the world religions substitute prayer or incense for their blood—to imagine what the Jerusalem temple was like: "The stench of blood and of roasting flesh can hardly have been drowned by the smoke of incense; nor can the cries of traders, or the uplifted voices of priests and pilgrims at prayer, have drowned the screeching of the beasts as they had their throats cut" (Wilson, p. 174). The temple economy was based on the selling, buying, and killing of animals. Whatever Jesus was doing, it had to be directly related to the animals that dominated the temple activities.

Given the enormity of the temple complex and its political as well as religious significance, it must have been hard for any Jew to imagine Jerusalem without it. Historian E. P. Sanders argues that Jesus would not have threatened the temple with destruction with-out holding out some prospect for its replacement with a new one. The temple, after all, was regarded as the dwelling place for Israel's

God. However, the temple was also the source of a purity system that created hardships for the poor and fostered illusory hopes of a restored nationalism. Jesus preached an inclusive message of peace that could only have been at great odds with the militaristic hopes that were associated with the maintenance of the temple. Sanders himself admits that Jesus thought that God was acting through him in order to offer sinners a direct and immediate place in the kingdom, thus bypassing the biblically sanctioned ordinances of the sacrificial system (p. 236). It thus seems likely that Jesus was making a symbolic statement about the eschatological, not immediate and literal, restoration of the true temple. He was announcing, by staging this dramatic conflict, his expectation that God would soon transform Jewish worship into something much more holy and pure.

We could even go so far as to say, with New Testament scholar N.T. Wright, that Jesus was offering himself as the new temple in the hope that the destruction of the old one would usher in the kingdom of God (p. 426). The new temple that Jesus envisioned had to do with the purity of our hearts and compassion for the needy—a temple "not made with hands" (Mark 14:58)—that left no room for the bloody killing of animals. The New Testament continues this emphasis on the need for a peaceful temple. The Letter to the Hebrews anticipates a heavenly Jerusalem where the blood of Jesus creates a new, nonsacrificial covenant (12:22–24), and the Book of Revelation envisions a future earthly city of Jerusalem that is shorn altogether of the temple (21:2, 22). These books look back to the decisive action of Jesus in the temple. They remember what Jesus came to bring to an end. Thus, the Gospel of John emphasizes that Jesus freed the doves and drove out the oxen and sheep from the temple (2:12–16). Jesus came to liberate the animals so that worship would not depend on the spilling of innocent blood.

Significantly, the attack on the temple traders is placed in Mark within the story of the cursing of the fig tree. Theologian Robert G. Hammerton-Kelly has argued that this warrants the conclusion that the fig tree represents the sacrificial system of the temple. According to the story, Jesus was hungry, saw a fig tree, and went to it to partake of its fruit. When he found only leaves, he said to it, "May no one ever eat fruit from you again" (Mark 11:14). This would be an odd story if it were really about figs because the story itself points out that it was not the right season for the tree to be bearing fruit. Indeed, it would be ludicrous to take the story literally; the story begs for an allegorical interpretation. It makes perfect sense as a warning about the sacrifices of the temple. The sacrificial system was no longer meeting the needs of the people, and, Jesus was saying, it must come to an end. It had its time, but the seasons change. By stating his hope that no one eat figs from the tree again, Jesus was saying that nobody needs to benefit from the animal sacrifices anymore. And since Jews in Jerusalem limited their meat consumption to animals that were properly killed in the temple, Jesus could be interpreted as advocating a vegetarian diet.

The temple was ultimately a place of violence that tied Judaism to a sacrificial ritual that excluded non-Jews from the presence of God. Judaism maintained its unity by a bloody ritual that channeled violence against animals. By using animals as scapegoats, Jews, like all ancient peoples, could alleviate feelings of guilt and control aggressive impulses. In Christianity, by contrast, as Hammerton-Kelly writes, "the sacrificial system is to be replaced by faith and prayer founded on the renunciation of violence" (p. 19). The most important and immediate beneficiaries of the religious revolution of Jesus were, then, the animals themselves, who no longer had to serve as mediators of our contact with the divine. Instead, Jesus himself took their place by being the victim who came to bring the need for victims to an end.

■ The Final Sacrifice

Unfortunately, there is no explanation in the Bible about the origin of or the reason behind the animal sacrifices. The Old Testament is not given to such philosophical speculations. The purpose of the sacrifices must be pieced together from the theology of the Hebrew scriptures. The basic fact of that theology, arguably, is that sinful humans cannot absolve themselves. They need some mediation in their relationship to God. The Hebraic sacrificial system is based on the idea that something has to bridge the gulf between humans and the divine. If animals were able to do that, it was because of their freedom from sin.

It is thus important to note that animals could be used for sacrificial rituals only because they are innocent and pure. Their very purity paradoxically permitted them to be killed in our place. The sacrificial rituals thus affirm the closeness of animals to God and to us. They are enough like us to take our place, yet in some ways they are closer to God than us, so that their substitution can move God to cancel our sin. Animals, after all, do not need sacrifices; only humans do.

Nonetheless, these very same rituals treat animals as a mere means to the end of human redemption and purification. Animals have spiritual value only to the extent that they can be used to repair the breech between God and humanity. The sacrificial system is thus inherently unstable. If animals are innocent and pure, why are they being killed and eaten? If they are close to God, why would God want their shed blood as a compensation for human wrongdoing? If humans are trying to repair their relationship to God, why do they scapegoat animals by transferring their guilt to an innocent victim? Finally, if humans need moral transformation, why must this be accomplished through the violent act of ritual killing?

Even in the ancient world, as documented by theologian Godfrey Ashby, animal sacrifices were often the subject of intense scrutiny and criticism. Philo argued that the true altar of God is the soul and that the true sacrifice is moral nobility (Winston, p. 159). Justin the Martyr, the second-century theologian, argued that God does not demand the destruction of God's good gifts but rather their proper use and distribution. Arnobius (c. 300 C.E.), an African Christian, passionately criticized pagan sacrifices by appealing to the innocence of animals and our sympathy for their brutal treatment (Roberts, vol. 6, p. 519). The Neoplatonist Porphyry stated in his *De Abstinentia* that killing animals is always morally wrong, so God would never have required such an act as a form of worship. A spiritual being needs only spiritual gifts. Clement of Alexandria even suggested that carnivorous eating habits were the origin of animal sacrifices, a common argument among philosophers. Sacrifice was thus nothing more than an elaborate means of justifying meat-eating.

Philosophers criticized the sacrifices as superstitious and irrational, but Christianity had a more fundamental interpretation of these rituals. From a Christian perspective, the human demand for an innocent victim is difficult to understand, except when that is seen in the light of the mission of Jesus Christ. Jesus came to end the sacrifice of animals because he was the final sacrifice—the culmination as well as the destruction of the sacrificial system. No longer does the blood of an innocent victim need to be spilled in order to please God. No longer must we use animals as a way of trying to work out our own salvation. The gravity of killing an animal was a dramatic way of symbolizing our guilt and our need to pay a price for what we had done. But now Jesus has paid that price in full. Only retrospectively, then, do the animal sacrifices make sense as an unsavory and grim expression of humanity's desperate need for deliverance.

In Jesus Christ, God becomes one with all living beings through a very terrible death. God experiences sacrifice firsthand, we could say, in order to take upon the divine being the pain and suffering that our sins cause. God accepts the consequences of our acts as God's own destiny, without complaint or resentment. God willingly becomes a victim in order to alleviate our need to find victims to take away our sin. As a result, the second Adam, Jesus, allows for the beginning of a return to the first Adam, and the state of peace that God first granted the world.

An animal sacrifice is a way of venting tension and anxiety—a cathartic release of violence onto an innocent victim, the animal. This may be why God accepted Abel's sacrifice of a sheep, rather than Cain's offering of the fruit of the ground. God knew that Cain had anger and hatred in his heart, and that he would make Abel a victim if he did not have any other way of releasing his emotions. Of course, that is precisely what happened. Without animal sacrifice in the ancient world, men turned against each other, and murder is the result. God thus allowed Noah to sacrifice animals in order to insure that the world would not fall into the same violence that had led to God's destructive anger. The killing of animals is thus an outlet for aggression. Put simply, ancient peoples killed animals as a substitute for the killing of humans, as the story of Abraham and his son Isaac demonstrates.

Christianity is about a further substitution, indeed, the ultimate act of a substitution. The Letter to the Hebrews makes it clear that the animal sacrifices were never completely successful in removing the stain of sin (Hebrews 10:1–18). Violence can never solve the problem of violence. In the ancient world animal sacrifices were the main way of controlling, channelling, and discharging aggression. According to the provocative theory of the French literary critic and religion scholar René Girard, sacrificial rituals were a highly refined way of maintaining order through an elaborately staged and regularly practiced spilling of blood. To say that Jesus came to save the world means not only that Jesus came to save us, but also that Jesus came to save the animals. Jesus quite literally took the place of the animals so that they would not have to take the place of us.

The result was a revolution in religious faith. When Christians rejected the practice of animal sacrifice, the Roman economy felt the impact, and the powers that be were not happy (Acts 19:24–27). When some locals complained about the Christians to Pliny, a late-first- and early-second-century Roman politician and governor, they might have been the butchers, who saw their sale of sacrificial meat threatened. Since nearly all festivals and holidays involved the ritualized killing of animals, Christians were exposed to persecution for their antisocial and unpatriotic behavior. When they refused to participate in the celebration of the imperial cult, they were hunted down like animals, becoming a substitute for the sacrifices they rejected. The Christian martyrs faced the wild animals in the arena with courage and tranquility, letting their bodies be broken as a sign of their faith in the saving blood of Jesus Christ.

Christians still talked the language of sacrifice, but they followed the example of Paul, who called the charity of the Philippians a "fragrant offering" (Philippians 4:18) and equated sacrifice with moral obedience and religious dedication (Romans 12:1; 15:16; Philippians 2:17; 1 Peter 2:5). The pagans thought the Christians were not very religious because they had none of the trappings of ritualized killing. The early Christians had houses, not temples, for worship and tables, not altars, for their ritual meals. They understood the temple to be the people of God and the altar to be the cross, where the faithful bring their sins only to find that God has already been there before them, so no more blood needs to be shed. Sacrifice becomes a spiritual transformation, a gift made possible not by what we bring to God but by what God has already done for us.

Consequently our lives are transformed so that we are liberated from the desire to use animals in any way other than the way God originally intended. Indeed, the suffering of Jesus should remind us of the suffering of animals, the very creatures whose place God took. After all, the Roman soldiers treated Jesus like an animal. As Cardinal Newman once preached, "Think of your feelings at cruelty practiced upon brute animals and you will gain the sort of feeling which the history of Christ's Cross and Passion ought to excite within you" (p. 138). The age of forgiveness that Jesus unleashed should empower us to feel the pain of animals as our own, precisely because God encompassed all pain through the cross. This theology is consonant with the vision of Colossians, "For in him all the fullness of God was pleased to dwell, and through him God was pleased to reconcile to himself all things, whether on earth or in heaven, by making peace through the blood of his cross" (1:19–20). The cross frees us from the need to make scapegoats out of animals, our tendency to project our worst impulses onto them in order to feel better about ourselves.

Christian vegetarianism raises the fundamental issue of who Jesus is and what his death accomplished. There is a flurry of activity recently among historians to try to find the "real" Jesus, that is, to use historical methods to discern what can really and truly be known about Jesus, above and beyond what the church believed and taught. These historical debates often emphasize the Jewishness of Jesus. The death of Jesus must have been interpreted by his contemporaries, at least in part, as a statement about the death of the animals in the temple. The language of sacrifice was originally applied to animals, and now it was being applied to Jesus Christ, and thus to God. How does this one death change the death of the animals? Is it a death that liberates Christians from all of the many legal requirements that restrict what we can do with animals and which animals we can eat? Or is it a death that puts an end to the entire system of using animals as a means of reaching God? Jesus died to bring an end to the culture of death, to the ancient idea that blood needed to be spilled in order to appease the gods. Jesus suffered on our behalf so that now we can live on the behalf of others. The only question is, who are those others, and do they include animals? To think about animals is to think through the central beliefs of the Christian faith, and to show compassion toward animals is to put those beliefs into practice in surprising and liberating ways.

5

Why Jesus Was (Probably) Not a (Strict) Vegetarian

■ The animal rights group PETA, People for the Ethical Treatment of Animals, is known for its media savvy. Recently they orchestrated a campaign centered around the claim that "Jesus was a vegetarian." They even created an icon for their media blitz: an image of Jesus framed by an orange-slice halo! PETA sells T-shirts with this image on its web site, and the image has appeared on billboards. One of the billboards was in Tulsa, Oklahoma, near the campus of Oral Roberts University. One can only imagine what the fundamentalist students of ORU thought about this attempt to use Jesus to spread the gospel of vegetarianism. How Christians have depicted Jesus has evolved over the centuries as the church has tried to convey the gospel to changing audiences, but is there any truth behind this marketing ploy? Was Jesus a vegetarian?

The PETA campaign is admirable for raising the issue with such passionate conviction. Unfortunately, much of the literature about Jesus and vegetarianism is full of speculation at best and inaccuracies at worst. There are many books and web sites that make all sorts of claims about Jesus that are without any historical foundation whatsoever. It is almost as if the vegetarian community, in its rush to recruit Jesus as one of their own, is creating a Jesus to fit their needs by rewriting history. The result is a conspiracy-theory view of history, not unlike the wild and paranoid theories that surround the assassination of John F. Kennedy, to take one contemporary example.

According to the logic of the conspiracy theorists (see, for example, the book by the Quaker medical doctor Charles P. Vaclavik, *The Vegetarianism of Jesus Christ,* as well as the work of Keith Akers), any glimmer from the Bible that Jesus was not a vegetarian must be the product of later additions to the text by meat-eaters who were trying to cover up the real Jesus. The real Jesus is an Eastern-sounding philosopher who belonged to a sect of Pythagorean Judaism. His true teachings are hidden in the biblical and post-biblical material. Indeed, "heretical" groups actually carried on his legacy far better than the Christians who would come to define themselves as "orthodox." The implication is that only vegetarians truly understand Jesus because they see through the conspiracy to cover up Jesus' vegetarianism.

This theory is circular and self-justifying. Any evidence that is contrary to a vegetarian Jesus is dismissed as the product of writers who were rationalizing their own meat-heavy diets. While all such debates about Jesus will ultimately prove inconclusive, still, by putting Jesus in his historical context, we can go a long way toward discovering not only what Jesus taught about food but also how Christianity came to terms with the vegetarian ideal that was so prominent in the ancient world.

The attempt to establish a vegetarian Jesus begins with the argument that those closest to Jesus were vegetarians. Animal rights groups argue that if his mentors and friends were vegetarian, then it stands to reason that Jesus was as well. They portray Jesus as a follower of a vegetarian John the Baptist. They also suggest that Jesus was a member of a vegetarian community called the Essenes; that Jesus' brother, James, was a vegetarian; that the earliest Christians, called the Ebionites, were vegetarians; and that many so-called "lost stories of Jesus" point to his true, vegetarian philosophy. Finally, they blame followers of Paul for trying to erase all traces of vegetarianism from early church practices. I will examine carefully each of these claims before turning to a more balanced analysis of the difficult question of what Jesus ate and why.

■ Was John the Baptist a Vegetarian?

Given the fact that Jesus was at one time a disciple of John the Baptist, it seems reasonable to assume that Jesus would have been influenced by John's diet. The question of John's diet, however, is vexing, to say the least. In Luke 7:33–34 and Matthew 11:18–19, John is described as the opposite of Jesus. John ate a frugal diet, while Jesus was sometimes called a glutton. Some vegetarians read these texts as part of the "carnivorous cover-up," because they assume that Jesus must have eaten a diet similar to John's. It is also tempting to read into John's diet later Christian notions about asceticism, but this temptation should be avoided. John probably took the Nazirite vow, a Hebrew word which means "consecrated" or "separated." A Nazirite would not cut his hair, come into contact with a corpse, or touch grapes or their byproducts (Numbers 6:1–21). A *nazir* was consecrated to God, sometimes for a brief, specific period of time and sometimes for life. To end the vow, a sacrificial procedure had to be followed. Both Samson and Samuel took this vow and were thus called *nazirim*. (There is some speculation that Jesus also took this vow, which might account for some confusion in the Gospels over references to Jesus as a Nazorean—see Matthew 2:23—which later tradition understood to refer to Jesus' home town in Nazareth.)

Why was the exclusion of wine part of the Nazirite's holy diet? This is a puzzling question because the Bible praises wine as a blessing from God, even though it recognizes the dangers of drunkenness (Genesis 27:28, Deuteronomy 7:13, Amos 9:14). Wine was such a staple of everyday life in Mediterranean culture that its abundance was a sign of the harbinger of the Messianic Age (Amos 9:13, Joel 3:18, Zechariah 9:16–17). When it was prohibited, the reason often had something to do with the animal sacrifices. Its red color alone suggested an association with the blood of the sacrifices, and the Israelites occasionally used it in their rituals (see Numbers 28–29). This association was even more clear in the pagan world, where wine almost always indicated the religious character of a meal. It was rarely drunk without a propitiatory libation, which means that some wine was poured out as a sacrifice to the gods. Because of this link between wine and idolatrous ritual, Jews were forbidden to partake of wine prepared by Gentiles, a rabbinic law that is still considered binding in orthodox Judaism.

Consequently, any diet that was meant to protest animal sacrifices or abstain from them by setting apart the eater from the rest of the community would usually exclude both meat and wine. For the ancient Cynics, for example, "Drinking water, the pure and natural drink, went logically with avoiding meat" (McGowan, p. 75). Thus, even though the Nazirite vow did not exclude eating meat (and it did not include being celibate, which later ascetic groups often connected to vegetariansim), it is possible that it was expanded in its later history to include this restriction. Much vegetarian literature makes this assumption, although it is speculative and without concrete historical documentation.

In point of fact, John was not a strict vegetarian. He ate locusts (grasshoppers), which were kosher and widely available for consumption. This is often denied by the conspiracy theorists, who argue that in the translation from Aramaic to Greek, the word for carob pods gets confused with the word for locusts. This argument was popular among vegetarians in the nineteenth century, but linguistic evidence weighs against it. All can agree, however, that John did eat a frugal diet, which would complement his Nazirite vow, but he also ate wild honey, a delicacy. The point of his diet seems to have been an attempt to live off the natural conditions of the wilderness. There is biblical precedent for a vegetarian wilderness diet in the example of Judas Maccabee (2 Maccabees 5:27), a revolutionary leader who protested corruption in the temple and ate nothing but wild plants. Judas was a messianic figure who, like John, wanted to inspire and challenge his fellow Israelites, so his lifestyle might well have influenced John's diet.

Yet Judas was most worried about pagan influences in the temple. His separation from the temple and from eating meat had to do with his desire to avoid pollution from impure people and impure practices. John, on the contrary, wanted to demonstrate, by returning to the theme of abundance in Genesis, that God had made more than enough for us so that we can enjoy God's creation and be frugal at the same time. John put his trust in God that God would provide him with all he needed, just as Jesus did when he went out into the wilderness for forty days. For this reason, John wore clothing made from camel's hair with a strip of skin tied around his waist (Mark 1:6, Matthew 3:4). The tie probably was made from the skin of some creature found dead (see Taylor, p. 35). John would not have eaten a carcass, but using whatever one could find in the wild to wear was another matter.

John can be seen, then, as a great dramatist, theatrically reenacting the plight of Israel. His entire way of life symbolized the situation of the Israelites when they were wandering in the desert, preparing to enter the promised land. He preached the power of repentance and demanded a confession of sins. He led his followers to the Jordan River as a symbolic border that they would have to cross in order to receive salvation. His message was urgent because he thought that the day of judgment was coming. He was a prophet who wanted people to change their lives in expectation of the coming end of the world.

There is no evidence that John advocated his own frugal diet for everyone, nor that he connected a semivegetarian diet with repentance and moral rebirth. It is not unreasonable, however, to suggest that Jesus might have been influenced by John's frugal diet, which was based on a trust in God to provide everything that is necessary for life.

■ Who Were the Essenes?

The conspiracy theorists further their claims by trying to connect John the Baptist to the Essenes and their writings, the Dead Sea Scrolls. The Essenes were a Jewish group that rejected the temple sacrifices and practiced water purification. Vegetarian conspiracy theorists often suggest that John spent time with the Essenes and thus shared their attitude about food and sacrifices. They even go so far as to speculate that he was adopted by the Essenes. To support this scenario, they point out that John was born to elderly parents who died when he was still a child (Luke 1:18). And they refer to Josephus who mentions that the Essenes practiced such adoptions. After the conspirators connect John to the Essenes, they then associate the Essenes with the Therapeutae, another ascetic community. In *The Contemplative Life,* the first century Jewish philosopher Philo described the Therapeutae as a Jewish group who lived near Alexandria and ate solemn meals of bread, hyssop, salt, and water—in stark contrast to pagan banquets (Winston, p. 54). The Therapeutae, however, based their utopianism more on philosophy than religion.

There are many similarities between John and the Essenes. Both preached repentance and expected the Messiah, but other connections fall apart upon closer examination. There is little evidence that John was hostile to the Jerusalem temple. Moreover, all Jews practiced some form of water purification, and John's own practice of baptism for repentance bears little resemblance to the water purification rituals of the Essenes. John baptized people once and sent them back into the world, whereas the Essenes practiced daily ablutions as part of an effort to maintain their separatist holiness in preparation for the coming Messiah.

The Essenes are a difficult group to understand. The word itself is simply an anglicization of a Greek transliteration of an Aramaic word that means "the pious ones." The Essenes were a group of Jews, mostly men, who separated themselves from other Jews. They scorned marriage, followed a strict regime of prayer and work, and lived in communities where they shared their resources, practiced ritual purification by water immersion, and ate a common meal of loaves of bread and wine. Although there is much debate on the topic, many scholars connect them to the sect that lived at Qumran, near the Dead Sea. That group left their library of scrolls in clay jugs in their caves, and these were discovered by some Bedouin shepherd boys in 1947. At first, many people thought the Essenes might represent a form of Christianity that preceded the institutional church, so there was a lot of excitement about the publication and study of the Dead Sea Scrolls. As more of these fragmented texts have been translated, it seems clear that they belong to a particular Jewish group that had little if any connection to Christianity. Most importantly, the scrolls include versions of some of the books of the Hebrew Bible, as well as ancient religious texts that were otherwise lost to history, so they tell us a lot about the diversity of Judaism during the time of Jesus but relatively little about the movement that became Christianity.

Much of what we know of the Essenes comes from sources outside of the scrolls, in the works of Josephus, Pliny, and Philo. The religious movement of the Essenes began in the middle of the second century B.C.E., and lasted until the end of the Jewish revolt against the Romans in 73/4 C.E. They were a tightly organized group, sharing their possessions, sometimes allowing marriage but usually practicing celibacy, and letting in new members only after a period of examination and testing. Significantly, they understood themselves not as religious revolutionaries but as guardians of Jewish tradition.

The origin of this group is difficult to piece together, but a standard theory has emerged. One problem is that the language of the scrolls is highly symbolic, and some of that language does parallel themes found in the New Testament. The Essenes were founded by a shadowy figure called the Teacher of Righteousness, who was opposed by the Man of the Lie and the Wicked Priest. Something happened to drive the Teacher and his followers into exile from Jerusalem. It has been suggested that the Essenes were the losing party in the internal politics of the battle for control over the temple. The Essenes, like many Jewish groups, rejected the Hellenization of Palestine, which arrived on the heels of Alexander's military triumphs in the Middle East. Greek customs and opinions spread in Palestine in ways similar to the diffusion of American influence around the world today. When the temple fell into the hands of a Hellenized Jewish party, a group of Jews led by the Teacher of Righteousness broke off their relations with the Jewish leaders of Jerusalem. They decided to await the Messiah to deliver them from their enemies. They founded a community in exile from the temple and its politics in Qumran, where they could copy their scrolls and practice their rigorous lifestyle.

At Qumran they waited patiently for the coming deliverance of God. They observed the rules of the Torah strictly, but they did not participate in temple activities or sacrifices. Philo tells us, for example, that the Essenes became holy "not by sacrificing animals, but by deeming it right to render their minds holy" (Winston, p. 249). Some scholars argue that this was mainly due to a dispute over what calendar—solar or lunar—should be used to determine when to celebrate the various holy days and rituals. The validity of the temple sacrifices depended in part on their being offered at the right time, something the Essenes thought was not happening. Thus, the Essenes did not reject the temple sacrifices altogether. They boycotted the temple by substituting their daily prayers and their morally rigorous lifestyle for the animal sacrifices. Indeed, the way they thought of their own community as a temple might be their closest parallel to Pauline Christianity (Wise, p. 126).

The important point is that the Essenes rejected the temple not on the grounds of compassion for animals but over disputes about the timing of the performance of the rituals. They expected the Messiah to bring about the descent of a heavenly temple to Jerusalem, more beautiful and perfect than anything made by human hands. In this temple the entire set of animal sacrifices would be restored in complete conformity to the Torah. Moreover, all foreigners would be banished from the Holy Land. The extent to which they did not regularly eat meat was due to the fact that they could not participate in the temple ceremonies. They did not embrace vegetarianism as a philosophical or religious ideal, as seems to be the case with the Therapeutae. There is included in the Dead Sea Scrolls a vegetarian Psalm, not found in the Bible, that portrays the last days as a time of wondrous fecundity, when the earth will offer up abundant fruit and crops and the poor shall eat and be satisfied (Wise, p. 199), but there is no evidence that the Genesis story of an original vegetarianism had any influence over them.

The evidence of their diet is contradictory and complex. Caches of animal bones have been found at Qumran (curiously buried in jars), which suggest that the Essenes were not strict vegetarians. However, the Damascus Document, the group's foundational text, states, "No one may defile himself with any creature or creeping thing by eating them," (Wise, p. 70), but it goes on to allow the consumption of fish and locusts. The most that can be said about their eating habits is that they ate, like John the Baptist, a simple and frugal diet, so that all the members of their community could have enough. They also probably ate only what they could grow, so that they could be confident in the purity of their food. If they were semi-vegetarians, it was a temporary state forced upon them by the disruption of temple politics, a state that would be reversed once the temple was restored by the Messiah.

■ James the Just, the First Christian Vegetarian

The next stage of the conspiracy theory is to connect the earliest Christian community in Jerusalem to the leadership of James the Just, the brother of Jesus, who was, evidently, a vegetarian. If James was a vegetarian, and if the Christian movement was influenced by John's diet and the antitemple attitude of the Essenes, then it stands to reason that the earliest Christians, who were Jews living in Jerusalem under James's leadership, might also have been vegetarian.

There are many debates about James, both concerning his relationship to Jesus (brother, cousin, or stepbrother?) and his role in the early church (first bishop, rival of Peter and Paul, founder of Christianity, or leader of a Jewish group that never fully accepted the divinity of Christ?). In the Gospels Jesus appears to keep his distance from his brothers, so that some scholars think that James became a member of the Jesus movement only after he became a witness to Jesus' resurrection. There is also the ongoing debate about whether he wrote the letter in the New Testament that is attributed to him (most scholars think not, although the theology of the Letter of James, which emphasizes the importance of good works for salvation, may well represent the outlook of the historical James). Finally, there are debates about his martyrdom and the relationship of his death to the outbreak of the Jewish revolt in 66 c.e. that led to the destruction of the temple.

The problem with any discussion of James is the paucity of the early sources. James was the leader of the Jerusalem Christian church, but when that church dispersed during the Jewish revolt that led to the fall of Jerusalem (66–70 c.e.), the most successful and thriving Christian traditions did not bear his beliefs. Without an orthodox Christian community that traced its lineage back to him, his role in the early church began to be diminished. The early Christians wanted to portray a unified origin, so Paul's influence began to eclipse the memory of James. Moreover, as the early church began to emphasize Mary's perpetual virginity, the idea that Jesus had brothers had to be ignored, denied, or rationalized away as cousins or as sons of Joseph from a prior marriage.

Robert Eisenman has done the most of any scholar to try to revive the significance of James. Unfortunately, his work is marred by a deep bias against Paul and orthodox Christianity. Eisenman sees Paul as the bitter enemy of James. Interestingly, the issue they most clashed over is whether Christians should eat meat. According to Eisenman, Paul was a man who compromised with Roman rule and thus turned Christianity into a Hellenistic mystery cult. If Paul sold out to Greek culture and Roman political power, which therefore enabled his version of Christianity to survive and triumph in the pagan world, James stuck to his zeal for the law, which made his version of Christianity anticosmopolitan and xenophobic. Eisenman connects James to the Essenes—going so far as to identify him with the righteous teacher of Qumran, a claim hotly disputed by most scholars—and their protest against the temple. He even sees James as the pivotal figure in the Jewish nationalism that led to the war with Rome. The upshot of his investigation is the claim that only through James can we obtain a realistic sense of who Jesus really was. (Eisenman seems to assume that brothers ordinarily hold the same views and rarely disagree with each other—a rather dubious assumption at best.)

It is true that James was the leader of the Jewish Christians in Jerusalem until his martyrdom in 62 C.E. He probably rose to power after many of the apostles were persecuted, killed, or dispersed in the early 40s. In the Book of Acts, where he appears out of nowhere in chapter 12, he is described only reluctantly by Luke (the putative author). Yet Paul never mentions any James other than James the brother of Jesus, and he is also prominent in apocryphal works, such as the Gospel of Thomas. According to Galatians 2:11–12, not only does Peter seem to take his orders from James (also see Acts 12:17), but James is the one who most clashes with Paul on the question of whether Jewish Christians should eat with Gentile Christians and whether Gentile Christians should be required to follow the kosher food laws. At the very least, as evidenced by his speech at the Jerusalem Council (in Acts 15) and the subsequent apostolic decree (see Acts 15:29 and 21:25), James thought that Gentile Christians should abstain from meat sacrificed to idols and from blood altogether.

Some vegetarians think that this ban on consuming blood meant that Christians were not to eat meat. But why would James regulate meat-eating with these rules when it would have been simpler just to ban the practice? More likely, James thought that animals should be properly killed and drained of their blood if they were to be eaten at all. In effect, he applied some Mosaic dietary regulations, but not circumcision, to Gentile as well as Jewish Christians. In doing this, James was being consistent with Jewish tradition. According to Leviticus 17:10, as well as the story of Noah, the regulations against consuming blood were meant to govern both Israel and outsiders living within Israel.

But there is also a case to be made that James came to the conclusion that even if meat-eating is permissible, it would be best for Christians to avoid meat altogether. In this regard, the most important piece of information about James comes from Eusebius (260–340), who draws from the otherwise lost works of Hegesippus (c. 90–180), a Jewish Christian who had access to the earliest sources on James. Eusebius writes that James "was holy from his birth; he drank no wine or intoxicating liquor and ate no animal food; no razor came near his head; he did not smear himself with oil, and he took no baths. He alone was permitted to enter the Holy Place, for his garments were not of wool but of linen" (quoted in Painter, p. 122). This is a puzzling set of descriptions, but it is clear that Eusebius describes James as a lifelong Nazirite (abstaining from wine) and vegetarian, demonstrating a possible connection between the two—a connection that could have arisen during the Hellenistic period. Regardless of whether James's vegetarianism resulted from or was in addition to his Nazirite vows, it is clear that, according to longstanding tradition, his vegetarianism was a significant aspect of his high standing in the early Christian community and one reason he continued to be revered by later Jewish Christians.

Early church accounts do portray James as an influential figure in temple politics. Eusebius says that he frequented the temple in order to pray for the forgiveness of the people. Moreover, Acts ends with James suggesting that Paul participate in a purification rite in the temple (some have suggested that this is a Nazirite vow), after which Paul was accused of bringing Gentiles into the temple and arrested. Significantly, Paul was not aided by the Jerusalem Christians after his arrest, but instead had to rely on his Roman citizenship and the influence of his sister's son to help him. Earlier some Jews had taken an oath to kill Paul (Acts 23:12), and historian John Painter thinks it is likely that James foresaw that Paul's presence in the temple would precipitate a riot (p. 57). It is possible, then, that James wanted Paul out of the way. If so, his ploy did not work. In fact, the triumph of Pauline theology accounts for the ways in which James was increasingly ignored as accounts of the early church were being gathered and written.

According to Eisenman, the issue that most divided them was the ongoing sacrifices at the temple. For Paul, the temple needed to be reinterpreted as the Christian body as a whole or the individual bodies of believers, so he did not revere the Jerusalem temple as a singular and exclusive place of holiness. He thus could teach Gentiles about Christianity in the temple, inviting foreigners into what Jews considered to be an exclusive space (Acts 21:28). If Eisenman is right, James represents a contrary view. James, like Judas Maccabee before him, wanted to purify the temple of any foreign influence or interference. For Eisenman, James's vegetarianism was based on his disagreement with how open the temple should be to Gentiles. James avoided temple sacrifices—and thus the consumption of meat—as a protest against the impurity of the temple.

Ancient vegetarianism was often the product of concerns about ritual and dietary purity, so Eisenman's speculations are plausible. If he is right, then the piety of James must have been quite different—much more moralistic, restrictive, and self-righteous—than the piety of his brother, Jesus. Nonetheless, Eisenman's entire thesis is built upon his connection of James to the Qumran community, an unlikely hypothesis that has received virtually no support from other scholars. What is more likely is that James shared his brother's attitude toward the temple. After all, as New Testament scholar Craig A. Evans has shown, both Jesus and James were critical of the temple, and both paid for their criticisms with their lives. In fact, Jesus and James were condemned by high priests Caiaphas and Ananus, who were related to each other by marriage (they were brothers-in-law). As Evans argues, Jesus and James "may very well have advanced the same agenda over against the temple establishment [since] they suffered the same fate at the hands of essentially the same people" (p. 249). James is thus closely associated with the temple in most accounts of his life precisely because he was so heavily involved in disputes over what the temple meant and what should take place there. It seems that early in his career as leader of the Jerusalem church, he thought that Gentile Christians should restrict their diets by respecting at least some Jewish food rituals. However, he personally practiced vegetarianism, and he also grew increasingly disenchanted with the temple sacrifices altogether.

It is thus possible to put James's vegetarianism in a context entirely different from Eisenman's. For example, it is tempting to argue that one of the reasons James was consistently called a *zaddik* or holy one was because of his vegetarian diet. Noah, it should be remembered, is the first biblical figure to be called a *zaddik,* and he earned this title by his compassion for animals. Moreover, although the precise reasons he did not eat meat are lost to us in history, it is not pure speculation to suggest that James was influenced by his more famous brother. He could have understood Jesus' message as a call for compassion for all life. He also could have interpreted Jesus' death as bringing an end to the need for animal sacrifices and thus nullifying the biblical justification for meat-eating. His belief in Jesus as the gateway to God—in effect, a new temple—would account for his conflict with the temple authorities, which led to his death. James's theology was thus not that far removed from Paul's, even though they drew different conclusions about the legitimacy of eating meat. If I am right, then understanding James's vegetarianism requires us to take a position on what we believe Jesus taught about the temple, diet, and animals. We cannot use James's vegetarianism to illuminate the teachings of Jesus because so little is known about James, so we have to work the other way around. We must reconstruct the teachings of Jesus in order to shed more light on the dietary practices of his brother.

■ Who Were the Ebionites?

Another piece of the conspiracy puzzle is the connection of the earliest community of Jewish Christians, led by James, to the later heretical group known as the Ebionites. The Ebionites are the favorite heretical group of vegetarians. Not much is known about them, which gives those who want to find a vegetarian Jesus a license to say all sorts of things about this group. Indeed, the less known about them the better, because that only validates the conspiracy theory approach to history. According to the conspiracy theorists, the Ebionites have been nearly wiped from history by meat-eating Christians who desperately tried to cover up their trail.

These exaggerations about the role the Ebionites play in church history are unfortunate, because they really were an important group and deserve careful attention. In a development that parallels the rabbinic response to the destruction of the temple in 70 C.E., the Ebionites raise a fundamental question for early Christianity. If Jews ate only meat that was properly sacrificed, what happens when Jesus annuls the purity laws and cancels the necessity of animal sacrifices for the forgiveness of sins? Moreover, what happens when the second temple is destroyed, so that animals can no longer be properly sacrificed? If Jesus came to abolish the temple, does that mean that all meat can now be eaten, or none?

The Ebionites lived in Syria but traced their origins back to the church at Jerusalem. The earliest Jewish Christians left Jerusalem at the time of its destruction by the Romans or after a second war, the Bar Cochba revolt (132–35 C.E.), after which all Jews, including Jewish Christians, were excluded from Jerusalem. Eusebius (in his *Ecclesiastical History,* 3.5.3) says that the Christian church in Jerusalem escaped the destruction by fleeing to the city of Pella, which is east of the Jordan river (Schaff, p. 138). Scholars today debate whether there really was an exodus to Pella, but it was in that region that the Jewish Christians first claimed to be the survivors of the earliest church. Evidence for their lineage comes from their name, which comes from the Hebrew word that means "the poor." According to Galatians 2:10, that is the same name that was used to refer to the Christians of Jerusalem. It is also possible that they received their nickname from their literal poverty, since they valued asceticism. In any case, their theology was never widely accepted by the growing church, which ridiculed them for being "poor in the faith." Whether or not they were direct descendants of the Jerusalem church, it is likely that they continued some of the teachings of that group. To make matters more complicated, the term *Ebionite* is sometimes simply applied to any Christian group with Jewish influences, and the Ebionites are sometimes confused with another Jewish-Christian group called the Nazarenes.

The Ebionites were vegetarians who fervently honored the memory of James, the first Christian vegetarian, so it is tempting to think that they represent a continuous religious history, beginning with the very brother of Jesus. Much of our information about their diet comes from Epiphanius, a fourth-century theologian who wrote extensively about heresy in the *Panarion* (or "medicine chest," that is, arguments that provide an antidote to the poison of sects). He quotes from the Gospel of the Ebionites, which survives only in fragments, in order to show how they portray a vegetarian Jesus who proclaimed, "I have come to abolish the sacrifices: if you do not cease from sacrificing, the wrath of God will not cease from weighing upon you" (Elliott, p. 15). The Ebionites even celebrated a bread and water communion probably because wine reminded them too much of the animal sacrifices that Jesus' death was meant to replace. Their gospel also suggests that John the Baptist ate bread, or manna, instead of locusts (James, pp. 8–10). Furthermore, it explicitly rejects the idea that Jesus ate animal flesh on Passover. Many scholars mistrust the historical reliability of these passages, but it is possible that they existed in a pool of traditional material that was passed over by the composers of the other Gospels. If this is so, then the Ebionites did not create these passages but instead chose them from a set of variants because they suited their purposes. These passages, then, could be as early as anything that occurs in the four canonical Gospels.

On the other hand, their continuity with early Christianity is not fully substantiated by the historical record. John Painter is not alone in suggesting the possibility that the Ebionites themselves were responsible for the idea that James was a vegetarian (p. 126). After all, vegetarianism in the ancient church is often associated with Jewish Christianity, and the Ebionites would have had an incentive to project their beliefs onto the brother of Jesus. They might have gradually exaggerated his holiness and importance in early Christianity in order to defend their own communal practices. It is hard, then, to judge the historical origins of their traditions.

As their theology evolved in relative isolation from other Christians, it became increasingly at odds with the developing tradition of orthodox Christianity. They taught that Jesus fulfilled the law in order to purify it and make it finally holy, a position that put them at odds with Paul. Indeed, they even claimed that Paul, prior to his conversion, physically assaulted James in the temple. They considered Jesus the adopted son of God, and thus they rejected what would eventually become orthodox Christology. They also rejected any idea that the cross of the crucifixion had an atoning or salvific significance. While it is possible that they thought of Jesus as the incarnation of an archangel, which would reflect Gnostic influences, they most typically portrayed Jesus as a great and final prophet. Jesus was the new Moses, who preached against the temple and called for a reformation of Jewish law. Because the Jews would not heed his message, the temple was destroyed.

Only through a complex reading of the Bible could they reconcile the radical nature of Jesus' message with their intention to be true to the Jewish law. According to Irenaeus (c. 130–200) in his *Against Heresies,* written around 190, "They use only the Gospel which is according to Matthew, and they reject the apostle Paul, calling him an apostate from the law" (Hultgren, p. 118). And Epiphanius accused them of altering the biblical record and telling lies about the apostles in order to defend their own heretical practices. They argued that the cultic portions of the Hebrew scriptures were late additions, falsifications, and distortions of God's revelation. They believed that Judaism was originally a vegetarian religion that became corrupt with Solomon's building of the temple. They thus could argue that Jesus was being true to Jewish tradition by calling for an end to animal sacrifices. Their vegetarianism, then, was at least in part a product of their strict Jewishness—it was, in one scholar's words, "an intensification of the Mosaic food laws" (Schoeps, p. 100).

Their vegetarianism was also an aspect of their ascetic way of life. They embraced poverty and, as pacifists, abhorred all bloodshed. They were also anxious about demons, which resulted in strict purity regulations. Epiphanius suggests that they avoided meat because animals are the product of sexual intercourse (Amidon, p. 103). They might have thought that animal sexuality was unclean, and thus eating meat made one vulnerable to demonic possession. Perhaps as a product of influence from the Essenes, they practiced regular bathing rituals—which seem very remote from the historical Jesus—in order to free themselves from demonic pollution and defilement.

The literature that is most associated with the Ebionites, and the only works of that community that have survived in forms other than as quotations in orthodox critics, consist of the *Recognitions of Clement* and the *Homilies of Clement.* They are attributed to one of the earliest popes, Clement of Rome (who is traditionally ranked as the second, third, or fourth pope). These books, which are actually two versions of the same work, are called Pseudo-Clementines, because their true author is unknown (see Jones and Danielou). They are usually classified as Hellenistic romance novels, because they represent a kind of travel literature, full of adventures and debates. They tell the story of Clement's conversion to Christianity and his travels with Peter. The author of the Clementines used a variety of sources that are now lost to us, though scholars try to reconstruct them. He also used his own vivid and creative imagination. Thus, the Pseudo-Clementines seem strange and curious to modern readers, blending fact with fiction in ways that are difficult to distinguish.

Nonetheless, these documents contain many theological themes that originated in the century after the life of Jesus, and they also refer to historical episodes that might reflect a continuous tradition of stories dating far back into the origins of Christianity. Most importantly, they portray a Christian community that was profoundly disturbed by the consumption of meat. Central to their theology was the belief that Jesus came to abolish the temple sacrifices: "For we have ascertained beyond doubt that God is much rather displeased with the sacrifices which you [Jews] offer, the time of sacrifice having now passed away; and because you will not acknowledge that the time for offering victims is now past, therefore the temple shall be destroyed" (Roberts, vol. 8, p. 94). To bolster their image of a vegetarian Jesus, they drew on the fear that demons can enter the body through the consumption of meat offered to idols as sacrifice. This fear was widespread in the early church, as demonstrated by the second century apocryphal *Acts of Andrew,* where the apostle explains the connection between demons and meat: "As long as the demonic nature lacks its bloody food and cannot suck up its nutrition because animals are not slain, it weakens and recedes to nothingness, becoming entirely dead. But if it has what it longs for, it strengthens, expands, and rises up, growing by means of those foods it enjoys" (Elliott, p. 262). Although *The Acts of Andrew* was used by Gnostic and heretical groups like the Encratites, it demonstrates that the Christian revulsion against animals sacrifices was widespread.

A key theme of the Pseudo-Clementines is the contrast of fire, which fuels the animal sacrifices and is connected to the burning of lust, with the water of baptism, which washes away sin. Water is the lifeblood of creation, flowing through the earth to sustain all life. Fire destroys, while water—pure, clean, and transparent—sustains. This stark opposition of water to fire implies a vegetarian diet, which Peter makes explicit in a speech to Clement: "I live on bread alone, with olives, and seldom even with pot-herbs" (Roberts, vol. 8, p. 158). Indeed, the Clementines argue that gluttony is at the root of sin. The excessive consumption of meat cannot be digested, and thus "curdles into a sort of poison, and it, flowing through the bowels and all the veins like a common sewer, renders the motion of the body unhealthy and base" (p. 138). Pagan medical philosophy thus agrees with theological argument that meat is as unhealthy as it is sinful. Only baptism and a eucharistic meal of bread and water can quench the violence of the fire that both burns animals and incites the passions.

Clearly, in this creative interpretation of the power of the baptismal and eucharistic rites, Christianity is seen as a peaceful religion that leaves no room for the cooking of meat. Whether these texts reflect traditions that reach back to the time of Jesus and the disciples, they show that some Christians were earnestly working through the logic of Christian faith toward a theology of vegetarianism. Today the Ebionites are often discussed more in terms of their position on Jewish-Christian relations than their views on diet. The Ebionites did not think Jesus was the incarnation of God, and thus they did not think that Christianity was an essentially new religion that should break from Judaism. Stuck between Judaism and Christianity (their reformation of the law was unacceptable to rabbinic Judaism just as their adoptionist Christology was unacceptable to orthodox Christianity), they were fated to disappear from history by the fifth century. Nevertheless, some scholars have speculated about their influence on Islam. Their dietary restrictions, conception of Jesus as a prophet, emphasis on works-righteousness, and tendency to correct ancient religious law in order to develop a more comprehensive revelation all could have found their way into Arabia and influenced the tradition proclaimed by Mohammed.

■ The Compromising Influence of the Apostle Paul

Those who believe that Jesus practiced and preached vegetarianism lay all the blame for Christian meat-eating practices at the feet of Paul. They love to point out, based on one New Testament passage, that Paul does not appear to have much compassion for animals. In a discussion of payment for church missionaries, Paul interprets allegorically the law of Moses that forbids a farmer from muzzling an ox while it is treading grain, suggesting that God is not really concerned for the oxen but for humans (1 Corinthians 9:8–10). In other words, missionaries, like oxen, should be allowed to eat while they work. Whether Paul seriously meant to downplay the original meaning of the law, which was to safeguard the health of working animals, is questionable. Yet this passage does show that Paul tended to dismiss a literal and rigorous interpretation of Jewish law. It is also evidence of the particular circumstances that Paul had to address. Although it cannot be argued, as does Robert Eisenman, that Paul intentionally betrays the mission of Jesus, Paul does deal with a lot of difficult situations brought about by the growing church—situations that could not all be anticipated by the stories and teachings of Jesus.

As the early church began to grow, its Jewish leaders in Jerusalem had to decide to what extent Gentile converts should be asked to follow Jewish law. In other words, was Christianity going to continue to be a Jewish sect, a religious movement that added to, but did not subtract from, Jewish beliefs and practices? Or was Christianity going to become a relatively new religion, somewhat independent of Judaism even though it had deeply Jewish roots? Eventually, Christianity became a Gentile religion, but in its earliest years the Jewish influence was still very strong. There were many debates about whether Gentiles should be circumcised and required to follow the kosher food laws. Some Christians began to argue, following Paul, that it is not what goes into your mouth but what comes out of it that really matters.

Peter, although reluctantly, followed this advice when, in a dream, he saw "all kinds of four-footed creatures and reptiles and birds of the air," and God's voice said to him, "Get up, Peter; kill and eat" (Acts 10:12–13). The main point of the story is not that God desires the killing of animals. The point is that Peter realized that God did not want the Jewish dietary laws to prevent the spread of Christianity. Peter dreamed that the distinction between clean and unclean animals had been overcome, just as the distinction between the Jews as the people of God and the Gentiles as outside the covenant had been overcome by a new covenant, more universal and inclusive.

Given these debates about food, it should not be surprising that in several of his letters, Paul deals specifically with the issue of vegetarianism. It is strange, then, that many Christians seem not to know that vegetarianism appears in the New Testament. It is sometimes argued that one clear mention of meat-eating appears in 1 Timothy 4:1–5, a letter that many scholars no longer attribute to Paul. Although the King James Version talks about hypocrites who advocate the abstinence from meat, the Greek word *broma* is better translated as the generic for food. The group in question probably advocated strict periods of fasting. Even if they were vegetarians, they were being criticized not because of what they would not eat but because they connected their diet to a prohibition of marriage. They were thus motivated by a denial of the goodness of the material world and by a fear of all things sexual. This group (as with the group that is criticized in Colossians 2:16–17) was probably composed of Gnostics, and I will go into Gnosticism in depth in chapter nine.

In 1 Corinthians 8, Paul deals with the tricky problem of whether one should eat meat that has been sacrificed to idols. This seems like an irrelevant problem to us today, but in the ancient world, nearly all meat would have been the product of a religious sacrificial ritual. Meat was the most desirable and least available of foods in the ancient world. Most meals for the poor did not include meat, but it was still available in meat shops or distributed as charity. As the primary product of the pagan religious cult, eating meat would not have been a merely mundane act of satisfying hunger; instead, it was a way of participating in the social customs and religious practices of the pagan world.

Eating is such an intimate act that, for many Christians, eating pagan-sacrificed meat was identical to consuming and internalizing the gods (which they took to be demons) of the pagan religion. Increasingly, during the time of the rise of Christianity, eating meat also became a political act, since the sacrifices were dedicated to the honor of the Emperor. Thus the question of whether to eat meat involved a complex set of issues that were of fundamental importance.

Early Christian leaders, in their effort to distance the faithful from the idol-worshiping of their pagan contemporaries, often warned believers not to eat meat sold in the market that had come from pagan worship practices (see, for example, Revelation 2:14–15). This would have prevented Christians from dining with their pagan friends, who might offer them meat that had come from a sacrifice. Many Christians must have come to the conclusion that nearly all meat-eating was an indirect way of affirming pagan religion, so they decided that it would be best to avoid meat altogether. Such a decision would distance Christians not only from pagan religion, but also from the social, political, and economic practices of the Roman world. Religious studies professor Stanley K. Stowers suggests how radical this vegetarian lifestyle was:

> Imagine a community in the contemporary United States that renounced not only television viewing but also any products, persons, and ideas promoted by television. The group would not vote in elections, drive automobiles, shop in supermarkets, watch athletic contests, or form conventional families. These people would remain citizens of the United States but to a large extent would have abandoned American and Western culture. Understanding what it meant for a Greek, Roman, or Syrian to renounce animal sacrifice requires some such act of comparative imagination (p. 293).

Vegetarian Christians were protesting against the entire Roman way of life, which would have made them a dangerous group in the Empire and vulnerable to persecution.

In his first letter to the church at Corinth, Paul argues that since the pagan gods do not exist, Christians should not worry about meat being contaminated by idols. Nevertheless, he concludes that if eating meat causes vegetarian Christians to stumble in their faith, it is best to eat no meat at all (v. 13).

Gerd Theissen has tried to penetrate the social situation behind Paul's advice. He argues that the poorest members of the Corinthian church would have eaten meat only at public religious functions, so they would have associated meat with pagan religion. The wealthier Christians would have linked meat to their social and economic needs to dine with their pagan friends. When Paul suggests that meat-eating is acceptable, then, he sides with the wealthy, because it would have been devastating for them to have given up the privilege of eating with their friends. In response to Theissen, some scholars argue that the poor had access to meat in cook-shops, but these establishments had notorious reputations and were still affiliated with pagan religion, since they were operated by the same guilds that organized the sacrifices. Paul's distinction, then, between eating meat in a temple and eating it in a home or a tavern was one of his own making. He was trying to separate the sacred from the secular, in order to carve out a public space where Christians could socialize with pagans without worrying about compromising their faith. What really seems to be at stake in Corinth is what kind of attitude Christians should take to Roman religion—indeed, to Roman society altogether. In this letter, Paul shows that his main focus is the growth of Christianity, so he hesitates to side with those Christians who want to separate themselves so radically from the Roman world.

The situation in the church in Rome is a bit different, but Paul's advice is the same. In Romans 14–15, Paul seems to be addressing a group of Christians who were fundamental vegetarians. Some scholars suggest that Paul is only dealing with a hypothetical situation of vegetarianism, but this argument does not take into account the popularity of vegetarianism in first-century Rome. Paul calls this group of Christians "weak," as opposed to the "strong" who will eat anything. Who were these weak Christians? Many hypotheses abound. Some scholars think they were Jewish-Christians who were still committed to the Torah, the Jewish law. Perhaps they could not find meat in Rome that satisfied the *kashrut,* the Jewish food laws. Or perhaps they did not want to call attention to their Jewishness by asking for kosher meat. It is actually not unusual for Jews to abstain from meat when living among Gentiles (see Daniel 1:16, Tobit 1:10-12, Judith 10:5, 12:1-2, and 2 Maccabees 5:27). Josephus reports that priests sent to Rome during Nero's reign took figs and nuts with them in order to avoid eating impure meat. It is also possible that the vegetarianism of James, who was well known for his righteousness, could have influenced the diet of this Roman group.

The weak Christians might not have been limited to a group of Jewish Christians, however. If the weak were a Gentile group, they might have been influenced by a neo-Pythagorean or Orphic community, or by a philosopher in the Cynic school. They also could have been influenced by a Gnostic group, since many Gnostics were vegetarian. All of these speculations, however, imply that only special groups were vegetarian, while the reality was quite different. Vegetarianism was widespread and popular in Rome. Mark Reasoner, in the best scholarly work on this topic, points out that there were many reasons to abstain from meat in ancient Rome. The Romans valued vegetarianism as part of their cultural heritage, an attitude that was often translated into sumptuary laws that restricted the sale of meat. For example, at the time when Paul wrote his letter to the Romans, Nero outlawed the selling of meat in taverns, though it was legal to cook it at home. It is, therefore, futile to try to find one particular motivation for this weak group. People back then could abstain from meat for as many reasons as people today do so.

The Roman vegetarians, therefore, probably restricted their diet for a variety of reasons, which could explain why Paul does not try to sort out the complex issues behind their food preferences. Instead, Paul goes right to the theological heart of the controversy, because his main concern is harmony in the church, and he knows that people must be able to eat with each other if they are to worship the same God.

The situation in Rome is not unlike today, when vegetarians are often chided for not getting enough protein and thus for looking pale and thin. This might be why the vegetarians of Rome were called weak. In addition, vegetables were considered then, like today, as a "weak" food when compared to meat. More fundamentally, the two groups disagreed about the relationship of faith and morality. The strong included gluttons and antinomians who thought that faith in Jesus freed them from all ethical constraints. They saw the weak as superstitious and timid. The weak probably thought that a meatless diet was more morally pure, an accomplishment in self-discipline. They probably looked down on the strong as much as the strong looked down on them.

Paul actually does not resolve this dispute, and those looking for a condemnation of vegetarianism will be disappointed. Paul is more interested in a practical settlement, bringing about enough peace between the two groups so that they can worship and work together. Paul spent a lot of his time traveling, eating, and socializing with countless non-Christians, and so he himself did not practice any dietary restrictions, which would have hindered his missionary efforts. But Paul does not condemn the weak group in Rome for their vegetarianism. He thinks both groups are right, as long as they do not judge each other.

What he most worries about is how stringent moral standards can lead to a schism in the church. The priority of church unity means that Paul did not think that dietary codes needed to become uniformly enforced in the church. Paul also, in reaction to his own legalistic past, wanted to emphasize the freedom that comes with Christianity. Nevertheless, Paul argues against the strong that "if your brother or sister is being injured by what you eat, you are no longer walking in love. Do not let what you eat cause the ruin of one for whom Christ died" (Romans 14:15). Paul's notion of freedom, then, was not absolute. Freedom is bounded by the greater value of love. The strong have an obligation to those they regard as superstitious.

Thus, although Romans 14–15 is often read as an argument against vegetarianism, Paul actually sides as much or more with "the weak." After all, Jesus gave up his divine privileges, and Paul made many sacrifices for the gospel. Even if meat-eating is permitted, it might not be for the good of the whole community. "It is good not to eat meat or drink wine or do anything that makes your brother or sister stumble" (14:21). Interestingly, a truncated version of this statement, "It is good not to eat meat or drink wine," was often used by the church fathers to defend vegetarianism. This is an example of how early theologians could play fast and loose with quotations that were removed—but perhaps not too far— from Paul's original intention. Paul certainly ate meat on his journeys when it was offered to him, but it also seems likely that he abstained when he visited and worshiped with vegetarian Christians. Paul can be read as the apostle of freedom who cleared away every ethical legalism from Christianity, or he can be read as an astute politician who sought harmony and compromise in the churches. Either way, it should be sobering to all who read this letter that Paul goes a long way toward siding with the weak Romans who thought that a meatless diet was essential for their faith.

■ Hidden Stories about Jesus and Animals

To bolster the idea that orthodox Christians covered up Jesus' vegetarianism, conspiracy theorists often appeal to apocryphal stories that they say reveal the true, even if long-hidden, Jesus. Many of these stories originated in heretical Gnostic communities, centuries after the life of Jesus, and thus they are meant to uphold the beliefs of a particular religious group, not to convey accurate historical information about the life of Jesus. In several important Gnostic texts that were found in 1945 in Egypt, called the Nag Hammadi library, James appears as an esoteric teacher who possesses the true wisdom of Jesus. Some scholars thus argue that the Gnostics are the ones who originated the vegetarianism of the Ebionites and the legend that James himself was a vegetarian.

Nevertheless, it is interesting that many stories about Jesus that have come down to us outside of the four canonical Gospels do emphasize his compassion for animals. It is possible that the early Christian movement, which eagerly and mistakenly anticipated the early return of Jesus and thus the immanent end of the world, did not think it was important to collect and distribute stories about Jesus and animals. Why worry about what Jesus taught about our obligations to animals when a new earth was fast approaching? In a time of great eschatological expectation, only the most essential teachings of Jesus concerning our relationships with God and each other would have been preserved. It is also possible that some of these stories were passed along in communities that had more at stake in the vegetarianism that is often their implicit message. The conspiracy theorists take this argument to an extreme by suggesting that orthodox Christians suppressed these stories in an attempt to deny the vegetarianism of Jesus.

Some of these stories are just as theologically powerful today as they must have been in ancient times. *The Gospel of Pseudo-Matthew,* for example, portrays Jesus as a new Adam who is adored by animals at his birth. They recognize him as their natural master.

Pseudo-Matthew emphasizes this point by telling the story of Jesus entering Jericho when he was a young boy. A family of lions runs up to meet him, and the lion whelps run around and play with him. The onlookers are frightened, but Jesus says to them: "How much better are the beasts than you, seeing that they recognize their Lord and glorify him: while you, who have been made in the image and likeness of God, do not know him! Beasts know me and are tame; men see me and do not acknowledge me" (Elliott, pp. 97–8). Jesus then tells the animals to go in peace, hurting no one and being hurt by no one in return.

This Gospel also tells the story of the lions and panthers who followed Joseph, Mary, and Jesus on their sojourn to the desert. The lions and panthers "showed their submission by wagging their tails" (p. 95). Jesus thus turned wild animals into creatures as compliant as dogs. The lions and panthers also befriend the oxen, sheep, and asses, and no animals eat or hurt each other, which fulfills, the Gospel states, the prophecy of Isaiah. At one point in the Gospel Jesus says, "All the beasts of the forest must needs be docile [or should grow tame] before me" (p. 95). Jesus brings peace to the animals, transforming their very natures.

In these portraits of Jesus he has the power to tame wild animals. This theme continues in works like the second-century *Acts of Paul,* where Paul is forced to face a lion in a Roman stadium. Instead of killing him, however, the lion recognizes Paul as the one who had previously baptized him and lets him go (Elliott, p. 379). In the *Acts of Philip,* a fourth-century work that borrows from pagan romances, this popular theme of converted animals is elaborated into a powerful story. On a mission journey Philip and his sister are worshiped by a leopard. The leopard tells them that he seized a goat intending to eat it, but the goat pleaded, "O leopard, put off your fierce heart and the beastlike part of your nature, and put on mildness, for the apostles of the divine greatness are about to pass through this desert, to accomplish perfectly the promise of the glory of the only-begotten Son of God" (Elliott, p. 515). The leopard is deeply moved by these words, and when he addresses Philip, he asks him to tame his wild nature. Philip prays, "Now therefore, Lord Jesus Christ, come and grant life and breath and secure existence to these creatures, that they may forsake their nature of beast and cattle and come to tameness, and no longer eat flesh, nor the kid the food of cattle; but that men's hearts may be given them, and they may follow us wherever we go, and eat what we eat, to your glory" (p. 516). The animals, then, become vegetarians, just like the apostles, and they give thanks to God for their transformation into domesticated creatures. They even ask for communion! This story was probably thought to be too fanciful to be seriously discussed and included in the orthodox church's memory of Jesus and his disciples, yet there is a more creative and systematic biblical theology of animals here than in most of contemporary Christian theology.

■ What Would Jesus Eat?

The PETA campaign plays into the hands of Christian fundamentalists, the very group that PETA most wants to combat. It assumes that morality consists of absolute rights and wrongs and that we should base our moral decisions on the exact details of Jesus' life. Therefore, if it can be proven that Jesus was a vegetarian, then we should eat likewise. Regardless of the historical record, this is a theologically difficult position to hold. Jesus was, according to orthodox belief, fully human as well as fully divine, so that Jesus was not some sort of superhero only pretending to be a man. He was fully a part of his world, taking on the language, customs, and habits of his contemporaries. The question of how to conceptualize the way in which he combined his divinity with his humanity is something theologians have argued about for as long as there has been theology. Some early Christians, called Docetists, thought that Jesus did not eat at all, because he was so perfect and otherworldly. They believed he did not have a real body, only an apparent one. The church rejected that position, but the question of what Jesus ate remains and is very difficult to answer.

The PETA campaign also raises the question of what vegetarianism is. There was no animal rights movement in the ancient world. Indeed, the very word *vegetarian* was not invented until the nineteenth century, so Jesus could not have called himself a vegetarian, even if he wanted to! Vegetarianism often originated, in the ancient world, in attitudes that were hostile to the natural function of the body. Some people denied themselves animal flesh because they wanted to starve the body in order to free the soul, or they did not want to eat anything that was the byproduct of sexual reproduction. Thus, even if Jesus wanted to make a statement about food, he would have been forced to be very careful about what he preached and how he ate.

Given these complexities, the question should not be about what Jesus ate but how Jesus lived. Christians today do not imitate every detail of Jesus' life. We do not speak the language he spoke, wear the clothing he wore, and follow many of the social customs he followed. Nevertheless, we do try to pattern our lives after his moral example, if not his daily habits.

At the very least, Jesus, as a Jew, did not eat pork, and yet Christians today show no regard for this basic fact about his diet. As a man of his time, he probably did eat fish, since all people in the ancient world believed that some animal flesh was necessary for survival. Does this mean that we should eat all the fish we want today? Should we try to find out what kind of recipes his parents cooked for him and follow them in exact detail for our own children? Should we limit ourselves to Middle Eastern cuisine? That idea is, of course, preposterous (even if it probably would improve the health of the average North American!). It would be better to focus on his teachings and see how they should inform the way we treat animals today. The question is not what Jesus ate two thousand years ago but what Jesus would eat today.

Having said all this, one can still ask the simple question, Did Jesus eat meat? One can ask that simple question, but one should not expect a simple reply. Biblical translations, for one thing, can be a problem. The King James Version of the Bible says that "Jesus sat at meat in the house," (Matthew 9:10), but the word translated as meat in that verse is the Greek word that usually simply means food. The word meat occurs over fifty times in the King James Version of the New Testament, but most of the time the proper translation should be just food, not meat.

■ An Aside on Fish

In point of fact, we do not see Jesus eating any meat in the Gospels except for fish. Growing up near the shore of the Sea of

Galilee, it is hard to imagine that he did not eat fish. He even worked miracles to help his disciples catch fish (Luke 5:4–6; John 21:6–8), and Matthew 17:24–27 tells how Jesus criticized the temple tax but paid for it by directing Peter to catch a fish with a coin in its mouth. He also, of course, called his disciples away from their occupation so that they could follow him.

In one of his most famous miracles, he multiplied the fish and loaves in order to feed the poor who had gathered to hear him speak (Matthew 14:13–21, 15:32–39). Technically speaking, in this story we see Jesus multiplying fish already dead, but we do not see Jesus eating fish. Some vegetarians argue that Jesus merely multiplied the bread. Interestingly, Irenaeus, in his *Against Heresies,* mentions only the bread and not the fish (Roberts, vol. 1, pp. 391 and 395). Moreover, when Jesus later refers to this miracle, he refers only to the bread (Matthew 16:9–10; Mark 8:19–20; John 6:26). Other vegetarians have argued that it is more likely that fishweed (a dried seaweed) was served in a basket with bread on a hot day, and that fishweed became fish through an editorial alteration. It is possible that fish were later added to the story because the Greek word for fish, *ichthys,* was a popular code name for Christianity. (It is a Greek acronym for the phrase, "Jesus Christ Son of God Savior.") Even today, a fish is still a symbol of Christianity. Thus, the multiplication of the fish may not have meant to be taken literally. Instead, it may represent the spread of the church and the increase in the number of Christian believers. However, the documented use of this acrostic is relatively late, dating to the fourth century, so this argument is speculative at best.

More concrete evidence comes from the stories of Jesus eating fish after his resurrection (Luke 24:42–3; John 21:13). It is interesting that in the King James Version of the Luke passage, Jesus eats honeycomb along with the fish. Most modern translations omit the honeycomb, because scholars think it was inserted into some Greek versions of the Gospel at a later date. If it is an insertion, it could be evidence of a debate going on in early Christian communities over the question of whether Jesus ate fish and thus whether Jesus was a vegetarian (see Akers, pp. 127–8).

In any case, most scholars argue that these fish-eating stories are late additions to the Gospels. Christians had to battle Gnostic groups who taught a Docetic Christology. Marcion, for example, used a truncated version of Luke as his Gospel, and he believed that Jesus arose only as a spirit, not as a body. In response, orthodox Christians responded with stories about Jesus eating real food as evidence of his bodily resurrection. What better way to show that Jesus arose as flesh than to show him eating flesh? Nevertheless, these passages would have originated in communities only one or two generations removed from the life of Jesus, so it is hard to imagine Christians passing on this tradition if Jesus had been a strict vegetarian. The evidence, then, seems slightly weighted toward the conclusion that Jesus did eat fish.

Further evidence that Jesus might have eaten fish comes from the hypothesis that the early church originally practiced a bread and fish Eucharist, not bread and wine. Paintings on the walls of early Christian catacombs show a group of males sitting around a table of loaves and fish (Crossan, p. 398). However, these paintings date from the third century, so their relevance for New Testament practices is limited. Most likely, they could be portraits of an eschatological meal, rather than literal descriptions of ritual meals Christians actually ate. There is some evidence that eating fish had an eschatological meaning in Judaism (see Ezekiel 47:9–10; also see Hiers, pp. 35–38). Fresh fish was a luxury for most city-dwellers (although salted fish and fermented fish sauce were more common), so it is understandable how fish came to represent the eternal banquets of heaven. (For this reason, the preferred food for the Jewish celebration of the Sabbath became fish rather than meat.)

If there was a tradition of Christian thanksgiving dinners of bread and fish, it probably originated in the miracle of Jesus multiplying the loaves and fishes and in his post-resurrection appearances. Some scholars have suggested that there are eucharistic elements in these Gospel scenes. Such a tradition, however, tells us less about Jesus' meal practices than about what some early Christians believed, since these eucharistic elements would have been read back into the text by later editors. If the eucharistic overtones of these fish scenes is the product of a later Christian community, then it was probably a community that did not eat meat other than fish. In the ancient world, fish was a common alternative to (other) meat, because it was never a part of the sacrificial cuisine. Consequently, as classicist James Davidson explains, "In an important sense, fish-consumption was simply not taken as seriously as other kinds of carnivorousness" (p. 12). To put it bluntly, fish did not have the religious baggage that came with the consumption of other kinds of meat. This meant that there were a variety of attitudes about fish in the ancient world. Eating fish could be held in suspicion, because it was a food that was not a part of established religious routines. Likewise, fish could be celebrated because they were regulated by the market and by personal taste and pleasure, rather than religious rules.

Most significantly, sectarian Christians could eat fish as a way of enjoying the gifts of God without resorting to pagan-sacrificed meat. Eating fish for a ritual dinner was nearly unheard of in Greece and Rome, so if Christians did so, they were making a pretty blatant statement about the uniqueness of their meal and their religious beliefs. To eat fish for a ritual dinner is to reject the (much more) bloody meal of an animal sacrifice.

■ Jesus the Glutton?

More so than the stories about fish, there is the problem that Jesus was known to his contemporaries as a glutton (see Matthew 11:18–19). This criticism of Jesus' character needs to be put into the context of Jesus' open table fellowship. As we have already observed, there were many reasons in the ancient world for restricting one's diet. Most of them were based on what we now recognize as superstitions. Jesus tried to cut through the ways in which diets could separate people from each other. He was concerned about the legalistic attitude that many people brought to their dinner. Jesus doubtless would have known self-righteous vegetarians, those who ate the most minimal diet in order to keep from being polluted by others. Even if he shared their concern about animals, as I have argued, he would not have been sympathetic toward their exclusive lifestyle. His own principle of eating was based on an inclusive and open community, where nobody was rejected and all life was affirmed. He thus transformed Jewish notions of holiness from external to internal purity.

The authors of the Gospels, which were written many years after Jesus' death, understood this transformation to mean that all animals were clean, that is, people could eat whatever they wanted to.

When Jesus said, "Do you not see that whatever goes into a person from outside cannot defile, since it enters, not the heart but the stomach, and goes out into the sewer?" (Mark 7:18–19), the author of Mark adds as an editorial comment, "Thus he declared all foods clean." It is almost as if Mark is taking a traditional teaching of Jesus and putting his own spin on it. The point that Mark wants to make is that Christianity has nothing to do with the restrictive food laws that characterize Judaism. That is not necessarily the point that Jesus wanted to make. If Jesus had meant by this comment that his followers could eat whatever they want, the early church would never have become so embroiled in controversies about diet. The Christians who collected his sayings were involved in polemical disputes with Jews, so they wanted to downplay any concerns Jesus had with dietary restrictions. Moreover, in their missionary travels, they secularized the production and consumption of food not because food is unimportant, but in order to permit the sharing of food across lines that traditionally separated people from each other.

So what did Jesus eat? Some vegetarians try to connect Jesus' diet with John the Baptist's, but the New Testament actually portrays them as having very different lifestyles. Of course, early Christians were anxious to argue that Jesus was superior to John, so it is possible that the Gospels magnify differences that might have been only slight. Mark 2:18 states that Jesus and his disciples did not keep the same fasts as the Pharisees and the disciples of John the Baptist. Elsewhere, Jesus does tell his disciples to fast (Matthew 6:16–18, where he advises them not to look dismal when they fast and to do it in private, secretly). In Mark 2:18–20, however, Jesus suggests that there is a time to fast and a time to feast, and as long as he is around, it is time for the latter. Just what kind of feasts he enjoyed, however, we do not know.

Jesus did eat at the homes of the wealthy, where meat was almost certainly served. Did he eat that meat? Again, we do not know. But we do know that it was important for Jesus to welcome everyone into his fellowship, so he would not have acted in such a way as to make someone feel guilty for their hospitality. He advised his disciples to eat whatever was put before them (Luke 10:8). Perhaps he behaved as some Buddhist monks do, who do not fix meat for themselves but do not turn it down when it is placed in their begging bowls. It is hard to imagine Jesus raising the issue of meat as a guest at a dinner table, which would be cause for disagreement and tension, when a major purpose of Jesus' ministry was to bring people together and to celebrate a shared humanity.

Robert Eisenman reads the Gospel portraits of Jesus as keeping table fellowship with all kinds of sinners as a reflection of later polemical battles in the church between Paul and James. That is, the Pauline communities wanted to portray Jesus as disregarding the food and purity rituals that James insisted all Christians, Gentile and Jewish alike, should uphold. How could the Christian community have been so divided about food issues so soon after Jesus' death? The only explanation is that Jesus was a revolutionary with regard to Jewish dietary laws, and revolutionaries are often misunderstood. James was more conservative than his radical brother and tried to keep the Christian movement within the Jewish fold. Paul was more liberal than Jesus because he spent his life on the road, eating at all times and in all places. Jesus wanted to rethink the whole notion of ritual purity and impurity, but this does not mean that he thought eating was unimportant. He ate and socialized with lots of people that the Pharisees would have considered unclean, but he did this precisely because he endowed food with a new significance, based on a communal sharing made possible by a hope in God's future. Does this mean that he ignored the differences between unclean and clean animals that is so much a part of Jewish tradition? Or did he avoid meat altogether, as the simplest way of dining with others without worrying about ritualistic rules?

My best guess is that Jesus was not a strict vegetarian, because the earliest Gospels do not mention this belief and, more importantly, Jesus was against erecting food rituals that separate people. However, since there is no mention of him eating meat (besides fish) in the New Testament (I will deal with the Passover dinner in the next chapter), it seems likely he avoided meat whenever that was consistent with his ministry. He was especially critical of self-righteousness, which would have made it difficult for him to defend his diet as superior to the alternatives. He was more concerned about preaching a message of love than passing onto his followers a new set of absolutist rules specifying what they should eat. He wanted everything his followers did to emerge from an attitude of trust in God. He was, in all probability, a "loose" vegetarian, one who abstains from meat without drawing undue attention to that dietary choice. However good this guess is, anyone who writes on this topic must, in the end, admit that we simply do not know the detailed answer to the question of what Jesus ate. The best guess must be informed by the whole shape and impact of what Jesus taught.

To be a disciple of Jesus today is to treat him as a full disclosure of God's purposes for our lives, but that does not necessarily entail treating Jesus as our exemplar in every detail. Christians are not like scientists who look to the Bible for proof concerning every decision they make. Reading the Bible involves the wisdom of discernment, which is a gift of the Holy Spirit. This gift enables Christians to apply ancient teachings and stories to contemporary situations by making analogies and comparisons between the experiences of Jesus and the early Christians and the very different context in which we live today. Such discernment is hard work—it involves a total dedication to understanding the presence of Jesus Christ in the world today based on the life he lived and the responses to his teachings as they are recorded in the New Testament.

Finally, we cannot detach Jesus from his surroundings and his culture. Jesus was not a divine spirit only pretending to inhabit a human frame. Jesus was wholly a part of his time and place, while at the same time he powerfully challenged his contemporaries. He was more successful at transforming later generations of followers than in changing the world in which he grew up and lived. His message was for the ages, but this does not mean he spoke about every single problem that all Christians confront in their daily lives. He spoke the language of his time and he met the problems of his day. To follow him is to listen to his stories and apply them to today. Discipleship is the creative act of fitting our lives into his. Such an enterprise no doubt will lead to frustrating challenges, but even more, it will result in surprising changes in the way we see the world and lead our lives.

■ Jesus as a Lover of Animals

The four Gospels do not explicitly put animals at the birth of Jesus, but Luke does say that Jesus was born in a manger, so the animals are implied even though not described. The Gospel of

Pseudo-Matthew, a compilation in Latin dating from the eighth or ninth century, fills in the details that the New Testament stories leave out: "And on the third day after the birth of our Lord Jesus Christ, Mary went out of the cave and, entering a stable, placed the child in the manger and an ox and an ass adored him. Then was fulfilled that which was said by Isaiah the prophet, 'The ox knows his owner, and the ass his master's crib'" (Elliott, p. 94). The tradition of animals worshiping Jesus at his birth is much older than this, although scholars cannot date its origin with any certainty. Clearly, though, Christians believed that the incarnation of God in Jesus Christ had significance for the whole world, including the animals. As St. Thomas Acquinas explains in the *Summa Contra Gentiles,* "The Word also has a kind of essential kinship not only with the rational nature, but also universally with the whole of creation, since the Word contains the essence of all things created by God" (IV. 42 [3], p. 198). Jesus, the new Adam, came to set the world right, and one of those tasks included bringing peace to the animals by ordering their relationship to each other and to humanity.

Regardless of whether Jesus ate fish, he certainly should be included in the long line of Hebrew prophets who showed compassion for all of God's creation. Indeed, his many references to birds indicate that he must have had a special affection for them. Jesus declared his Father's love for the sparrows (Matthew 10:29; Luke 12:6), portrayed God as feeder of birds (Matthew 6:26; Luke 12:24), and compared himself to a hen gathering together her brood under her wings (Matthew 23:37). In a story about a poor man named Lazarus, he depicts dogs licking his sores (Luke 16:21). Jesus also states that it is acceptable to pull an animal out of a pit even on the Sabbath (Luke 14:5), suggesting that the Jewish law should not get in the way of treating animals with compassion. In fact, although Jesus criticized certain aspects of the Jewish law that made it overly rigorous and sectarian, he expected from his followers more than, not less than, the law. If the Jewish law was a means of protecting the welfare of animals, Jesus would have proclaimed nothing less.

Not everything Jesus ever said was recorded, of course. Indeed, it is remarkable that these sayings were preserved, because the early church tended to write down those sayings of Jesus that were most relevant for its situation. The writers of the Gospels were most concerned about differentiating Christian from Judaism and in reaching out to the world of Gentiles, so Jesus' attitude toward animals would have been a marginal concern. But enough of that attitude comes across in the New Testament to justify calling Jesus a lover of animals. Christianity grew primarily in urban trading cities, so it is reasonable to assume that some of Jesus' more agricultural teachings were not highlighted by early Christian writers. As a general rule, we tend to remember most those things that are most useful for us. Even more significant was the Christian polemic against Judaism, which had the result of putting topics like diet and animals outside the realm of religious concern.

The New Testament as a whole, by the way, seems to favor gentle and domesticated animals over wild ones. God descends twice as a dove (once to Mary and again at Jesus' baptism), and one of the great symbols of the Bible is the portrait of Jesus as the Lamb of God, a vision that dominates the Book of Revelation. It was natural to choose a animal that is helpless and defenseless to represent Jesus because he himself was an innocent victim who gave his life for others. By attacking the temple, he proclaimed that God no longer had any need for the spilling of blood in order to justify sinful humans. Instead, God gave of God's own life in the death of God's Son.

■ What Jesus Preached

Jesus announced the coming of the kingdom of God. That kingdom is made possible because God is working through history and has not relinquished God's authority or intentions. The kingdom is not an inner state, something like a warm, fuzzy feeling or peace of mind. It is a worldly peace, a peace that will destroy the old ways of the world based on violence and hatred and erect a new social order based on mutuality and compassion. We can see the kingdom breaking into history in the life of Jesus. Jesus is the new King of the world, but the world knew him not, and they crucified him. Even so, his life is the paradigm for the world that is still to come.

That world should not be constricted to the church or to the souls of Christian believers. The good news is for the whole world. Peace will reign when God's authority is established again and the Spirit reunites the world on the basis of the resurrected body of Jesus Christ. The glorified body of Jesus is the firstborn of all creation, a body that still has the marks of the wounds and torture that were inflicted on him. Yet that body is the sign that God will not stop in God's plans for peace. God who created the world can create it anew, and has begun doing precisely that in Jesus Christ.

The kingdom that Jesus announced and embodied, then, is a world that affirms life, that liberates the world from the forces of death. Death will be no more, nor suffering or tears. And in that new world all that has suffered, all that has been unjustly deprived of life, all that has been taken away by greed will be returned by the mighty hand of God. What God will return, surely, will include not only us but the animals as well. To say anything less is to limit God and to deny the very material reality of the resurrection.

Jesus asked his followers to press ahead toward the kingdom, even when the path looks bleak. He did not want his disciples to settle for anything less than God's full plan for the world. He thus wanted to capture the true meaning of the Torah, the Jewish law. Meat-eating is permissible, but it is hardly the best that God has in mind for us or for the animals. The kosher laws were an attempt to regulate the human consumption of meat, but an even better idea would be to go without meat altogether. Although God's self-revelation is definitive and final in the Bible, the human capacity for that revelation does change as humans grow in wisdom and as entire cultures and civilizations become more influenced by and open to the Gospel teachings. The disciples were often confused by the teachings of Jesus, and it has taken the church centuries to clarify its interpretations of every aspect of Christian belief. Perhaps it is time, then, to announce that vegetarianism is the diet of the kingdom of God.

■ The Humble King Riding on the Donkey

One of the most moving stories about Jesus is his entry into Jerusalem, which the church celebrates on Palm Sunday. The people of Jerusalem greeted him with jubilant cries, and in order to honor him, they laid down palm leaves for his donkey to tread upon. The Gospel writers saw this as a fulfillment of the prophecy in Zechariah 9:9. What is fascinating is that the people wanted to soften the step of his donkey as a way of showing respect to Jesus. This story is mostly about Jesus, of course, and that is the way it should be, but there is also a moral here about our relationship to animals. We should revere animals today not because they are as smart as us or because they share in the notion of universal rights. They aren't and they don't. We should revere animals today as a way of showing respect to Jesus.

When God became embodied in Jesus Christ, God shared not only in the plight of humanity but also in the life of animals. Anything that Jesus touched and showed compassion for should also be respected by us. The animal world served Jesus, just as animals continue to serve us, and there is nothing wrong with that unless we take their service for granted. When we think of Jesus sitting on a donkey, we naturally want to honor that animal not only for its proximity to God but also for its humble service to the humble Savior. It seems natural to us that Jesus rode into Jerusalem on a donkey, rather than a chariot pulled by horses, because Jesus came to serve us by sharing in our sufferings and sorrows. Earthly kings do not have to have any contact with working animals. Somebody else does that for them. But Jesus was not a king in that sense. Rather, Jesus redefined what kingship means. Jesus was a king who rode a lowly donkey, which should change both our conception of royal power and our notion of how power should be used in relation to animals.

The animals that most represent Jesus are not the lions and eagles of the world, but the lambs, donkeys, and doves, animals that are gentle and easily abused. Note, for example, how the Book of Revelation plays on our expectations about the relationship of power to the animal world. The author has a vision of a scroll with seven seals, which nobody can open. "Do not weep. See, the Lion of the tribe of Judah, the root of David, has conquered, so that he can open the scroll and its seven seals" (Revelation 5:5). But the very next verse surprisingly switches to the image of the slaughtered lamb, not the carnivorous lion. It is inappropriate, Scripture is teaching us, to imagine God as exercising divine power like a vicious lion. God identifies not so much with the power of the lion but with the vulnerability of the lamb. God works in the world more like an animal who is defenseless than an animal who eats other animals.

When the people of Jerusalem laid out palms and spread their cloaks for the donkey, they were making a statement about how worshiping Jesus should change the way we think about nature and the animal world. Jesus shows us what true servanthood means, and in that process we learn to treat our animal servants in a new light. "The last will be first, and the first will be last" (see Matthew 20:16) is a principle that applies not only to the human world but also to all who suffer and are mistreated. Following Jesus means giving up our privileges and serving those who ordinarily serve us. It means taking seriously the idea that God identifies with all suffering flesh, siding with those who suffer, even the lowliest of animals, the lamb or the donkey, who desperately need our tender care.

The story of Jesus riding a donkey should remind us of another story from the Old Testament. Balaam was riding on his donkey when the donkey saw the angel of the Lord standing on the road, so the donkey turned off the road and into a field. Balaam struck the donkey, and God gave the animal the power of speech to ask what he had done wrong. Balaam wanted to kill the donkey, but the donkey protested, "Am I not your donkey, which you have ridden all your life to this day? Have I been in the habit of treating you this way?" (Numbers 22:30). Finally, God intervenes and asks Balaam to account for his cruelty. This folk story is a powerful statement of the covenant between humans and animals. It upholds the moral principle that animals who labor for us should be rewarded with respect. It also supports the theological understanding of a God who is on the side of all creatures who are the victims of unfair treatment.

Early Christian theologians made precisely this set of connections. *The Acts of Thomas* is a fictional and romantic treatment of the legends surrounding the tradition that Thomas brought Christianity to India. It probably originated in Syria in the third century, but scholars continue to debate its composition and authorship. At the very least, it contains stories that attest to the intimacy with animals that was associated with the early Christians. In one such story, Thomas encounters a talking colt of an ass who tells him, "I am of that family which served Balaam, and to which also belonged that colt on which sat your Lord and Master. And now I have been sent to give you rest as you sit on me" (Elliott, p. 464). The message is clear. God gives us animals as a gift, and we should treat them as such. They are creatures to be cherished and employed with respect and compassion.

6

The Lord's Supper as a Vegetarian Meal

■ Food is not just essential for our survival. How and what we eat is a way of defining who we are. Even the bland diet of meat and potatoes that comprises what historian Daniel Sack calls "whitebread Protestantism" is a social construct that has its own particular history. Christians, of all people, should know that food shapes belief because their religion is defined by a dinner. When the disciples reclined around Jesus, each of them raised on his left elbow in the manner of the Romans at a banquet, with John leaning on the chest of Jesus, Christianity was born. True, the Eucharist today looks like an abbreviated or pretend meal. So little is eaten, and there is so little talking! Nonetheless, this ceremony signifies how rooted Christianity is in the simple act of sharing food. Sharing food is one of the most fundamental gestures of what it means to be human, and remembering this particular meal is the most fundamental determination of Christian identity.

Because eating is usually a social affair, how we behave when we eat tells others something about who we are. That is why Miss

Manners is right when she insists that etiquette is so important. Just as most rituals, from weddings to birthdays, are marked by the sharing of food, eating itself is a ritual with rules, traditions, and customs. Just setting aside certain times during the day to eat makes eating a special activity. Of course, we ordinarily take our own eating customs for granted. When we travel to a foreign country, however, one of the first things we notice is differences in eating habits and food preferences.

Etiquette is a way of regulating social relations. Manners curb violence and aggression by teaching people to control their instincts and to take other peoples' needs seriously by obeying social customs. Although manners can be an expression of social class and thus a way of legitimating wealth and elitism, manners can also create social solidarity. If there were no coherent rules about how to behave during meal times, chaos would ensue, and eating would degenerate into laborious negotiations rather than joyful celebration.

If sharing food is one of the most direct ways of establishing friendship and community, it can also keep people apart by reinforcing the status quo. People tend to eat only with those who share their same station in life, because accepting an invitation to dine implies an endorsement of one's dinner companions. Moreover, when the arrangement of guests around the table reflects social hierarchy, the dinner becomes a microcosm of the social order.

Jesus was very critical of hypocritical or false food rituals. Food was used in his day (as it still is today) as a way of claiming privilege and excluding those who are not socially acceptable company. When someone would clean himself through ritual ablutions before dinner and then act in an arrogant and self-righteous manner throughout the meal, Jesus protested. Rituals can be ways of keeping people apart and asserting one's superiority. Jesus wanted food rituals that would bring people together. That is why he was called a glutton (Matthew 11:18–19). He would eat with anyone, not because he did not believe in good manners, but because he believed in an open table fellowship, where no one is excluded from the presence of God and good food. In fact, one of his most common images for the kingdom of God was a banquet (Matthew 22:4; Luke 14:16). Christian worship is like a feast that includes "both good and bad" (Matthew 22:10). He blessed the hungry (Luke 6:20) and asked God for our daily bread (Luke 11:3). Simply put, Jesus used food to teach the most basic lessons concerning his announcement of the coming kingdom of God.

Democratic societies today do not foster strict and elaborate rules of etiquette and social behavior. They are too egalitarian for that. They suspect excessive politeness of hypocrisy. Democratic societies do have rules, but they are used to hide economic distinctions, not display them. Restaurants, for example, are hospitable places where people are invited to share a meal with perfect strangers. But what kind of community do they promise? Historian Rebecca L. Spang has shown how the restaurant is a fairly recent invention, a bourgeois institution that began in France just prior to the French revolution. Restaurants appear to be public meeting places open to all. In reality, they protect our privacy by enabling us to focus on our own individual tastes without being encumbered with any unpleasant interaction with our neighbors. They are designed to hide the work of the messy and hot kitchen from the customers, and those who work there must act like they are happy to see you, even though they do not know you. The listing of prices and the exchange of money is discrete in order not to ruin the illusion of domesticity and friendship. The point of a restaurant is to let people feel at home in public, while imagining that their homes are really like those of people who are much wealthier than they are, with servants and cooks. Such experiences can lead us to think that we live in a world that does not privilege class distinctions, yet we are still surrounded by economically disadvantaged people who are often deprived of a healthy diet. Moreover, wealthy people still feel uncomfortable eating with poor people, and whites and blacks rarely eat together in school or work cafeterias. The sharing of food, then, remains a very sensitive and politicized activity.

In the ancient world, when people (usually exclusively men) ate outside of the household it would have been in groups—sitting at a common table, sharing the same food, and thus building community. Today we have lost much of the meaning that comes with sharing meals. We are so used to eating privately in public that it is hard for us to imagine the power of the Eucharist in the early church. Nevertheless, the communion service can still be a potent reminder of the peaceful kingdom that Jesus preached. In this meal, people of all races and classes come together to celebrate the life of Jesus and give thanks for God's blessings. This very public meal manages to be deeply personal without being merely private.

■ Learning to Eat Like Christians

How Christians relate to the rest of the world is determined, in part, by how they eat, and how they eat is constituted by the paradigmatic meal of the Lord's Supper. In a book about the origins and evolution of table manners, food historian Margaret Visser has some very perceptive comments about the importance of the Lord's Supper for Christians. Just as children learn to behave and to act like adults at the dinner table, Christians learn what it means to be a Christian at communion. We learn what Christian behavior is by sharing a meal with each other, a meal that is a communion with God made possible by the death of Jesus Christ. All Christians are invited to the Lord's Table, and thus this is the most concrete expression of what it means to be a part of the body of Christ. Sharing the bread and the cup, no matter how it is done in the different Christian traditions, is the single act that demonstrates what Christian community is all about.

It is important, then, to reflect on what this meal actually is. Perhaps the most striking characteristic of the Eucharist is something that is often overlooked precisely because it is *not* a part of this meal. That is, the Eucharist does not include meat. Is this omission a mere accident of history, or does it say something fundamental about who Jesus was and what he taught? Visser calls communion a meal of peace, which makes sense because Jesus rejected the militaristic nationalism of many of his contemporaries and instead anticipated a more radical kingdom of God, where the whole world would be returned to an Edenic state of harmony and love. Meals of peace do not serve dead animal flesh for obvious reasons. Of course, the Eucharist operates on many different levels, and I am not suggesting that vegetarianism is its most fundamental message. The message of the Eucharist is that God is one with us through the life, death, and resurrection of Jesus Christ. Nevertheless, the medium of that message—the actual food eaten—is not irrelevant to the content of what the Eucharist conveys.

The question for us today is the same one that confronted the earliest Christians: How do we best remember, celebrate, and follow Jesus? Think about how inappropriate it would be to receive meat with the wine or grape juice and bread. As Visser explains, "In it [the Eucharist], animals are not killed because one message of the Eucharist is that, for believers, it reenacts the conclusive sacrifice; neither human beings nor animals need ever be immolated again, because the thing has been done" (p. 36). Moreover: "No animal and no new death is needed, no bridges required: God enters directly" (p. 36). It takes a food critic, perhaps, to understand how the Eucharist is a meal that comments on every other meal.

Meat could not be a part of the Eucharist not only because the death of Jesus puts an end to the need to sacrifice animals, but also because the whole ritual of eating meat is so different from the ritual of eating a vegetarian meal. When an animal is served for a meal, decisions must be made about how to carve and distribute it. The quality of meat varies from cut to cut. Moreover, meat could not be preserved very well, so it had to be passed out all at once, and thus when an animal was killed there would be a feast. The pieces of meat that were more desirable than others would be given to honored guests or people of merit and distinction. Thus, serving meat has always been one of the most visible signs of hierarchy, rank, and wealth.

Meat not only reflects and upholds class distinctions; it also creates gender differences. As religion scholar Nancy Jay has argued, sacrificial rituals serve to distinguish the roles of men and women by putting male priests in charge of the rituals that ancient people thought did the most to uphold social and even cosmic order. Throughout history men almost always have been in charge of the meat. This continues today, as any barbecue will demonstrate. Cooking meat on a fire, as with the ancient sacrifices, is a male-dominated activity. Killing animals was thought to be not dissimilar to going to war, and cutting meat involved the use of dangerous tools and knives. There are many ancient rituals that suggest that sacrificing animals is the only way to keep peace with the gods and promote social stability, and these rituals take for granted that the only people who can perform such serious duties are men.

A vegetarian meal has a totally different dynamic. As Visser explains, the preparation of vegetables in the ancient world, as today, was a more feminine activity. "Vegetables, on the other hand, were most often the result of the steady, unexalted, cooperative, and often mainly female work required for collecting them, or for tending them in the fields" (p. 231). Preparing vegetables has none of the drama of killing animals. In killing animals, men express their dominance over nature, their skill at using knives and controlling fire, and their willingness to shed blood for the good of their families. In preparing vegetables, women express their closeness to the earth and the equality of all those partaking of the meal, since there is no single portion of a vegetable dish that is better than any other portion.

Certainly the death of Jesus was very dramatic and bloody. But it is interesting that we remember that death in a vegetarian meal of fruit and bread, not in the further slaying of animals. The Bible often associates meat eating with gluttony, as is clear from the story of the sons of Eli, who were in a hurry to eat their meat before it was properly sacrificed on the altar (1 Samuel 2:12–17). It makes sense, then, that the Eucharist is a simple, frugal, and vegetarian meal. As Visser comments, "A joint of meat served for dinner restricts the number of guests invited; vegetarian meals permit far more elastic arrangements because they are easily shared and extended" (p. 231). Serving meat is a sign of wealth and power; thus, in remembering the humility and suffering of God in Jesus, meat would be out of place.

Unfortunately, today we eat meat with a regularity and passion that was unheard of in the premodern world. One consequence of our meat-heavy diet is that Christians no longer look at the communion as a real meal. Communion seems like a play meal, a ritual with nominal meaning, precisely because it does not include meat. In many churches today, Christians sip some juice from thimble-sized glasses, often made of disposable plastic, and they nibble a tiny, tasteless piece of bread, as if eating too much would be a sacrilegious act in the presence of God's holiness. In other churches, they carefully tear off a small piece of bread to dip in the chalice or hold out their cupped hands for a bread crumb or a pressed wafer. The Eucharist provides hardly enough food to constitute a snack, let alone a meal. Solemn music plays in the background, and everyone keeps their heads bowed. At family meals, people look at each other, but at this ceremonious meal people act like they are in a fancy restaurant, where they shun each other's eyes and try not to make a sound. It is almost as if Christians are ashamed of their need for food.

Certainly reverence is a part of this central Christian ritual, but the Lord's Supper should also be a festive occasion. We can only be embarrassed to eat before the Lord if we do not think that our bodies as well as our souls are saved by Jesus' death. The Lord's Supper tells us that all who come to the Lord's Table will not be turned away, that all who come to Jesus will be given sustenance and life. Communion is the heart of Christianity because in it we know and experience the fullness of God's abundant gifts to us. There is enough for all, the Eucharist proclaims. Meat is the food of the wealthy and the powerful. A meatless diet, by contrast, says that everyone can be cared for cheaply and without bloodshed. After all, a vegetarian diet can quite literally feed more people than a meat diet.

Bread, then, and not meat, is the staff of life. In many languages, the very word *bread* means simply food, and "breaking bread" means eating. We want bread with every meal. The word *companion,* from the Latin, literally means a person with whom we share bread. Jesus broke bread with the disciples on the road to Emmaus, and only then did they recognize him. When we eat the bread of communion we should be reminded that the essence of food is not a life that has been taken but a substance that gives life. Anthropologist Mary Douglas has recently suggested that the bread of the Eucharist could have reminded the early Christians of the cereal offerings that are detailed in Leviticus. She even argues that the existence of a cereal offering as a kind of alternative or parallel to the animal sacrifices in Judaism prepared the way for the early Christians to have a vegetable, not animal, sacrificial meal. Perhaps bread is treated as such a special food item throughout history precisely because it has always represented an alternative to animal sacrifices, something women would bake and share at home while the men were dividing up the meat.

In the middle of the nineteenth century, many Protestant churches, with Methodists in the lead, were so committed to the temperance movement that they changed the cup of wine to grape juice as a protest against the way alcohol can be easily abused. Abstemious Christians wanted the Eucharist to address a devas-

147

tating social problem not just in terms of its meaning but also in terms of what it literally serves. Putting a social statement above the biblical account of the Last Supper, however, forced them into some fancy biblical hermeneutics. They developed a "two wine" theory, arguing, without any evidence, that the biblical word for wine could mean either an alcoholic or nonalcoholic drink, even though, as religious studies professor Robert Fuller has shown, the Bible is basically very positive about the value of wine as a gift from God. Later in that century many churches began substituting individual cups for the single chalice out of concern for hygiene. They made the liturgy a more individual experience because they were worried about new theories concerning germs and the spread of disease. They made this change even though the use of one cup, which symbolized the unity of the body of believers, was the clear practice throughout Christian history.

By contrast, to think about the Eucharist as a vegetarian meal does not involve any changes in what is served or how it is served. It would involve a change, however, in what we take away from this meal. It would ask Christians to think much more seriously about what they actually eat on Sunday mornings. John 4:34 says, "Jesus said to them, 'My food is to do the will of him who sent me and to complete his work.'" The will of God should be in our food, something that we are reminded of when we partake of the body and blood of Jesus Christ. Jesus is the perfect embodiment of God's will, so we should eat in a way that celebrates his life and what he represents. Perhaps today the bread and juice together can be thought of as a vegetarian meal that witnesses to the sacrificial presence of Jesus Christ while also protesting against the way factory farms and slaughterhouses abuse animals.

◼ Was Meat Served at the Last Supper?

Jewish law forbids the consumption of blood. This law dates back to the covenant God made with Noah, and it was meant to be enforced even on foreigners (Leviticus 17:10–12). Saul even built his first altar for God because his army, faint with hunger, ate meat with the blood still in it (1 Samuel 14:31–35). Blood, as the very essence of life, belongs to God alone. Therefore, when Jesus presented the cup of wine to his followers at the Last Supper as the blood of a new covenant, his companions must have been startled. If his fellow Jews did not imagine themselves as literally drinking blood, what did they think they were doing? What kind of meal had Jesus prepared?

Did Jesus serve meat at his dinner while talking about the wine becoming his very own blood? Did he serve animal flesh while stating that the bread was his very own body? Wouldn't the presence of real blood and flesh at this meal have confused the issue? How could the Jewish disciples have been eating meat while talking about the soon-to-be-tortured body of Christ?

To answer these questions, we need to know what kind of meal Jesus served. Some scholars doubt that a Last Supper ever took place. However, there is good historical reasoning in its favor. Because Jesus used meals as a means of proclaiming his message, it is likely that, knowing that his public ministry was drawing to a close, he held a final meal with his disciples in order to give them a special foretaste of the kingdom (Koenig, p. 16). He had already chosen twelve disciples as a symbolic expression of his desire to restore Israel. Now he was going to use one of Judaism's most sacred rituals in order to redefine God's covenant with the nations.

Many scholars think that the Jewish holiday of the Passover was the context for the Last Supper. The synoptic Gospels (Matthew, Mark, and Luke) place the event on the same evening as Passover. However, the Gospel of John has the death of Jesus coincide with the slaughter of the lambs in the temple (they were killed there and then eaten at home), thus placing the Last Supper before the Passover meal. This discrepancy can probably be resolved by noting that John has a theological point to make: the crucifixion of Jesus replaces the killing of the lambs. Paul further emphasizes this point when he calls Jesus the Paschal Lamb in 1 Corinthians 5:7.

Clearly, in gathering his disciples together on Passover, Jesus was trying to place his own ministry in the context of the struggles of the people of Israel. Jesus could thus draw on the knowledge of his disciples of Jewish history while reinterpreting that history in provocative ways. The Passover celebrates the liberation of the Israelites from slavery in Egypt. According to Exodus 12, God ordered each Jewish household to kill an unblemished male lamb, sprinkle some of the blood on the doorpost, and eat the flesh with bitter herbs and in haste. God then passed over those houses while he plagued the Egyptians. In the time of Jesus, the Passover was celebrated again in a situation of bondage, this time to Roman rule. A large goblet was kept for the prophet Elijah, in the hope that he would pay a visit, since he is the prophet who will announce the arrival of the Messiah. When Jesus and his disciples ate their dinner, their thoughts must have been on the dire situation of their people, who once again needed liberation from an oppressive foe.

Jesus was not simply repeating the Jewish tradition of Passover; instead, he was transforming it (Chilton, 1994). In fact, there is no biblical evidence that the Passover lamb was served at this meal. Some might argue that the lamb is not mentioned simply because it was widely known to be a part of the Passover meal. That is, why mention the obvious? The Gospels, however, were written for a Christian audience that did not always know the details of Jewish rituals and that commemorated the Last Supper with a meatless meal. The way the Last Supper was remembered and recorded was crucial for the development of early Christian ritual. The Gospel writers knew that every detail of their description of this meal was important, and their silence concerning the lamb spoke volumes to the early Christians. The temple rituals were being condensed into the very person of Jesus Christ, making this meal the foundation for a new religious movement. The Gospel writers did not just forget about the lamb when describing the Last Supper, nor was it a convenient omission, since the early Christians were trying to distinguish themselves from the Jews. Instead, they remembered the true lamb, the one necessary sacrifice who came to end all unnecessary sacrifices.

Given what Jesus said during the meal, the lamb would have been redundant. Rabbi Lawrence Hoffman has argued that during the early Christian era Jews had also begun thinking about the bread (*matzah*) as a substitute for the lamb. If this tradition dates back to the time of Jesus, then Jesus would have made perfect sense to his disciples when he substituted the bread, as a symbol of his body, for the lamb. Jesus was offering himself as the final sacrifice, a death that would break the very bonds of death and violence. God saw what Jesus had done and God passed over not just the homes of the elect but the whole world, announcing the good news of forgiveness. Jesus took a meal that represented the necessity of spilled blood and transposed it to preach a message of hope for a peaceful kingdom. He was using food to make a theological point. Serving lamb would have confused the issue of how his path of deliverance differed from the temple rituals.

John Koenig has speculated that Jesus and his disciples might also have had the story of Moses from Exodus 24 on their minds during the Last Supper. After Moses read the covenant to the people, he dashed the blood of a slain oxen onto the crowd, sealing God's promises. Then the people ate and drank. This scene from the Old Testament brings together the shedding of blood, a meal, and the celebration and ratification of God's covenant. Likewise, Jesus used the wine to demonstrate a new liberation, one based on the overflowing of God's grace from the covenant with Israel to include the whole world.

The crucial question is, what kind of liberation did he offer? There were many Jews, called Zealots, who thought that a military conflict with the Romans would hasten the coming of the Messiah. They were willing to spill their own blood (and the blood of Roman soldiers) in order to drive out the infidels who were polluting the temple. Jesus had other ideas. Jesus thought of himself as a kind of nourishment for his followers that would put an end to the unnecessary spilling of blood. In the Gospel of John he identified himself with the vegetarian manna, the "true bread from heaven" (6:32–35 and 49–51). By remembering Jesus' death, we are really celebrating the abundance of God's good gifts, which sustain all life. Christians appropriately remember this death by eating a vegetarian meal. Indeed, throughout most of its history, the church honored the day of Friday, the day on which Jesus was killed, by asking all Christians not to eat meat on that day. (Because fish was not classified as meat, that day quickly became a day of eating fish, but the point was not to eat meat; fish-eating was permitted but not required on that day.)

■ Is Communion a Real Meal?

For many Christians, the celebration of the Lord's Supper, variously called communion, Eucharist, or the Mass, is not thought to be a real meal for the simple reason that not enough is eaten to satisfy our hunger. It is an act of worship where the elements often seem like props in a play without enough budget to create the illusion of a real meal. To break off too big of a chunk of bread or take too large of a swallow from the cup would somehow mock the gravity of the occasion by reducing it to the function of meeting basic bodily needs. The problem is that this ritual is treated as so special—indeed, it is the ritual that makes Christians Christian—that it is connected to what we think or feel rather than to something as mundane as eating dinner.

The fact that the Eucharist today is not a real meal that satisfies our hunger does not mean that it has always been that way. Many scholars today think that the Eucharist took a variety of forms in the early church. The liturgy was not standardized until several hundred years after the death of Jesus. Until the fourth century, Christians gave thanks and remembered the life and death of Jesus through a variety of ritualized meals. In a very real sense, these meals provided the foundation for the emerging church.

When early Christians would gather together for the Eucharist, eating bread and drinking wine would function for most of them as a real meal. The earliest Christians probably ate this meal on Saturday nights, which would have functioned as a kind of extended Sabbath (which took place from sundown on Friday to sundown on Saturday). This would have permitted them to observe the commandment to honor the Sabbath as well as to honor the day, Sunday, on which Jesus was raised from the dead (Koenig, pp. 69–70). Cheap wine or wine mixed with water was the normal drink for many people in the ancient world, and bread, perhaps with some relishes like oil, salt, and vegetables, was the staff of life. Those were the most basic elements of any meal, so that sharing this food for the early Christians was really an act of satisfying everyone's hunger, not just a symbolic statement about the death of Jesus.

The Eucharist sometimes even included food other than the bread and wine. Andrew McGowan has done more than any scholar to identify various eucharistic meals in the early church that included items such as cheese, milk, honey, oil, salt, fruits, vegetables, and fish. As he points out, there were many communal meals of thanksgiving in the early church that are difficult, in retrospect, to distinguish from Eucharists proper. If you begin with the assumption that any food other than bread and wine rules out a meal as being a Eucharist, then you solve a lot of problems in the historical record. But then you are reading history backwards from the vantage point of an orthodox Eucharist that emerged, some scholars think, only gradually in Christian history.

In fact, some early Christians did not think that the Eucharist should be only a symbolic meal. Instead, they tried to make every meal they ate a Eucharist. The distinction between secular and sacred meals, after all, derives from a modern rather than an ancient set of categories. These communal meals of thanksgiving that resembled the Eucharist but included other food were based not only on the memory of the Last Supper. Some of these meals might have looked back more to the New Testament meals of the resurrection appearances or the miracles of Jesus feeding the multitudes, rather than the Last Supper. These meals were also influenced by various Roman and Jewish customs. They included what early Christians called *agapes,* "love feasts" that included a variety of food. Clement of Alexandria defined the *agape* as "in essence heavenly food," and argued that it should not include the smell of roasting meat (Leyerle, p. 138). Such meals indicate that a lively and vigorous sense of God's abundance was a guiding theme in the life of the early church.

The most important alternative to the bread and wine tradition was the celebration of a bread and water Eucharist. (Sometimes wine and water were mixed as a symbol of the dual nature of Jesus Christ, but I am discussing here evidence that water alone was used in the cup.) Eucharists that avoided wine were not an innovative modification of an early orthodox consensus—arising from ascetic concerns over the consumption of alcohol—but were instead creative attempts by early Christians to figure out what kind of meal was the most appropriate setting for the act of remembering Jesus Christ. McGowan suggests that it is possible that the advice given in 1 Timothy 5:23 against drinking water alone reflects a Pauline argument against Christians who would not drink wine in the Eucharist.

To eat a meal of bread and water would not have been uncommon, but to choose to make that your most basic meal as well as the fundamental expression of your relationship to God was distinctive. Philosophers who belonged to schools like the Cynics, who often did not eat meat in order to show their indifference to social customs and their freedom from thoughtless practices, also ate frugal meals of bread and water. Their dietary dissent from society could have influenced the eating habits of early Christians. The Cynics were critical of institutional religion, which meant animal sacrifices, and this was probably the same motivation behind the early Christian bread and water meals. Wine was closely associated with feasts of animal flesh, and it has obvious connotations of blood, which is why Jesus could use wine to symbolize his blood. For some early Christians, the Eucharist was a meal of thanks that was meant to replace the animal sacrifices of Jews and pagans alike, so drinking wine seemed as inappropriate as eating meat with such a meal.

Among many groups that were later deemed heretical there seems to be a common trait of celebrating the Eucharist with foods that were not a part of the sacrificial cuisine. Montanists and Marcionites, for example, probably used a kind of soft cheese or curd in their Eucharist, which, as a form of milk, might have been a substitution for the wine. Likewise, milk and honey meals were an explicit attempt to conjure an original golden age of innocence and plenty, when animal sacrifices were unnecessary. Christians would have associated milk and honey, of course, with the story of the promised land in Exodus—although milk and honey were also used for initiation rites in pagan religion, which might be the reason for their decline in Christianity. In Africa (and elsewhere), there was a custom of giving milk (or a milk and honey mixture) to the newly baptized. It should be remembered that early Christians were in danger of being martyred for their faith. They were turned into sacrifices simply because they would not participate in the pagan animal sacrifices. Thus, milk was a potent (and maternal) symbol of a life-sustaining liquid that is the opposite of the blood of the pagan sacrifices, just as honey was a foretaste of the joys of heaven. If Romans wanted blood, in both their games and their meals, then it makes sense that Christians, who were often the victims of Roman bloodthirstiness, would turn to a food like milk to articulate their alternative vision of a peaceable kingdom.

The groups that ate an explicitly vegetarian Eucharist had in common a sectarian tendency to separate themselves from pagan society. That is, they did not want to participate in the animal sacrifices in any form, so they worked hard to eliminate the vestiges of sacrificial cuisine from their own ritual meals. They wanted the Eucharist to be more than a symbolic meal. Consequently, they placed a lot of emphasis on the details of what was actually served in communion.

■ The Compromising Influence of the Apostle Paul, Again

These full-meal Eucharists did not long survive in Christianity. When the Eucharist was moved to Sunday morning, from Saturday or Sunday evening, it became a symbolic meal. Christians no longer gathered around tables to eat and worship. Only the bishop or the presbyter needed a table to preside over the breaking of the bread and the pouring of the wine. This table could be construed as an altar, which would make the Eucharist look something like the pagan and Jewish sacrifices.

Indeed, Paul set the stage for what would become orthodox eucharistic practice when he emphasized the similarities between the Lord's Supper and pagan sacrifices (see, for example, 1 Corinthians 10:16–22). The Christian ritual was to be a new kind of sacrifice, a bloodless dramatization of the ultimate sacrifice, the sacrifice to end all sacrifices. This means not just that Paul had a more complacent or tolerant attitude toward the pagan sacrifices. More importantly, it means that Paul, to make sense of the Eucharist, placed it in a narrative context, in continuity with the religious practices that he saw all around him, in Judaism and paganism alike. He did this in order to demonstrate the superiority of Christianity, but as a result, he also cast the Eucharist in a sacrificial mold. He used the logic, language, and even the elements of animal sacrifice—bread/body and wine/blood—to build a bridge from pagan religion to the new religion of Christianity. His main concern was the spread of the gospel, and he wanted to be able to preach a message that made sense to his audience. To say that the Eucharist was completely anti-sacrificial would have been to risk alienating the very people Paul was trying to convert. Instead, Paul represented the Eucharist as counter-sacrificial, a ritual that both continued and disrupted the logic of pagan sacrifices.

Every theologian has to try to tell the good news of Jesus in a way that people can understand, and Paul was very successful in planting new churches. Paul wanted to uphold the final sacrifice, while the sectarian groups wanted to reject sacrifices altogether. Did Paul try too hard to compromise with his audience? By preaching a new sacrifice that renders old ones redundant, he risked continuing the very thing that he was trying to replace. By perpetuating the language of sacrifice, even in a new key, his message tended to mute the implication of Jesus' death for the animals. In other words, he was not able to clearly articulate how the death of Jesus had brought an end to the religious justification of the spilling of innocent blood. Moreover, he was unable to include in the transformation demanded by Christianity the social practices of eating.

The point that the "bread and water" Christians wanted to emphasize is that the Lord's Supper is a frugal meal. It is not a pagan banquet, a carnival that gives the participants permission to do whatever they want. That kind of feast erases all boundaries and limits in order to probe the infinite possibilities of human desire. Such festivals always end up with somebody getting hurt, because our desires inevitably run up against the limits of other people and their own wants. The Eucharist, by contrast, does not let people enjoy the forbidden fruits of unbound passions, but rather asks people to do the right thing, to pursue justice and equality before the majesty of God. Paul criticizes those who partake of the Eucharist while disregarding their hungry brothers and sisters (1 Corinthians 11:17–34). In the Eucharist (which literally means thanksgiving), we give thanks to God for giving us everything that we need, rather than all that we want and desire.

Like the Passover celebration of the Exodus from Egypt, this meal should urge us to remember what God has done for us. It should also, however, remind us that God's work of liberation is not yet complete. Not until the Messianic banquet, which will be inclusive and peaceful, will the ministry of Jesus find its conclusion (Revelation 19:9). The Eucharist thus looks forward, as well as back to the past. As Jesus said, "I have food to eat that you do not know about" (John 4:32). A meal of meat that wastes God's resources by using grain, land, and water in tremendously inefficient ways—not to mention the suffering of the animals—is hardly an appropriate way to remember the death of Jesus. Such meals will be as bad for the body as they are for the spirit. We need to learn to eat in ways that are complementary to what we believe, and we can start by letting the communion service shape both how and what we eat.

■ Rethinking Transubstantiation

Partly as a result of Paul's theology, the Eucharist began to look more and more like an animal sacrifice, as evidenced in an Easter hymn from the fourth to sixth century: "We are looking forward to the supper of the lamb . . . whose sacred body is roasted on the altar of the cross. By drinking his rosy blood, we live with God . . . Now Christ is our Passover, our sacrificial lamb: His flesh, the unleavened bread of sincerity, is offered up" (Bynum, 1987, p. 49). This process of animalizing the Eucharist reached its peak in the Middle Ages with the doctrine of transubstantiation, which portrayed the Eucharist as an reenactment of Christ's death. Some scholars have suggested that this doctrine was formulated in reaction against the vegetarian diet of various heretical groups. These groups, which I will discuss in greater detail in chapter nine, challenged church hierarchy and rejected priestly authority. By making the Eucharist look more like a sacrifice, the Roman Catholic church could enhance the power of the priesthood and denounce a nonbloody diet at the same time.

This does not mean, however, that the doctrine of the real presence of Christ in the Eucharist is incompatible with an interpretation of the Eucharist as a vegetarian meal. On the contrary, a very traditional understanding of this ritual makes its actual contents more important, not less. What the doctrine of transubstantiation highlights is how the bread and wine are not arbitrary signs of faith but instead fitting vehicles of the nourishment given by God's outpouring in Jesus Christ. In explaining St. Thomas Aquinas's position on transubstantiation, theologians John Milbank and Catherine Pickstock have noted how he "places great stress on the analogical appropriateness of the elements of bread and wine right down to the details of the multiplicity of grape and grain being compressed into a unity. He also stresses how the elements of the Eucharist taste and smell good, and regards this as part of a complex rhetoric whereby the Eucharistic presentation of Christ is made attractive to us" (p. 104). God's presence in the bread and wine during the liturgy is not incidental to God's plan for redemption. Just as Jesus Christ is God's embodied encounter with humanity, the bread and wine are all that we have of Christ's body after the ascension.

Indeed, there is a perfect harmony established between God's descent in Jesus Christ and our ascent in the Eucharist. The incarnation shows us that salvation concerns the whole person, body and soul, while the Eucharist demonstrates that the senses are the medium through which we begin our reception of grace. It is not the head or the heart that most basically encounters God. We can believe or feel in private, but eating is a social activity that draws us out of ourselves and demonstrates how dependent we are on nature and other people. The eating of the eucharistic elements goes even further by revealing how everything material is dependent on the supernatural.

If the incarnation is the way in which God touches and thus knows the world, then we best know God through that most intimate touch, the taste of the tongue in consuming the bread and wine. As the very substance of our communion with God, this food becomes the paradigm for all food, just as Jesus defines our true humanity. The modern world, obsessed with novelty, can never understand the repetition of rituals, but we can receive the Eucharist repeatedly without ever getting enough because our desire for God is endless. That desire is not futile, however, because in this meal we have a foretaste of the heavenly banquet that is to come.

It is easy to think that the Medieval saints who lived on a diet of the Eucharist alone were fanatics, but they were guilty only of impatience. They wanted their bodies to become transformed by what they ate, so that their flesh could experience the glorification made possible by Christ's resurrection. They knew that this ritual is more than a symbolic meal or a moment for meditative reflection. God chose to use the biological metamorphosis of fruit and grain into wine and bread as the occasion to enact Christ's own transfiguration of matter into spirit. In this good food we come to know the goodness of all of God's creation, because the body we are and the body we eat—as well as all bodies, represented by the particles of grain and fruit—are all part of the sacrificed body of Christ.

■ God Bless This Meal

The most obvious Christian practice in the area of diet is the customary prayer before the meal. Because Christianity is a religion all about sacrifice, it can seem to make sense that Christians pray before meals that include meat. As Karl Barth has written, "The slaying of animals is really possible only as an appeal to God's reconciling grace, as its representation and proclamation" (1961, p. 354). The logic goes like this: When Christians pray before a meal of meat, they are thanking God not only for the sacrifice of God's Son but also for the sacrifice of the life of the animal that they are about to eat. God had to give up something for us, just as animals give their lives for our benefit. Sacrifice might be a nasty business, whether it is the crucifixion on Golgotha or the animals packed into the slaughterhouses, but it is something that simply must be done, and we should be grateful to God for both the gentle obedience of God's Son and the tender morsels of meat on our plates.

Vegetarian Christians, however, see the death of animals differently. If an animal needs to be eaten to keep humans alive, then such a tragic choice must be made. But most of us live in a society where animals do not have to die for us. We have plenty of nonmeat alternatives for our protein. Thus, when Christian vegetarians say grace before a meal, they are thanking God that Jesus Christ came to end unnecessary suffering and to teach us how to live in peace with each other and with the world. The whole meal of the vegetarian is a supplication to the extent that it is an expression of confidence in God and an act of solidarity with the all-encompassing suffering of Jesus Christ. Christian vegetarians find the good in what they eat not by turning their diet into a new religion but by turning every meal into a plea for the good of all God's creatures.

7

Will All Good Dogs Go to Heaven?

■ Too often, when theologians write about nature, they do so in very abstract terms, arguing that God loves nature and thus we should too. Such talk about nature is theoretical and vague. It is much more practical to address the more concrete and more demanding question of animals than nature in general. It is too easy to speculate about how we should respect the world as God's good creation without specifying what our obligations to animals are. The theological issue that most reveals what we think about those obligations is, paradoxically, the doctrine of heaven—the very doctrine that often seems the most removed from all of our worldly concerns. If we are to transform our attitude toward the lowest and most defenseless forms of life on earth, then we must lift our vision to the highest and most glorious purpose beyond this life. Only by thinking about heaven and the ultimate destiny of all animals can we bring an ambiguous theology of nature down to earth.

■ Pet Theology

When a child tells us her dog has died and asks us if her dog will go to heaven, we are usually quick to respond with a yes, and then we hope the conversation ends right there. But then the child might ask us if all dogs go to heaven, and that should stop and make us think very hard about what we think heaven is. If heaven is the place where God will redeem and restore all that God values, then is it really so childish to think about animals being there? If God is omnipotent and God's love knows no limits, is it really so innocent to think about God loving animals enough to make them a part of heaven? If humans have always shared their lives with animals, indeed, if our bond with animals has been so important throughout history that it in part makes us who we are, then is it naive to think that this bond will survive death and that we will not be separated from our animal companions in the life that is yet to come?

People are desperate to conceive of their pets as having an afterlife. There is a new company, PerPETuate Inc., that will take a genetic sample of a living or dead pet and keep it frozen in their lab. They will store the DNA until science perfects the cloning of companion animals. One woman who uses the service said, "It's a comforting feeling to know that maybe someday we can have her back." Rather than adopting one of the millions of stray animals that are put to death each year, some people choose to trust in futuristic technology to give them a glimmer of hope that their pet might one day return to life for a few more years.

Pets have always been pampered. That, indeed, seems to be what pets are for. They are there to be an outlet for extravagant emotions and exuberant affection. It is natural that we do not want to see those relationships come to an end. This is beautifully captured in Paul Auster's recent novel *Timbuktu,* which is about a dog's unwavering loyalty to his homeless master. It movingly portrays a steadfast bond that is strong enough to survive death. Even when the dog, after his master's miserable death, finds a home in the suburbs with a loving family, he never gives up longing to be reunited with the one who needed him most. "When the moment came for him to part company with this world, it seemed only right that he should be allowed to dwell in the hereafter with the same person he had loved in the here-before" (p. 49). If God is love, then God will preserve every loving relationship in the world, turning our feeble and desperate attempts at attachment into something true, good, and everlasting.

St. Augustine defined sin as disordered love, that is, loving things with more passion than they deserve. And it is true that pets can get in the way of our love for other people and even our love for God. When do we know that our love for a pet has gone too far? Doesn't all love make us foolish in our attempts to aid and benefit the loved one? Perhaps the most controversial aspect of pet-keeping is the practice of pet burial. There is a famous pet cemetery in Los Angeles that is used by Hollywood stars. The Pet Memorial Park was satirized by Evelyn Waugh's 1948 novel, *The Loved One,* where it was referred to as the "Happier Hunting Grounds." Started in 1928, it is operated by Sophie Corp., an acronym for Save Our Pets' History in Eternity. One board member explained their purpose, "We give the same kind of service as if Uncle Harry died in the living room. We give them respect." The message on a marker at the entrance states: "When a beloved pet dies, the pet goes to this place. There is always food, water and warm spring weather. The old and frail animals are young again. Those who are maimed are made whole again. They play all day with each other." With suburban sprawl and the decline of farmland in our country, the idea of all pets being buried is enough to make any environmentalist panic, but surely the sentiments behind the gesture are deeply Christian. All bodies matter because God became embodied and Jesus rose as a body from the grave.

Burying a pet has the same motivation as burying people. We want to know where the pet's body lies so that we can honor its memory and respect its life. Some people will think that burying pets is crazy, but that is because they have no sense of the ultimate worth of animals. To think about animal resurrection is to acknowledge the absolute value of all animal bodies, even those we eat. Many dead pets are rendered (made into tallow), rather than buried, hardly a practice conducive to thinking about the value of animals. Of course, honoring the memory of a beloved pet can go too far, especially when resources need to be prioritized. After all, the love of pets can become a distraction from our responsibilities toward all people and animals. What is unfortunate is that when religious people experience the loss of a pet, they rarely have a sympathetic pastor to turn to or church rituals to sustain them.

Perhaps if the churches were more clear about the idea of pets being in heaven, then people would not seek such desperate ways to honor their memory here and now.

■ The Need for a New Boldness about Heaven

In the modern world, heaven is not considered a serious topic of conversation. Heaven might be fine for sentimental movies or old-fashioned stories, but busy, practical people do not take it seriously. Even people who entertain the idea of an afterlife are reluctant to think in concrete terms about heaven. There are two reasons for this, one epistemological and the other moral. I will deal first with the epistemological reason, which has to do with how we think about the limits to human knowledge. In the next section I will deal with the moral worry that heaven functions as a disincentive for people to try to change the injustices of this world by leading people to expect that everything will be taken care of in the next one.

In the ancient world, people thought that the Earth was at the center of the cosmos, surrounded by the stars, which were themselves the portals of the divine light. Just above that, it was agreed, lies heaven. Copernicus changed all of that, of course, by telling us that the Earth is just another planet, not even at the center of this solar system. Modern physics makes everything even much more complicated than that by talking about black holes and reversible time, but even though nature seems stranger than we can possibly imagine, most people are still committed to an empirical outlook on life: something is real only if you can actually see it. Before we ask what something is, we want to know where it is. Since heaven is commonly thought to exist in a dimension of reality that we cannot presently perceive, many people have trouble thinking of the afterlife in terms of anything more specific than floating spirits and bright lights. Astronomers keep searching for new planets and talking about an infinite universe, expanding the limits of human knowledge, so there is no room in our collective imagination for depicting a place that exists in an utterly different mode of reality and yet is a perfect version of what we already experience here and now.

It is not clear, then, when we do talk about heaven, what we are talking about. We have limited our imaginations to what is, rather than to what could be. We think it is silly to think about animals being in heaven, and yet that very skepticism has led to a crisis in our theology of the afterlife. We think of heaven as the opposite of our earthly existence, rather than the fulfillment of our deepest desires and needs. If we are so embarrassed to be too explicit in our portrait of heaven, then heaven becomes some vague notion that has little meaning in our everyday world. Imagining animals in heaven is a good way of remembering that the Christian notion of the afterlife emphasizes the restoration and completion of this world, not the substitution of material life with something less concrete and real.

A heaven without animals is a heaven without those relationships that bring so much meaning and pleasure to our lives. It is the kind of heaven that atheists make fun of when they reject the idea: a bunch of pious people standing around and singing hymns forever and ever. Who would want to go there? And wouldn't even the most faithful of us get bored by that? Only by putting animals back in heaven can we save heaven from our own lack of imagination.

There is a great thirst in our culture for a fuller account of the afterlife than modernist, liberal theology has been able to conjure. When theologians cannot deliver, Hollywood films try to fill the gap. When the character played by Robin Williams dies and goes to heaven in the movie *What Dreams May Come,* the first being he meets is his dog, who had been put to sleep years before. There are many ancient myths about dogs greeting people in the afterlife, and why not? Dogs have a way of making us feel at home with their loyalty and affection, and they guard the doors to our homes, intent to let in only our loved ones. They have long accompanied people on their various journeys in the world, so why wouldn't they be there on the final and most important journey of all?

Theologians are often afraid that specific descriptions of heaven will promote a naive and crude literalism. The Bible, however, shows no signs of such timidity. As Psalm 36:6 states, God "save[s] humans and animals alike." Both humans and animals share the same origin and thus the same destiny in God: "All go to the same place" (Ecclesiastes 3:19–21, NEB). When the Old Testament prophets picture the new Jerusalem, it is full of animals (see, for example, Zechariah 2:4 and Ezekiel 1:5, 10), a theme that is continued in the final book of the Bible, Revelation, where living creatures with animal forms join in the heavenly chorus around the throne of God (Revelation 4:6–11).

Nonetheless, we certainly need to keep in mind that the language of heaven is symbolic and not descriptive. It is much easier to imagine hell than heaven, because we experience more suffering than perfect bliss in this life. The good in all of its simplicity is always more difficult to picture than the endless layers of complexity that comprise moral evil. Moreover, heaven is nothing more than intimacy with God, and God lies beyond our categories and our constructions. God is wholly other than us, a being who is totally different from the various beings we see all around us. So thinking about heaven means, in a way, negating all of our experiences and all of our knowledge. To imagine heaven is to try to picture God, and for that we can rely only on metaphors, stories, and symbols. In the words of Martin Luther, "We know no more about eternal life than children in the womb of their mother know about the world they are about to enter" (Althaus, p. 425). We might not know more, but we know enough to hope for more. Imagining heaven is to risk thinking not about the utterly unknown but about the eagerly anticipated "not yet."

Christianity has a heritage of rich language about heaven, but we seem afraid to use that language today. Even if we cannot take that language literally, we need to be confident that what it points to is more true than we can presently know. When we know what heaven is like, we will realize that this language was the most appropriate one available, but we will also know heaven in ways that we never could have imagined on earth. The language that puts animals in heaven, then, is true and trustworthy language. It refers to a reality that will indeed be all-inclusive. But it is still merely human language, an attempt to describe the indescribable, so we must be humble when we use it. The point is that we should be humble not about what that language points to but about our ability to describe fully what only God can reveal. In sum, we need to be confident that God will do what God has promised, and thus we are free to use the most vivid language to try to imagine something that lies beyond even our wildest dreams.

■ Is Heaven a Bribe to Encourage Morality?

Another reason why we have a very minimal view of heaven today has to do with morality, not epistemology. Reading Marx, we are aware that the idea of heaven has been used to oppress the poor and needy. Promising the oppressed a happy ending to their lives—"pie in the sky when you die"—keeps them from demanding better conditions here and now. It also releases the wealthy and powerful from addressing the injustices that led to their misery in the first place. Even the most traditional among us does not want heaven to be used as an excuse not to do something here and now. After all, why put off until tomorrow what we can accomplish today? We spend so much time and money improving our lives in this world—building a heaven on earth—that it does not make much sense to dwell on what life will be like in the next world. As a result, the afterlife becomes nothing more than an afterthought.

Indeed, it is popular today among theologians and philosophers to argue that the hope for eternal reward in heaven can only contaminate moral action here on earth. If we do something good for somebody else because we want to get to heaven, then we are hardly acting in a self-sacrificial manner. If we give something to somebody only because we expect it to be returned, then what we have given can hardly be called a gift. Such an act looks more like entering into a contract (I will do something for you only if you do something for me) than an act of generosity or gift-giving. To give something away only because we expect its return is to do the right thing for the wrong reason. Thus many theologians and philosophers today argue that the belief in heaven is incompatible with being a morally good person. Heaven turns morality into a sham, replacing the best intentions with mere selfishness.

Consequently, most liberal theologians ask their readers to be very frugal and modest in their expectations of heaven. They subscribe to a kind of eschatological minimalism. For these theologians, imagining heaven in too much detail is childish and greedy. Such desires reduce religion to the level of selfish fantasy and wish-fulfillment. By implication, if we truly believe in God we will not worry about heaven. A heaven replete with the things of this world can only reinforce our natural tendency toward materialism and consumerism, rather than help us to cultivate a spirituality that reaches out to the needs of others.

Other theologians with a more conservative bent acknowledge the importance of heaven, but they insist that it should be conceived in moralistic terms. That is, heaven is in radical discontinuity with this world. Heaven is about the ultimate denial of human desires, not their fulfillment. Heaven rewards those who turn away from the things of the flesh. Heaven is all about God, not us, and the world is so fallen that heaven could not possibly resemble it.

Both the liberal modesty about heaven and the conservative portrait of an ultra-moral heaven miss something fundamental about the human longing for fulfillment and completion. God is not in need of our worship like a despot who demands continual entertainment. Heaven is not a form of forced labor for those who are willing to submit to God's infinite needs. Moreover, theologians do not need to deny heaven in order to protect faith from selfish distortions. Our longing for heaven is not the sign of an immature faith that needs to be chastised. On the contrary, hoping for more life, especially for more life for all those who suffer and have incomplete lives here and now, is not something to be ashamed of. Choose life, the Bible says (Deuteronomy 30:19). Hoping that our deepest and dearest relationships will continue into the next life is nothing to regret or repress. Such hope is the very basis of this life in the midst of all of its sorrows and tribulations. In fact, heaven is the very place where such hopes for happiness coincide with justice. Heaven is a place not of pure pleasure but of a restoration of what should have and could have been in this life. Heaven is nothing less that the completion of God's intentions for the world.

To imagine heaven today, when there is so much emphasis on this world rather than the next, takes a lot of courage, but that is precisely why we need a more robust, rather than a minimalistic, view of the afterlife. If imagining heaven is a way of imagining what this world should be like, then heaven is a radical, not an oppressive, idea. A full portrait of heaven would remind us that we do not need to strive for perfection and bliss in this world. A robust belief in heaven would tell us that the abundance we seek cannot be satisfied by the accumulation of consumer goods. Only an idea of a true heaven can compete with the false heaven that the North American way of life promises us.

To compensate for the greediness that pervades modern life, sometimes heaven is portrayed as an austere place, where the desires of the flesh are completely obliterated. Yet that does not cohere with the biblical promises. Heaven is neither the place where we can get everything we want, that is, everything that was denied to us during our earthly existence, nor is it the place where we learn to want nothing by giving up every desire and happiness. Heaven is where our distorted and twisted desires, burdened by our need to prolong every pleasure by controlling and manipulating its source, become sorted and straightened by the love of God. By being in the light of God's love we learn to love things in the proper way and with the right intentions. In heaven we do not sacrifice or satisfy our desires. Instead we learn to let God shape our desires so that we can flourish most fully.

The moral critique of heaven sounds persuasive because it appeals to the Christian sense that morality should be self-sacrificial. We should do the right thing even if it means giving up our lives. But on further reflection, this critique of heaven has several shortcomings. I will offer three arguments in defense of heaven as a place where the good and the beautiful become true.

First of all, many of those who make this criticism are middle-class professors with well-paid jobs and enough leisure time to consider what role heaven plays in moral activity. The critics of heaven can afford to reject the afterlife because their lives here and now are so rewarding and challenging. For most Christians throughout history, however, heaven has been a powerful belief because this world does not seem to be all that God has promised to give us.

Second, the belief in heaven is rarely so crude as the caricature in the account of the critics. People do not do good things in order to get into heaven, but they do hope that their good deeds will actually make a difference in the world. Unfortunately, most good deeds do not seem to change the world very much. If the good is not validated in eternity, then it would be tempting to become cynical about the possibility of moral improvement in this world. Heaven is needed as the place where the good is ultimately preserved and rewarded in spite of all of the ways that the good does not win out on earth.

Another way of stating this argument is to observe that good people frequently suffer for their goodness. It does not seem just or fair that self-sacrificial acts end in suffering without some hope for self-fulfillment. Heaven is not a place where an account is kept so that every good deed is rewarded. It is the hope and dream of the completion of all that is incomplete in this world. Heaven is our hope that charitable deeds are not mere phantom acts in the world, because the good is eternal. In heaven the good coincides with justice.

Third, the critics of heaven often exercise almost a puritanical rejection of pleasure. If an act is good, they assume, it should be painful. But shouldn't the pursuit of good ultimately lead to pleasure, not pain? Heaven confirms our intuition that the good and the beautiful should ultimately coincide. To do good for others without the hope in resurrection is to surrender oneself to the void, where the consequences of one's actions are indeterminable. The hope in heaven is not a crass desire to be paid for good moral service. Instead, it is the hope that good actions now will lead to a world where gifts will be given and received mutually—a festive sharing made possible by the ecstatic communion of God's trinitarian nature.

■ How Can Animals Benefit from Heaven?

Even if heaven is not a bribe to encourage morality, surely it is a place where our moral character is judged and then brought into conformity with Christ. If the shape of our moral lives plays a determining role in our transformation in heaven, then how can animals, who are not moral creatures, benefit from the afterlife? There is much truth to the idea that animals are beyond the human categories of morality. In the Middle Ages animals were put on trial and held responsible for intruding into human affairs, but we now look at those trials as the height of medieval superstition. Animals are, by and large, morally innocent, and it is their very innocence that guarantees their intimacy with God. It is a slippery slope, however, from saying that animals are morally innocent to asserting that animals have no capacity for reflection or self-consciousness. Indeed, since the Middle Ages, we have slipped too far down that slope, treating animals as machines that have virtually no sensitivity or intelligence whatsoever.

Surely our ability to make demands on animals is evidence that they are more than bundles of instincts and thoughtless habits. Animal training, whether it be of dogs, horses, or the many other animals that can be trained by sensitive experts, is predicated on the idea that animals can learn to be responsible participants in human society. Pet lovers especially know that their animals are responsive to the rules and limits that interspecies interaction demands. Farmers also ask a lot of their animals. If scientists in their labs see only unfeeling machines when they experiment on animals, that is because that is what they expect; they do not let themselves become emotionally involved with their animals, and thus they limit the range of activities in which humans and animals can both participate.

Animals are shaped by their genetic heritage just as humans are, but they also take delight in their existence and exercise freedom in making decisions. As the philosopher Stephen R. L. Clark has written, "To be a 'good dog' is to have those virtues of character that must be fairly widespread in a natural population if creatures of that kind are to survive and reproduce. A good dog is discriminating in her choice of a mate, faithful to her cubs, prepared to spare her rivals and to accept her place in the social hierarchy of her group with good grace" (p. 50). And, we might add, a good dog is eager to share her life with a human companion. Although it is unreasonable to imagine God holding animals to the same high moral standards as humans, it is also unreasonable to picture animals as mechanical gadgets without any personality or creativity.

The more important point that needs to be made, however, is that we should not think of heaven as a place solely where morality is rewarded and immorality judged. God is full of grace, and if we were all accepted by God only on the basis of our moral actions, all of us would be in trouble. Heaven is not the idea that God only gives us what we deserve, weighing our virtues against our vices. Heaven is the idea that what is wrong with the world will be corrected and that God will fill the cosmos with the divine presence. Heaven thus does not just restore what was lost in Eden but also brings creation to its fullest maturation. That which separates humans from animals—and all of creation from God—will be abolished in heaven. Possibilities for relationships that were interrupted by the fall will be resumed in new and surprising ways.

Precisely because animals are more morally innocent than humans, they are in some ways closer to God. They have not consciously turned against the divine order, so their suffering is hardly their fault. They also cannot make sense of their suffering, so that their very innocence makes them more of a victim of the disorders of this world. If heaven is for all who suffer and cry out for redemption, then heaven is for animals just as much as it is for humans.

Sometimes the argument is made that dogs will be in heaven only because they are so much a part of human life. That is, heaven is for humanity, and dogs (and other pets) will be there as an appendage of human existence. "Man is to be understood only in his relation to God," wrote C. S. Lewis. "The beasts are to be understood only in their relation to man and, through man, to God" (p. 138). There is some truth to this argument. Humans do have a special role in the world. God gave us a higher level of freedom than other animals precisely because God wanted a higher level of companionship with us. God feels toward us in ways that are similar to how we feel about our companion animals. We are dependent on God just as they are dependent on us.

Nevertheless, God loves animals not just because they serve us but also because God takes pleasure in all the things God has created. Moreover, heaven is for all creatures who have suffered, so that not only pampered dogs will be there. If God is most compassionate toward those humans who have no home on this planet, who go without food and family, then likewise God will be most compassionate toward those dogs who have missed being a part of a human family, wandering the streets in search of scraps of food. Although we do not know the limits to God's patience, and we do not know if some people will eventually reject God and thus be excluded from heaven, we can say, as a general rule, that all dogs will be in heaven for the same reason that all people will be there: because there are no limits to God's ability to redeem and liberate what God has created. Indeed, it seems much more likely that humans have the freedom and power ultimately to reject God, as irrational as that would be, than that animals would be able to turn against their Maker, since they were endowed with the gift of a certain level of moral innocence.

■ The Matter of Souls

One of the most striking and distinctive Christian beliefs is the resurrection of the body. The ancient Greeks believed in something very different from this, namely, the immortality of the soul. They defined the soul as that which is self-moving. The soul does not move due to any external cause. Since the soul has the essence of motion within itself, it is immortal, having no beginning and no end. The soul thus precedes and outlives the body, which is but a temporary home for that which never decays or changes.

This is a beautiful portrait of the soul, and many people are inspired by it to this day, but it is hardly Christian. The idea of an immortal soul puts a limit on God's power and grace. It is as if the soul is a necessary precondition or prerequisite for the idea of heaven. We have an afterlife because that which is in us never really dies; we are immortal. Christians believe that humans are not comprised of eternal souls that are only temporarily visiting our bodies. Our bodies are not transitional soul homes that can be demolished once the occupant departs for heaven. Instead, heaven restores us completely, so that our very physical existence matters to God.

Sometimes theologians have argued that animals do not have souls, and that since only humans have souls, only humans will be in heaven. The biblical view of the soul is that it is nothing more than the breath of life, given to all living creatures. The Hebrew word *nephesh* is used in Genesis 1:20, 21, 24, and 30 to describe living creatures as having the breath of life, and the word is also used in reference to humans. Adam became a living being (*nephesh*) because God breathed life into him. God does not create souls and then plant them into bodies, using the flesh as a container that can be discarded when it has served its function. God creates material beings who can think, feel, suffer, and worship. In all creatures flows the breath of God's invigorating spirit (the Hebrew word for spirit, *ruach,* means breath). God gives life, God can take life away, and God will restore all life in the end. Death is real and final, yet God conquers death as demonstrated by the resurrection of God's Son, Jesus Christ.

The whole issue of whether animals have souls, then, is misleading. God does not need something called a soul in order to save us. The orthodox Christian doctrine is that God saves the whole person, body and soul. The idea that the soul is eternal is a pagan idea because it assumes that something in us will live forever regardless of God's sustaining activity. The Christian idea is that the afterlife, just as with this life, is a gift of God's grace. This gift can include animals because God intends to put all of creation right in the end.

We have a renewed appreciation for our bodies today, our gender, ethnicity, personal appearance, sexuality, family history, and on and on. We cannot imagine ourselves as bodiless souls, wrapped in flesh which can be peeled off like a winter coat and left at the door of death. If there is an afterlife, it must involve who we are in terms of our most embodied experiences. The resurrection of the body, according to historian Caroline Walker Bynum, is "a concept of sublime courage and optimism. It locates redemption there where ultimate horror also resides—in pain, mutilation, death, and decay" (1995, p. 343). The moral impact of this idea is tremendous. If our bodies will be resurrected some day, then what we do to our bodies, and to the bodies of others, is of incredible importance today.

■ We Are What We Eat

It is fascinating to think about the fact that if our bodies will rise some day, then we really are what we eat. If all flesh will be raised by God, then bodies count; matter is not mere matter, dead and immaterial, but the essential stuff of existence. The molecules we are made of are the handiwork of God and will not perish. To eat dead animal flesh is not to weigh down our souls but to insult God's own compassion and consideration for all physical bodies. The orthodox doctrine of the resurrection of the body should at the very least give us pause about what we put into our own bodies and how we treat other bodies, even the bodies of those, whether human or animal, who cannot think as clearly as we can. We should treat our bodies as temples of the Lord that will one day be in God's full presence, glorified and renewed. We can anticipate that day by refusing to eat the bodies of dead animals that will also one day be redeemed by God.

Theologians have long argued whether we will eat in heaven, which raises the same problems as whether there will be gender differences and the continuance of marriages in heaven. Augustine argued that Adam and Eve, before the fall, had to eat for nourishment, even though their bodies did not begin to grow old until after the fall. Eating, then, in moderation and with self-restraint, is good; eating is not a defect of human nature. The resurrected body will be even better than the sinless bodies of the first couple. Heavenly eating will be for pleasure, not to satisfy hunger and thirst. Resurrected saints "will eat only if they wish to eat; eating will be for them a possibility, not a necessity" (1984, pp. 535–6). For biblical support, Augustine could have referred to Revelation 22:1–2, which portrays the river of life flowing through heaven and the tree of life producing plentiful fruit, as well as Luke 14:15.

These issues can seem obscure and needlessly speculative. Such speculation reached its zenith in the Middle Ages when theologians tended to believe that the resurrection was a matter of reassembling the component parts of the body. People worried about how human bodies could be restored after they decayed in the grave or, worse, were consumed in fire or eaten by an animal. They decided that animals who had eaten humans would be forced to vomit up their remains on the day of judgment. But if human bodies that pass through animals can be resurrected, then animal bodies that pass through humans can also be resurrected.

Such discussions suggest that we must be reserved and modest about that which we do not know. To demand a literal description of the afterlife is both naive and arrogant. However, the argument over what heaven will be like does have important implications. If there is a resurrection of the body, and if we are not just souls who shed our bodies upon death like snakes shed their skin, then the idea of eating in heaven is not the fantasy of gluttons who enjoy imagining heavenly feasts, where you can overindulge your appetite without any indigestion. Eating in heaven is one way of affirming the afterlife as fundamentally in continuity with the life we have here and now. It is a way of saying that heaven is not ethereal and unreal. Heaven is full and rich. And if we eat there, as the prophets of the Old Testament insist in their portraits of the new creation, we surely will eat the original food of God, the manna of the Israelites and the bread that is the body of Christ. Indeed, in the ancient world both Jews and Christians believed that the gift of manna would be repeated in the messianic age (see the Syriac

Apocalypse of Baruch 29:8—a book which was written by a Jew around 100 C.E. and was on occasion included in the Syriac Bible— and Revelation 2:17). Our heavenly diet will not cause any suffering or harm. It most certainly will be vegetarian.

■ The Diet of Hell

The most striking image of hell that can be seen repeatedly in texts and paintings throughout much of Christian history is the act of being devoured by wild and demonic beasts. Perhaps this reversal of the natural order reflects a deep feeling of guilt about how humans treat animals. The victims of hell are dismembered and digested, their tongues ripped out, their flesh pierced and tortured, and their hands and feet cut off. Hell is a feast that has gone terribly, terribly wrong. As Caroline Walker Bynum explains, "The greatest horror is the corruption of fertility and nutrition themselves: milk from women's breasts hardens into vipers, which turn on them to consume them. Resurrection is regurgitation: God will force the beasts that have eaten human flesh to vomit it up again" (1995, pp. 291–2). Clearly, carnivorous eating is a mockery of all that God works toward and desires.

If hell is the worst that humans can imagine, it is interesting that the most concrete image of hell is a fire that treats humans like meat. The victims of hell are boiled alive in huge pots and eaten by demonic animals intent on revenge. While heaven is the very image of growth and fertility, hell is an endless cycle of creatures who gnaw, vomit, excrete, and putrefy. To become meat—chewed, spit out, digested, defecated, and chewed again—for other creatures to feed on is the fate of all those who reject the grace of God. In heaven, the opposite of hell, clearly there is no meat. The mutilation and mastication of the human body, which reflects the horrors of the decaying body in the grave, is a fundamental image of the punishment of evil, as can be seen in Dante's *Inferno*. Hell is a mouth that literally swallows the damned.

These sordid images are not just the product of medieval fantasy. If paradise is portrayed as a vegetarian feast, then damnation is depicted as a sacrifice of humans, not animals, as in Jeremiah 46:10 and Ezekiel 39:17. God's judgment in the Bible is thus connected to images of the consumption of flesh. Indeed, Micah condemns the wealthy rulers of Israel as cannibals: "You who hate the good and love the evil, who tear the skin off my people, flay their skin off them, break their bones in pieces, and chop them up like meat in a kettle, like flesh in a caldron" (3:2–3). Finally, Revelation 19:17–18 pictures the wrath of God as a summons to the birds to dine on the flesh of the mighty. Such meals of destruction and violence are the opposite of the peaceful meals of the kingdom, as foretold by the prophets and as practiced in that most simple meal of all, the Eucharist.

■ The Garden of Paradise

If hell has often been imagined as a carnivorous nightmare, heaven is most often depicted in Christian tradition as a garden. People in the ancient world had to struggle to come up with the most appropriate metaphor for heaven. Originally, in Jewish and Greco-Roman cultures, death was thought to lead to a shadowy existence. Later the afterlife became a happier place where heroes were given their just reward. For the Greeks and Romans, the afterlife repeats the golden age of justice and harmony. Similarly, in the Jewish tradition the kingdom of God recapitulates the Garden of Eden. The Book of Daniel (probably written in 165–4 B.C.E.) contains the first clear reference to resurrection in the Jewish Scriptures. Christianity adopted the Greco-Roman idea of the Elysian Fields or the Isles of the Just, where the virtuous receive what they merit. The idea of a garden, though, exercised the most power over the Christian imagination.

A garden is full of life, so the image of a heavenly garden forced theologians to think in very specific terms about what kind of life God will resurrect. Thomas Aquinas insisted that neither plants nor animals will be in heaven. Martin Luther, however, believed in a heaven that was full of life. "You must not think that heaven and earth will be made of nothing but air and sand, but there will be whatever belongs to it—sheep, oxen, beasts, fish, without which the earth and sky or air cannot be." Moreover, "Ants, bugs and all unpleasant stinking creatures will be most delightful and have a wonderful fragrance." Heaven will be a return to Eden, so that every man will be like Adam who "was stronger than the lions and the bears, whose strength is very great. He handled them the way we handle puppies" (quoted in McDannell and Lang, p. 153). We will play with all the creatures as if they were our pets. Calvin agreed with Luther about the role of animals in heaven. He thought saints would live apart from the new world, in communion with God, but the new earth would be full of plants and animals. They would live there in perfection for eternity, and the saints would enjoy contemplating them even if the saints do not live among them.

■ Making Animals Matter

The Holocaust—the destruction of Europe's Jews—is often described in animalistic terms. The Jews were herded into boxcars like cattle and given no food or water as they were transported to their deaths. However, as J. R. Hyland has written, "With very few exceptions, there has been no attempt to understand the moral/ethical relationship between a claim that animals can be tormented and slaughtered in the best interests of the human race and the Nazi claim that prisoners were brutalized and murdered because that served the best interests of an emerging super race" (Hyland, 2000, p. 92). The Nazis thought that the Jews were another species, more like animals than humans, and they used a utilitarian logic to justify treating them as a means to their own glory. Historian Boria Sax is one of the few writers to try to sort out the Nazi view of animals, and his conclusion is troubling: "By blurring the boundary between animals and human beings, many Nazi practices made the killing of people seem like the slaughtering of animals"(p. 150). There were many factors that contributed to the twisted and tragic racism of the Nazis. What is often overlooked is that the Jews could never have been so brutalized if humans had not long practiced similar cruelty toward animals.

The Nazi ideology was odd and paradoxical. Their mystical technocracy passed laws against cruelty to animals but reduced morality to the most basic biological law of survival. They used predator animals for symbols of the Nazi elite and drew on the imagery of ancient scapegoating practices to rationalize their slaughters. They believed in the salvific power of pure racial blood, rather than the redeeming grace of the holy blood of the lamb. Many German Christians were seduced by their highly ritualized nationalism, and they turned their backs on the God of Abraham, Moses, and Jesus by failing to do all they could to help the Jews.

The slaughter of the Jews could have been carried out only by a people who had rejected the biblical God. The Germans were able to build a hell on earth because they did not believe in a real hell. They could not imagine being held accountable for their actions by any power higher than the nation-state. If they had recognized God's continuing covenant with the people of Israel, they never would have singled out the Jews for such treatment. If they had believed in divine judgment, they never would have tormented the Jews on such a grand scale.

Much the same can be said about our treatment of animals today. We can only treat them as disposable nonentities if we think that their transient lives have no ultimate standing in the universe. How would we treat them if we thought that they shared our eternal destiny? How would we treat them if we thought that what we do to them, the least among us, could rebound on us in the afterlife? How would we treat them if we knew that they would be our eternal partners in the new world that God will create to redeem the suffering in this one?

To dream of heaven is to envision the world in new ways. Critics of Christianity like Karl Marx argued that heaven was a distraction from everyday problems and that the belief in heaven keeps people from changing the world, since it leads people to expect a perfect world in the afterlife. Such criticisms assume that only misery is a motivational force in life, and that the hope that God will provide something better is always a diversion from the here and now. On the contrary, the more real heaven seems to us, the more it will affect us here and now. Only a heaven that is fully imagined can change the way we think about animals. Anything less than that—a heaven that is a mere idea about disembodied souls moving vaguely toward an ethereal light—can only reinforce our notion that only humans matter, and that animals are merely material.

8

The Church Fathers on Fasting as a Form of Vegetarianism

■ The word asceticism is from the Greek (*askesis*), and it refers to any activity of self-discipline, as an athlete would train for a competition or a soldier for battle. But the term goes farther than this. Any regimen of exercise for the purpose of improving oneself could be an ascetic practice in the ancient world. The early Christians borrowed their ascetic ideas and practices from their Greek and Roman contemporaries. Those practices included the renunciation of sex, the voluntary embrace of poverty, and the restriction of diet. Vegetarianism is a key to this set of practices, because a meatless diet was an emblem of poverty, just as a meatless diet was thought to diminish the sexual drive.

In previous chapters, I have noted the connection between animal sacrifices and social order. This connection gave asceticism a social and political dimension. To reject meat and wine demonstrated a disdain for both everyday social intercourse and for long-established religious customs and traditions. Philosophers who belonged to the Cynic school, for example, held social authority in contempt, and thus they were frequently critical of banquets in general and, more specifically, meat-eating. They wanted to lead a more natural life, so the most basic foods—bread and water—were their preferred diet. By rejecting the institutional religion of the temples, the Cynics put themselves outside of society.

Along with the Pythagoreans and Neoplatonists like Porphyry, whose treatise *On Abstinence from Animal Food* was read by many Christian theologians, the Cynics helped establish the idea in the ancient world that vegetarianism was essential for the philosophical life. The connection between vegetarianism and philosophy relies, in part, on the ancient preconception that only meat can sustain hard, manual labor—which philosophers tried to avoid! Christian theologians would later make the same assumption by teaching that meat might be useful for those who are pursuing unseemly activities, like athletics or war, but for those seeking the kingdom of God, which only requires a submissive and peaceful spirit, meat is neither needed nor appropriate.

The Cynics probably had a significant influence on a lot of early theologians, and some scholars have tried to show their influence on Jesus himself. The Cynics and early Christians were both socially rebellious and even eccentric in the eyes of their contemporaries, and they put all of their energy into a search for personal transformation. It is this latter dimension of asceticism that became more important for Christianity as it grew and developed. As Christianity became more established, asceticism became connected less to an effort to separate the church from the world and more to an attempt to achieve spiritual perfection. When Christians were in danger of martyrdom, their vegetarianism was a form of social protest, but when Constantine began promoting Christianity as the official religion of the Roman Empire, Christian vegetarianism became more focused on inner transformation. In other words, the purpose of vegetarianism shifted from social to individual concerns.

The ancient Greeks based their understanding of asceticism as a means of self-improvement on a dualistic understanding of the constituents of the human person: the body and its unruly desires needed to be ruled and ordered by the mind or the spirit. Bodily desire had to be conquered in order to liberate the self from immoderate attachment to the passing things of this world. Christians challenged this dismal view of the body, which was a staple of pagan philosophy, by connecting acts of self-denial to the doctrines of the incarnation and resurrection. One of the great themes of ancient theology is that God became human so that we might become more like God. Asceticism was thus based on an optimistic, not pessimistic, assessment of human nature. The incarnation has broken the bonds of human nature to death and decay. And the resurrection reveals the exalted destiny of all human flesh. The body would not be left behind by death. Instead, it would be transformed. Acts of self-denial were thus a preparation for greater things to come. Christians had the audacity to believe that the body could be reshaped in expectation of a new creation. This meant that disciplining the body was not merely an attempt to live the good life, as with the pagan philosophers who wanted to free their minds from bodily distractions. Instead it was an effort to live the life of Jesus Christ, a life utterly free of worldly ambition and thus humbly able to serve others.

■ Rethinking Self-Denial as the Testimony of the Holy Spirit

In the modern world, we are taught that satisfying our bodily desires is not only a basic human right but also the only way to attain true happiness. We tend to see the ascetic practices of the ancient and medieval worlds through Freudian eyes: self-denial is a prudish and puritanical approach to life that reflects an uptight personality or, worse, an irrational fear and hatred of oneself.

Americans think about religion in pragmatic and therapeutic terms, as a means of enabling people to solve problems by finding inner peace and happiness. In this light, ancient forms of Christianity seem distorted by a prejudice against the pleasures of the body. Since most people think that religion today should be life-affirming, not life-denying, they view fasting as a futile and extreme means of self-punishment that could only arise from an unhealthy obsession with feelings of guilt and worthlessness.

The prejudice against ascetic acts is hypocritical, because asceticism continues in our society, only for different reasons. We starve ourselves to look good, and we punish our bodies to extend our life expectancy. These acts of self-denial are thus really a way of maximizing pleasure. This is also the motivation behind a new movement that is gaining in popularity, sometimes called simple living, that emphasizes the peaceful rewards of a frugal lifestyle. Frugality is portrayed as a quiet island in the midst of the boundless sea of the ceaseless quest for consumer goods. It seems as if we have reached the limit of the idea that glorifying the body is a good thing, but we are not sure what the alternatives are. We no longer know how to place acts of self-denial in anything other than a very vague spiritual context. Can the early Christians, who have been stereotyped as masochists who sought pain and martyrdom as an end in itself, help us rethink the relationship between body and soul?

For the Greeks, ascetic practices were all about the careful training of the body in order to enhance the mind's control over unruly desires. As with the Cynics, individual autonomy was the goal. Asceticism, then, was an art or technique intended to maximize human freedom and happiness. Being wise meant exercising one's mental discipline to its fullest capacity. Although ancient Christians often adopted the rhetoric as well as the actual practices of the ancient Greeks, they also thought about asceticism in new ways. Most distinctively, denying the body was a way of following Jesus Christ, and thus it was a means of becoming a part of a larger body, the body of Christ called the church.

Especially after the earliest period of the church, when some Christians were persecuted and martyred for their faith, acts of self-denial became a kind of metaphorical martyrdom, a way of continually reminding oneself of the cost of discipleship and the price that was paid by the crucifixion of Jesus Christ. Self-denial was not born out of a hatred for the self as modern people tend to think, nor was it merely a set of exercises meant to enhance self-control, as it was for the Greeks. It was a response to the grace of God, which calls us out of ourselves and into communion with others. The early Christian ascetics can teach us that, at its best, self-denial is the testimony of the Holy Spirit, who works through our acts of restraint in order to create an ever widening community of love. Ultimately, self-denial is a way of anticipating the coming kingdom of God, when bodily wants and needs will be transformed by the spiritual satisfaction of being filled with the Holy Spirit.

■ Fasting for Others

Fasting in the ancient world cannot simply be equated with vegetarianism, although the association is very close. In the strictest sense, it meant an absolute avoidance of eating (with minimal water to drink) for a specified period of time. More ordinarily, though, it meant making do with a reduced amount of food, which usually included abstinence from particular kinds of food. Fasting for the early Christians could be an act of mourning, a way of preparing for an exorcism, part of personal hygiene, a method of increasing self-control, or a way of sharing in the pains of Jesus Christ and thus growing closer to God. The foods most frequently restricted during a fast were alcohol and meat.

There are several reasons for this. Meat was readily available but not easily affordable for poor people, and thus it was a sign of luxury, privilege, and power. Not eating meat was a way of protesting against the wealthy and the powerful with their luxuriant lifestyles. Christians honored those who were humble and lived more like the poor than the rich. Jesus, after all, had few material possessions, and many of his followers were drawn from the lower classes.

Theologians frequently advocated a meatless diet, therefore, simply because meat symbolized the powerful elite of the Roman Empire, the very people who persecuted them. Rejecting meat meant embracing a humble lifestyle, and Christians could be assured of a future reward that was greater than any earthly pleasure. Cyril of Jerusalem, for example, wrote in 348 that "We abstain from meat and wine while we fast, not out of any abhorrence as though they were evil in themselves, but because we are looking to our reward: that by foregoing sensual pleasure we may be able to enjoy that spiritual and supernatural table: that, sowing in tears in this life, we may reap in joy in the next" (quoted in Musurillo, p. 41). Such self-denial runs the danger, of course, of looking like a calculated trade-off, where one pleasure is postponed only for a better deal in the future. It also tends to play into cultural assumptions about meat by agreeing to the premise that meat is precious and good. The conclusion that is drawn, however, is that Christians should not revel in such luxuries here and now.

There was another motivational factor for fasting that had to do with sexual continence. Because people thought meat aided in physical strength, they tended to associate it with sexual lust and virility. As a hot and moist food, meat was thought to be productive of both blood and semen, so one way of controlling sexual desires was to cut down on the consumption of meat. By controlling the intake of food, especially meat, the ancients thought that one could reduce the buildup of seminal fluid and thus reduce or eliminate the nocturnal emission of semen, an involuntary act that, to many ancients, disturbingly demonstrated the power of the body over the mind.

Christians used this line of thinking, but they combined it with another set of ideas. Most fundamentally, a meatless diet was associated with the original peace and harmony of the Garden of Eden. It seemed clear to many early Christians that eating meat was ultimately not in harmony with God's intentions for the world. Fasting for Christians, then, was not just a matter of becoming more disciplined; fasting was primarily a way of getting back to paradise. This is the protological argument for fasting (from the Greek *proto,* meaning first or beginning). One who fasts imitates the diet of Adam and Eve.

Fasting also has an eschatological side. It is a diet that anticipates the world that is yet to come and the powers that are still unseen. More specifically, fasting imitates the life of the angels, who have no need to eat at all and spend all of their time in the worship and service of God. The monastic life was often characterized as the life of the angels, who are not weighed down by having a body.

Distinguishing between the backward and forward orientation of fasting is difficult, of course, because the Garden of Eden serves as the most vivid image for the future paradise. Thus, fasting could simultaneously look backward and forward. Indeed, the church fathers taught that the end time will be like the beginning of time. Salvation will be (minimally) a restoration of what was lost. Retracing Adam's steps by reversing his decisions is a necessary procedure to return to the point where humanity departed from God's plan.

In fact, many ancient theologians—Ambrose, Tertullian, John Cassian, and John Chrysostom among them—equated Adam's original sin, stealing the forbidden fruit, with gluttony. After all, the very first rule that God gave humanity was a command of abstinence, so that controlling one's diet was the necessary prerequisite to staying in the garden. These same theologians often took the next step of connecting the sin of fornication with gluttony; if there had been no gluttony, then sexual disorder and excess would not have entered the world. Fasting is thus often paired with that other pillar of Christian virtue for the church fathers, virginity. The two went hand in hand, though in some sense fasting was more important because it was a necessary prerequisite for a chaste life, since eating too much of the wrong foods could only incite bodily desire. A study at the University of Minnesota in 1944 (Shaw, p. 125) confirmed the ancient belief that severely limiting food consumption can have physical effects that include a diminishment of sexual desire (even though the ancient association of meat-eating and sexual appetite is not borne out by scientific evidence).

Early theologians were also influenced by a common ancient argument concerning another problem aggravated by meat-eating and gluttony. Gluttony, everyone agreed, could only lead to laziness and obesity. As Proverbs 23:20–21 warns, "Do not be among winebibbers, or among gluttonous eaters of meat; for the drunkard and the glutton will come to poverty, and drowsiness will clothe them with rags." It was repeatedly said in the ancient world, as it is today, that meat is a heavy food that weighs down the body. Early Christians believed it also weighs down the soul, because whatever dulls the senses of the body also keeps the mind from operating with clarity and freshness. Meat takes longer to digest than other foods, and it feels heavier in the stomach. Gluttony in general slows and thickens the body and thus makes it almost impossible for the soul to exercise authority over the senses. More specifically, eating a lot of meat can make you sluggish and can disturb your sleep, whereas fasting helps you wake up alert and refreshed. Thus, a light diet is best for those who want to keep alert and vigilant as they diligently pursue the truth.

In the ancient world, then, the pursuit of perfection involved practices that kept the body in check, and one of the most important of these practices was fasting. Christians took this one step further by insisting that the soul is linked to the body, so that the soul cannot be refined without exercising the body. Lifestyle issues cannot be separated from morality. To spend time in devotion to God and in community with others, free from the continual obsession with ever richer meals, one had to eat simply. And the simplest diet began with the abstention from meat.

The early theologians could thus conclude that gluttony is the root of all sins, a position we find hard to entertain today. But it makes some sense: those who seek out fine delicacies and rich foods are too committed to the things of the world. Today, with so many restaurants and so many readymade food products in grocery stores, we think nothing of eating out every day and trying different foods, but in the ancient world the craving for heavy meals was a sure sign that you were more committed to satisfying your own desires than living in community with those who barely have enough to eat. Since the production of food took more time in the ancient world, those who spent a lot of time pursuing rich food were usually rich themselves, with time to waste on the luxuries of elaborate meals. Those who ate a frugal meal were more likely to have prepared it themselves rather than being dependent on a bunch of servants to do their cooking. A frugal and just life had to begin with what you ate. To eat in such a way as to live a life of Christ-like love for others, one had to eat less so that others could have more. The consequences of this line of thought reached a logical conclusion for the church fathers: If Adam brought sin into the world through his wanton appetite, then God's kingdom can be established only through the restriction of that appetite.

■ The Diet of the Desert Fathers

These arguments for vegetarianism were doubtless convincing to many Christians, but to promote these ascetic standards and publicize the church's message, the church needed role models or heroes. These ascetic virtuosos were found in the desert fathers, the first Christians to flee the world and to practice a way of life that would later become organized in the great monastic traditions. The beginnings of monasticism could be seen as a narrowing of the vegetarian tradition in Christianity, since it now becomes equated with a saint who is, in practical terms, a specialist in the ways of faith. On the other hand, these early monks can also be seen as preserving a dietary ideal precisely at that time when Christians, after their perseverance and triumph in the Roman Empire, were tempted to reap their reward by adopting the luxuries of a pagan lifestyle.

To maintain the intensity of their faith, the desert fathers, by all accounts, ate bread with salt for the most stringent fasts, but they also ate vegetables, fruits, legumes, grains, and cereals. Doubtlessly, stories about them exaggerated their feats of fasting. As historian Veronika Grimm explains, people in those days were as fascinated with monks as we are with movie stars today: "Since starvation is universally dreaded, the spectacle of self-imposed starvation usu-ally strikes the beholder with awe" (p. 160). Nevertheless, beneath the hyperbole was a grain of truth: these holy men (and, increas-ingly, women) took it for granted that the pursuit of righteousness was incompatible with a diet of meat. They ate plain foods in order to live simply, but they also avoided meat because it was the diet of savage beasts, hardly fitting for humans created in the image of God. They would consume meat only when seriously ill, as a kind of last resort to restore their strength.

For many of the desert fathers, controlling food was more impor-tant than controlling sex as the chief means for cultivating Christ-ian virtue. This is understandable when one realizes that living in or near the desert would make food a central preoccupation. In the desert, overeating was a symptom of a lack of self-control. It was also a potential social disaster, because, in a world of very scarce food resources, fasting was a necessary means of making sure that everyone had enough to eat.

While many ancient vegetarian groups avoided meat because they thought it would pollute their bodies, the Desert Fathers seem to have avoided meat because it was incompatible with their ide-alistic venture. They went into the desert in search of perfection, which involved taming not only their unruly appetites but also the wild animals. Abba Paul, who had a particular gift of mastering snakes, explained this authority by tracing it back to Genesis: "If someone has obtained purity, everything is in submission to him, as it was to Adam, when he was in Paradise before he transgressed the commandment" (Burton-Christie, p. 231). Gaining control over your own body and exercising compassionate responsibility for animals went hand in hand.

Generally speaking, then, fasting was taken for granted as an essential aspect of holiness in early Christianity. Indeed, it was one of the chief signs of being close to God and following in the steps of Jesus Christ. When St. Benedict made his rules for monastic living, chapter 39 forbade the eating of meat for all monks in his religious community except the sick. (He forbid the eating of "quadrupeds," terminology that led to many differences in later communities over what precisely constituted meat.) Such extreme testing of the body prepared the soul to become open to an immediate relationship with the divine. Fasting both weakened the body, thus reducing the energy available for sin, and disciplined the body, giving the saint energy to focus on God alone.

Yet it is not always easy to discern the motivations behind vegetarianism in the early church. Celsus, the second-century critic of Christianity, thought that Christians avoided meat only because it was associated with sacrifices to pagan gods. Why, he asked, didn't they go further by abstaining from meat altogether, like the followers of Pythagoras? In his reply to Celsus, Origen was quick to argue that Christianity respects only rational souls and thus defends the superiority of humans over animals. Origen interprets the Jewish distinction between clean and unclean animals allegorically as signs of the sinful state of humanity. "And therefore, so far as we are concerned, the followers of Pythagoras, who abstain from all things that contain life, may do as they please; only observe the different reason for abstaining from things that have life on the part of the Pythagoreans and our ascetics. For the former abstain on the account of the fable about the transmigration of souls [. . .] We, however, when we do abstain, do so because we keep under our body, and bring it into subjection, and desire to mortify our members that are upon the earth, fornication, uncleanness, inordinate affection, evil concupiscence; and we use every effort to mortify the deeds of the flesh" (cited in Roberts, vol. 4, p. 565). Origen could not reconcile the Bible's emphasis on the uniqueness of human nature with another biblical theme—the need to treat animals with compassion. In his rush to distinguish Christian diet from a belief in the transmigration of souls, he connected vegetarianism to moral discipline alone, severing it from a biblical foundation. Other theologians would do a better job of showing how biblical faith shapes the daily act of eating, making it at once the most material and spiritual of practices.

■ Tertullian

Tertullian, who lived from about 150 to 220, was a North African Christian who had a tremendous influence on subsequent theology. He became especially interested in diet during his involvement with Montanism, a heretical movement that proscribed or restricted the eating of meat, but all of his arguments for vegetarianism are carefully grounded in orthodox beliefs. Montanus, who taught sometime between 135 and 175 C.E., emphasized the efficacy of the Holy Spirit and expected Christ's immediate return. Filled with charismatic enthusiasm, the Montanists demanded high ethical standards from their followers, and this is what attracted Tertullian to them. They also granted women leadership roles, which is probably not unrelated to their rejection of meat and animal sacrifices. According to Hippolytus, an early heresiologist who wrote *The Refutation of All Heresies,* the Montanists "introduce, however, the novelties of fasts, and feasts, and meals of parched food, and repasts of radishes, alleging that they have been instructed by women" (Roberts, vol. 5, p. 123). While men traditionally controlled the animal sacrifices and thus the distribution of meat, women traditionally have been associated with the preparation of vegetables (indeed, historically, women have eaten far less meat than men, since part of the mythology of meat is that it is a man's food). So it makes sense that a movement led in part by women would result in a less meat-oriented diet.

What is fascinating is that Tertullian wrote a treatise, *De Ieiunio* (*On Fasting*) that builds on pagan assumptions by laying out nearly all of the biblical arguments for Christian vegetarianism. He was very critical of gluttony and saw fasting as a way of drawing closer to God. His rhetoric was as avid as that of any modern-day animal rights advocate: "For to you your belly is god, and your lungs a temple, and your paunch a sacrificial altar, and your cook the priest, and your fragrant smell the Holy Spirit, and your condiments spiritual gifts, and your belching prophecy" (Roberts, vol. 4, p. 113). Tertullian advocated a diet called xerophagy, which consisted of the eating of dry food only. This was presumably followed for only specific periods of time. The aim was to dry out the body so, it was thought, there would be no sexual fluid left and thus less sexual temptation.

But not all of Tertullian's arguments were based on a negative attitude toward sex. He thought that humans were originally vegetarian and that meat-eating began only after the flood. He believed that Adam's sin was gluttony, and thus fasting is the key to salvation. He even suggests that more slender and lighter bodies will more easily squeeze through the narrow gate of heaven. Tertullian wrote before the rise of monasticism, so he thought that a restricted diet was incumbent upon all Christians, not just those who were willing to strive for perfection. Later, acts of renunciation like fasting were reserved for the spiritual elite of the monasteries, but in Tertullian's time all Christians were called to be perfect. He argued that God let people eat meat only after they had demonstrated that they were not capable of following all of God's laws. He also used the story of Daniel as an example of how healthy vegetarianism could be. Finally, he insisted that Christians not eat meat with the blood still in it—a Jewish regulation that Christians followed from the beginning of the church through the Middle Ages (see McNeill, p.133).

■ Clement of Alexandria

Clement of Alexandria (c. 160–c. 215) formulated an art of living for the church in which lifestyle choices and forms of behavior are conduits for Christian virtues and witnesses to Christian faith. In a book called the *Paidagogos* (the tutor or instructor), he set out the daily conduct that should be expected of all Christians. Clement was not a theological innovator. Instead, he appealed to the most traditional pagan sources concerning proper behavior. When it came to the ethics of eating, he followed the dominant tradition established by the best ancient thinkers—Stoics like Seneca, essayists like Plutarch, Platonists like Porphyry, and medical philosophers like Galen (see Walters)—by arguing that heavy food binds the soul with an unnecessary burden, while a light diet, which he defined as meatless, can better help the Christian to fend off evil thoughts. He did not insist on a strict vegetarianism, but he did think that eating less meat was a Christian duty: "We must guard against those articles of food which persuade us to eat when we are not hungry, bewitching the appetite. For is there not, within a temperate simplicity, a wholesome variety of eatables? Bulbs, olives, certain herbs, milk, cheese, fruits, all kinds of cooked foods without sauces" (Roberts, vol. 2, p. 241). This popular passage sounds very clear, but the rest of it, which goes on to permit meat in moderation if it is really wanted, is rarely quoted by vegetarian activists.

Clement based his diet on the example of the first disciples. Indeed, he thought that "the apostle Matthew partook of seeds, and nuts, and vegetables, without flesh" (p. 241). Clement also greatly admired Pythagoras for his vegetarianism, but he claimed, mistakenly, that Pythagoras got his ideas about diet from Moses. According to the Mosaic food laws, he argued, "altogether but a few [animals] were left appropriate for their food" (p. 242). In sum, frugality in diet for Clement was just a matter of good Christian etiquette, the kind of manners that were needed if pagans were going to take Christianity seriously.

■ Novatian

A fascinating treatise by Novatian, a third-century Roman presbyter, demonstrates the complex set of issues that Christians had to work through in order to develop a position on fasting. In a letter, *On the Jewish Meats,* Novatian admits that the first humans were vegetarian. After the fall, however, men needed something more in their diet. "And since now it was no more a paradise to be tended, but a whole world to be cultivated, the more robust food of flesh is offered to men, that for the advantage of culture something more might be added to the vigor of the human body" (Roberts, vol. 5, p. 646). He then argues that the law of clean and unclean animals had nothing to do with the animals themselves, because God could not have made something that was unclean. Instead, God was using the animals as a mirror for humans to reflect on their own virtues and vices. Calling some animals unclean was actually a way for God to teach humans about their own sins. Moreover, God wanted to restrain the intemperance of God's chosen people. Frugality is a necessary precondition for the service of the Lord. Novatian then cites the relevant New Testament texts that declare the Christian's freedom from Jewish dietary law. Yet he ends his treatise by suggesting that it is not possible to pray to God if the mind is stupefied by meat and wine. Finally, he argues, contrary to Paul's position, that meat sacrificed to idols really is polluted by demons. Most of the issues that the early Christians had to deal with concerning meat are present in Novatian, yet they do not add up to a consistent and comprehensive vision of diet. One could say that Novatian wants to defend the right of Christians to eat meat, but he does not think it is right for Christians to eat too much meat.

■ Athanasius

Athanasius, an important theologian who lived from about 298 until 373, took the lead in popularizing fasting with his biography of St. Anthony, who is credited with being the father of Christian monasticism. After the age of the martyrs, Athanasius felt the need for new Christian heroes, and he looked to St. Anthony to lead the way. Rather than encouraging a spiritual elitism, however, Athanasius holds up Anthony's fasting as a model of asceticism that anyone could practice. It was the simplest way of withdrawing from the world; you did not have to leave your family and go out into the Egyptian deserts in order to fast. Interestingly, Athanasius read the story of Lot's journey out of Sodom in Genesis 19 as a movement away from feasting and gluttony (see Brakke, p. 315). Although we associate the sins of Sodom with sexual excess today, Athanasius clearly made the connection between Sodom and gluttony, and he based this on Ezekiel 16:49: "This was the guilt of your sister Sodom: she and her daughters had pride, excess of food, and prosperous ease, but did not aid the poor and needy." Instead of feasting like the Sodomites, Athanasius argues, we should be well-fed in the ways of poverty so that we can better serve others as well as God. Simple meals are the first step in the ascent toward God and away from the world. When Athanasius gave advice about diet in a treatise on virginity, he instructed these young women to eat bread, vegetables, and oil, and he suggested more broadly that only nonanimal food is pure and acceptable (Shaw, p. 8). The *Canons* attributed to Athanasius, Egyptian regulations regarding monastic life written between 350 and 500 C.E., instruct male and female monks to keep a perpetual fast by avoiding meat, fish, and wine.

■ Jerome

Jerome (c. 342–420) was a great scholar who founded monasteries, translated the Bible into Latin, and offended many people with his rigid and extremist views on morality and standards of behavior. He was probably revered in the Middle Ages as much for his reputation for kindness to animals as for his scholarship, a reputation that was based on widespread stories, drawn ultimately from pagan sources, about how he befriended a lion by healing his wounded paw. His arguments about meat, some borrowed from Tertullian, illustrate the complex variety of issues that were involved when the church fathers were thinking through the implications of diet. Jerome grew up in a world ruled by Christian emperors, where many people became Christians just because it was the socially acceptable thing to do. For Jerome, there had to be a higher standard distinguishing true Christians from those who were merely following the crowds into the church. He found it in the virtue of virginity. While Tertullian saw fasting as a religious duty and a way of regaining human nature's lost innocence, Jerome based his apologetic for fasting on the claim that it preserved chastity. Meat especially heats the body, he insisted, which leads to sexual lust. Thus a dry and cool diet is the most moral diet.

Jovinian, an opponent of Jerome's elitism, argued that animals were created for humans to use and thus meat-eating is acceptable in God's sight. Jovinian referred to New Testament passages suggesting that all foods are clean and that anything can be eaten as long as it is consumed with gratitude to God. He thought that the pursuit of a perfect life was illusory and that on the day of judgment all baptized Christians would enjoy an equal blessedness, regardless of how self-denying they were on earth, just as the baptized participate equally in the unified and holy church today. Jerome dismissed him as a voluptuary, calling him the Epicurus of Christians, but Jerome's sarcasm could not completely cover up what was a serious theological disagreement (see Kelly, p. 180).

Jerome responded to Jovinian by arguing that although animals were made for man's benefit, they were not necessarily made to be eaten. Adam fell through eating, and in point of fact, Adam did not

193

eat meat. Only after the great flood were humans allowed to eat meat. Jesus himself consecrated fasting by doing so for forty days. Jerome took his defense of fasting to the highest levels of polemical rhetoric. Meat for him became a symbol of every kind of self-indulgence and lustful desire. "Let them eat flesh who serve the flesh," he writes (Shaw, p. 102). Jerome assumes that the human race was originally vegetarian, an assumption that was widely shared in the ancient world. Meat could be included in the diet of the very old or the very young, but the rest of us should avoid it if we want to draw as close to God as possible. Although Jerome seems very pessimistic about human nature and its sinfulness, he actually is very optimistic about transforming the body now in preparation for the resurrection. The body can be remade by following an ideal that belongs at once to the most ancient past and to the most anticipated future.

When Jerome's dear friend Blesilla died in 384, many blamed Jerome. She was the daughter of his patroness and friend, Paula. She had converted to asceticism at age twenty after suddenly losing her husband, and died four months later, killed, people said, by fasting. Although Jerome won many of his arguments at the time (through the sheer force of his personality), the extremity of his rhetoric, the elitism of his theology, and the practical consequences of his advice could lead only to a devaluation of his obsessive insistence on a meatless diet. In other words, he probably did more harm than good for vegetarianism. He allowed his critics to equate his position with Manicheanism, so that vegetarianism seemed to be more in tune with a distaste for the material world than with traditional Christian beliefs about the goodness of creation. By establishing vegetarianism as one of the main criteria for Christian faith, his position could be dismissed by later theologians as too demanding and schismatic.

■ John Cassian

The great monastic theologian John Cassian (c. 360–c. 435) is representative of a surge of interest in fasting in the fourth century. He is clear that fasting (which he equates with an austere and meatless diet) is a way of learning how to share with others, not to find some state of moral purity: "You see, then, that fasting is by no means considered an essential good by the Lord, inasmuch as it does not become good and pleasing to God by itself but in conjunction with other works" (Ramsey, p. 731). He thus defends a vegetarian diet because it is cheap and easy to prepare and more suitable for the common life of monastic communities. Cassian argued that the church sets aside special days for fasting as a way of reminding monks that fasting is not an end in itself, and thus keeps fasting from becoming a habitual practice without any deeper meaning. Cassian is aware that the Pharisees and the disciples of John the Baptist fasted, while Jesus, during the time that he was with his disciples, did not. He addresses this by suggesting that fasting has its time and place. When Jesus was with his disciples, it was like the bridegroom being surrounded by friends, so it was not a time for mourning but for joy and celebration. Cassian does not say whether he thought that the festive eating undertaken by Jesus and his disciples included meat.

■ John Moschos and the Spiritual Meadows

Some of the best stories about the early monks and their treatment of animals come from a classic of Eastern spirituality, John Moschos's *The Spiritual Meadows*. After spending many years training as a monk, Moschos (c. 550–619) and his disciple Sophronios journeyed to Egypt to collect the lore of the great elders of the desert, the monastic leaders who had proven themselves faithful and obedient guardians of ascetic tradition. After many years of traveling, Moschos left the Holy Land during the terrible years of the Persian raids at the beginning of the seventh century. He finished his great work recording the wisdom of the fathers in Rome, where he died.

Several of Moschos's stories demonstrate the widespread belief in the ancient world that the spiritual elite had the power to restore peace to the animal world. The monks not only practiced kindness to animals; they also could reverse the consequences of the fall by the boldness of their intercourse with animals. There is the story of the monk who took two lion cubs to church, arguing that if we obeyed the commandments of Jesus Christ, we would have no fear of the wild animals (p. 13). There is also the story of the holy man who fed the lions from his lap (p. 5).

One of my favorite stories from *The Spiritual Meadows* involves Abba Gerasimos, who was walking by the banks of the river Jordan one day. There he met a lion with the point of a reed stuck in its paw, causing much pain. The lion approached the elder, begging and whimpering, and the saint lanced the paw, removed the point, and cleaned the wound. The healed lion thereafter would not leave Gerasimos, following him like a pet dog. Gerasimos thus took to feeding him bread and vegetables. The monastery used an ass to fetch water from the Jordan, about a mile away, and the lion would keep watch over the ass while it pastured. One day some camel drivers from Arabia saw the ass and took it away to their country. The lion returned to Abba Gerasimos very dejected and dismayed. The Abba immediately assumed that the lion, who was being fed a vegetarian diet, had eaten the ass. For his punishment, the monk told the lion that he would have to perform all the duties the ass had performed. The lion began carrying the saddlepack with the water vessels to the Jordan and back. Later the camel driver who had taken the ass returned to sell some grain, and he brought the ass with him. When he came upon the lion, he fled in terror, and the lion seized the rein and led not only the ass but also three camels back to the monastery. The elder realized that the lion had not eaten the ass, and so he named him Jordanes, and the lion lived with Gerasimos for five years, never leaving his side. The story does not end there. When Gerasimos died, the lion would not eat and roared with grief. The other elders showed the lion where he was buried, and the lion promptly died on top of Gerasimos's grave. Moschos ends his account of this story with the following commentary: "This did not take place because the lion had a rational soul, but because it is the will of God to glorify those who glorify him—and to show how the beasts were in subjection to Adam before he disobeyed the commandment and fell from the comfort of paradise" (p. 88). Animals are not our rational equals, but we can extend charity toward them. Living in peace and harmony with the animals is a sign of faith. Before the fall all animals were our pets, and in the end, when God restores the world to its original intentions, even the wildest animals will become our pets once again.

Moschos tells another story about how Abba Sergios saw a lion on his path, and instead of fleeing in fear, he fed the lion some of the eucharistic bread. The lion took the holy bread of Christ and went on his way. In yet another story, Abba Paul was in the habit of feeding a lion bread and peas. When asked why, he said, "I have required of it that it harm neither man nor beast; and I have told it to come here each day and I will give it its food" (p. 134). When the lion visits Abba Paul with a blood stain on its muzzle, the elder sent him away, vowing never to feed him again. Only a lion that can lay down in peace with a lamb, as Isaiah prophesied, can share the home of the saints.

The desert fathers often lived alone, in austere and abandoned countryside, so it is not surprising that there are many stories about how they would feed the animals and turn carnivores into trusting friends. Moschos writes about Abba John the Eunuch who "had more compassion than anybody we ever saw, not only for men, but also for animals" (p. 151). He would rise early every morning to feed the dogs, leave flour for the ants, and throw biscuits up on the rooftops for the birds to eat. He seems like a quixotic character, or like one of those retirees who sits on park benches feeding the birds. However one pictures him, his very actions bespoke the belief that God has provided food for all if only we have the foresight to distribute it to those in need.

■ A Diet for the New Millennium

Most modern books about fasting in the ancient world do not make the connection between fasting and vegetarianism, but there is plenty of evidence to show that when Christians thought about limiting their food intake, they mostly thought about not eating meat. Historians talk about the asceticism of the early church, but they rarely specify what was actually practiced in these revolutionary diets. By talking about self-denial in such vague terms, historians contribute to the amnesia of the church with regard to our duties toward animals. The very word *fasting* is a way of speaking in general and vague terms about something that is really very specific. When we hear the word *fasting* today, we should think about giving up meat. For most of Christian history, fasting has been defined as, at least in part, the voluntary refusal of meat.

Giving up meat is one of the longest Christian traditions and one of the most visible signs of being a saint. In the ancient church, fasting was frequently connected to prayer and almsgiving as one of the three pillars of the faith. Charity and prayer remain as staples of the Christian life, but fasting has fallen into disuse as an ancient practice with little contemporary meaning or relevance.

Nonetheless, people are looking for spiritual practices that can shape one's prayer life and promote a better world. Spiritual practices today should not be about self-denial alone. Such practices should enable us to reach out to others. Spirituality needs to be a way of both finding peace within and promoting peace for others. Fasting, interpreted as the voluntary abstention from meat, not only focuses our hearts on God but also reminds us of all those who do not have enough to eat and all the animals who must suffer for a meat-centered diet.

Fasting is also a way of recovering the dangerous memory of Jesus Christ. Like the death of Jesus, the self-denial of fasting is practiced not as an end in itself but in the interest of affirming the dignity of others. It is not self-punishment, because a vegetarian diet can be just as rich and delicious as a meat diet. But it is a matter of giving up something that most of us have been raised to desire and expect. It is also a matter of eating in such a way that will inevitably draw the attention of others, so how we explain our diet and present it to others is utterly crucial. If we lord vegetarianism over others, then the whole point of the act of self-denial will be lost.

Fasting seems to be making something of a comeback in recent years. Increasingly, it is a word that Christians honor today, even if they do not themselves practice it. On the other hand, vegetarianism is a word that has little or no respect in Christian circles. Books on fasting have become best sellers, and a recent Campus Crusade for Christ conference on fasting attracted thousands of readers on the Internet. Fasting has become especially popular among teenagers, who are looking for concrete ways to practice their faith. Unfortunately, books and programs on fasting often treat it as a trial that tests one's physical endurance when deprived of all food. They thus strip fasting of its specifically Christian heritage. John Julius Norwich, the historian of Byzantium, tells the story of the deposed eleventh-century emperor who was forced into the monastic life. When a friend visited him and asked how he was, the old man answered, "Abstinence from meat is the only thing that worries me; the other matters give me little concern" (p. 9). Deprived of all of his privileges, the emperor missed meat the most. Surely, then, that was the one sacrifice he most needed to make.

9

How Christianity Lost this Biblical Ideal

■ One might well wonder why, if so many early Christian fathers defended vegetarianism, it did not become a more widespread part of church custom and tradition. Much of the answer to that question has to do with the association of vegetarianism with groups that were considered heretical by the orthodox Christian church. In chapter five I discussed the Jewish-Christian group, the Ebionites, who advocated vegetarianism. Many orthodox Christians reacted to the Ebionites by rejecting all dietary restrictions as an attempt to Judaize the church. In this chapter I will discuss three further stages in the distancing of the church from an official endorsement of vegetarianism. First, some monks connected vegetarianism to the denial of marriage and wanted this diet required of all Christians. This was rejected at the Council of Gangra, held in the middle of the fourth century in Asia Minor, which is *the* turning point in the history of Christian vegetarianism. Second, many heretical groups embraced this diet, which made it look guilty by association. Third, the Protestant reformers connected vegetarianism to superstitious and authoritarian forms of piety and practice, which resulted in dietary restrictions being thought of as medieval and inappropriate for the modern church.

■ The Turning Point of the Council of Gangra

A vegetarian diet allowed monks to practice asceticism all year long. Such a diet could be healthy and life-sustaining and yet self-disciplined. Unfortunately, church authorities were not always willing to support vegetarianism, because it sometimes seemed to deny that the world is a gift from God to humanity. The line between advocating a meat-free diet and condemning the world altogether was difficult to draw, and thus the church was worried that the one position would blur into the other.

The problem came to a definitive climax and resolution in the middle of the fourth century. The followers of Eustathius of Sebaste evidently condemned all meat-eating. While such condemnations were common among many church fathers, the Eustathians must have voiced their views in such a way as to draw the suspicion of the authorities. They were zealous reformers who criticized the church and separated themselves from the ordinary clergy. Some historians see Eustathius (who was a mentor of Basil of Caesarea) as trying to transport the strict asceticism of the Egyptian monks to the very different customs and climate of Asia Minor (see Duchesne, pp. 410–11). In the more northern climate of Asia Minor, the weather would be colder, so that diet could not be as restricted. Moreover, asceticism in Asia Minor was different from Egypt, where monks fled the cities for life in the desert. According to historian Peter Brown, ascetics in Asia Minor frequently stayed in or near cities, drawing leadership away from the church and challenging the authority of the ordained clergy (p. 288). It is one thing to advocate austere living in the desert and quite another to make such dramatic gestures in the city for all to see.

The heart of the problem, therefore, seems not to concern what Eustathius advocated, but to whom he addressed himself. He pushed a meatless diet, among other things, too far—arguing that such ascetic practices were for everybody, not just the monastic elite.

The beliefs of Eustathius and his followers were anathematized at the Council of Gangra, thus establishing a precedent in the church for drawing the line against strict vegetarianism as an essential part of the faith. The Eustathians were mainly condemned for their teachings concerning marriage, which encourage women and men to leave their spouses, and for encouraging women to wear men's clothing and to cut their hair in order to show that they had transcended the limits of their gender. (It is interesting that a group that so insisted on vegetarianism also advocated an early version of the equality of the genders.) They also were accused of ignoring traditional church fasts and fasting on Sundays (as the day on which Christ arose, the early fathers thought Sunday should be a day of rejoicing, not fasting). They followed, then, their own fasting calendar rather than abiding by more established church customs.

The second canon of the council addresses the issue of vegetarianism: "If any one shall condemn him who eats flesh, which is without blood and has not been offered to idols nor strangled, and is faithful and devout, as though the man were without hope [of salvation] because of his eating, let him be anathema" (quoted in Percival, p. 92). What is striking is that the Jewish prohibition of eating meat with the blood still in it continued in force in early Christianity, as this statement suggests. The church accepted this limit on the enjoyment of meat, even though Augustine argued that the apostles followed this rule only in their failed attempt to convert the Jews. Indeed, as late as the eighth century Pope Gregory the Third could still forbid the eating of bloody meat or strangled animals.

The mistake Eustathius made was to connect the condemnation of all meat eating to the condemnation of all sexual activity. The church could not, of course, allow all sexual activity to be seen as bad. Sex within marriage had to be defended as a gift of God; otherwise, celibacy would have become so widespread as to threaten the very survival of the church. The church was thus struggling to affirm certain virtues, like perpetual chastity and vegetarianism, while at the same time limiting them to a spiritual elite in order to make room in the church for all those who could not live up to such a strict ethic.

Vegetarianism, of course, did not raise the same problem as lifelong virginity. Everyone can be a vegetarian without threatening the continuity of the human race. Nevertheless, vegetarianism was increasingly seen as something, like vows of chastity, that should be assigned to a select few—who, through a special calling, pursue a vocation that is not obligatory for most ordinary Christians. Moreover, vegetarianism was also regulated by being assigned to certain periods of time, like Holy Week, where a vegetarian diet could be used to put a special stamp on a religious season.

What the bishops were most worried about was a schismatic attitude that arrogantly rejected ordinary practices and set up new standards for determining true Christian faith. In their Synodical Letter, the bishops wrote that the Eustathians were "fomenting separations from the houses of God and of the Church; treating the Church and its members with disdain, and establishing separate meetings and assemblies and different doctrines and other things in opposition to the Churches and those things which are done in the Church." What the council makes clear is that vegetarianism is itself not heretical. Rather, the condescending attitude that some vegetarians had toward meat-eaters was not acceptable. Indeed, an earlier council, at Ancyra, demanded (in Canon XIV) that all those who abstain from meat should at least taste it, and should not disdain to eat herbs and vegetables that were cooked and seasoned with meat!

As Teresa M. Shaw puts it, "Vegetarianism becomes a focal point for concern over ascetic elitism, divisions among Christians, and questions of individual and ecclesiastical authority" (p. 233). The question this council leaves us is what it means for vegetarianism to be a counsel of perfection (Matthew 19:21), rather than a divine commandment for all Christians. Is it something that God desires of us but not something that God directly demands that all of us should do, presumably because it takes more moral discipline than most of us are capable of? If so, the question then becomes: Can Christian theologians find a way to advocate vegetarianism that does not deny the goodness of creation and does not result in a schismatic heresy or in an elitist understanding of what it takes to be a Christian?

■ How the Gnostics, Cathars, and Other Heretics Ruined Vegetarianism for Orthodox Christians

Dualism is the term scholars give to any religious group that posits two principles of absolute authority and power, one good and one bad, while arguing that the evil principle is in control of the physical world. In such a scheme creation is not a good thing, and the good God did not create the world. Matter is the result of some freak cosmic accident or some evil plan by an evil god. Dualists make the case that they have common sense and empirical observation on their side. Look around you, they argue, and you will find nothing but death, disease, pain, and suffering. Would God create all of that? The only way to be saved, therefore, is to escape this world by denying the value of everything connected to matter, including the material of our own bodies. The good God created only our souls, not the world, and thus we need to free our souls from being trapped in our bodies, which are full of disease and decay. Since sex, even between a married couple, leads to more physical life and thus more suffering, dualists often reject marriage.

Dualists also are frequently vegetarian in their diet. Animals are a part of bad matter, and so they should not be eaten. Orthodox Christians thought that animals, as created by God, were good, but ironically, in their rush to distinguish themselves from the dualists, this often meant that the orthodox argued that animals were good to eat. What they forgot is that good eating requires not only good tasting food but also food that is made for the common good of all God's creation.

One of the earliest dualist groups were the ancient Orphic communities that existed before Plato. They based their practices on the myth of Dionysus, who was killed and eaten by the Titans, resulting in a stain on human nature. Humans were born from the fragments of the Titans after they were struck by lightning by Zeus. Thus humanity is the result of a cataclysmic crisis in which a divine being is consumed and then dispersed into shambles. To expiate this sinful state, a frugal lifestyle was necessary that included vegetarianism. The Orphic communities also believed in reincarnation, which further reinforced their vegetarianism. Whether or not this group is a precursor to Gnostic forms of religion that were popular during the history of the early church, they are evidence of a fairly common pattern of linking vegetarianism with dualism and reincarnation. In some of the animal rights vegetarian literature, arguments are made that Jesus was influenced by the Orphic mysteries, a claim which is purely speculative and highly unlikely.

Gnostic groups were popular just as the Christian church was beginning to spread and grow, and there are many scholarly debates about the relation between the two. The term *gnostic* comes from the Greek word for knowledge. Gnostics were elitists who believed they possessed the secret knowledge of how the world came into being and how we can escape from it. They are hard to categorize, because they emerged before the church agreed about the hard boundaries that define orthodox Christianity. Like the Encratites, an early Christian group, they often combined a critique of marriage with an emphasis on vegetarianism. The specific reasons for the vegetarianism of the Encratites, as with many such groups, is lost to history, although Hippolytus blames the Cynics for their rejection of meat. Their orthodox critics thought that they were being ungrateful to God by denying the pleasure of meat-eating. What is striking is just how many Gnostics were vegetarians— especially Gnostic-influenced Christians from Syria and Asia, where asceticism was strongly practiced (like Saturninus, Tatian, and Marcion, who nonetheless ate fish).

One of the most powerful Gnostic groups was Manicheanism, which for many centuries was an influential competitor of Christianity for converts. Manicheanism was founded by Mani, who lived in Babylonia and Persia in the 200s. For a time it was a major world religion with adherents from Europe to China. It combined elements from many different traditions: from Christianity a belief in Christ as savior; from Buddhism an order of ascetic monks; and above all, from traditional Persian religion a dualism of good and evil. The Manicheans believed that this world, with all of its evils, could not have been created by a good God. Therefore, there must be two deities: an evil one who created the material world, and a good one who made souls or spirits. Every human being struggles between these two forces of darkness and light, and our task is to try to purify ourselves of material desires, a task pursued most fervently by an inner circle of elect monks (see BeDuhn).

The elect, the inner group of monks who had achieved a state of salvation, were strict vegetarians. Some scholars trace their vegetarianism to their belief in reincarnation (see Couliano, p. 178). They evidently believed that human souls that did not succeed in overcoming the weight of the world would be reborn in plants and animals, and thus the world is alive and even agriculture should be avoided if possible. Other scholars note that they had a complex view of the value of plants and animals (see Passmore, p. 197). The world is full of the divine spark, and divinity is released from the soil into plants and then into the animals that eat the plants. Animals should not be eaten because they are born as a result of the defiling act of sexual intercourse. Plants, however, have a divine substance that is more innocent and pure than animals. The elect can heighten their spiritual powers by extracting the divine substance in its purest form from plants, which is released when the plants are ground, cooked, chewed, and digested. Meat, however, is inherently evil.

When early Christians thought about vegetarianism, they inevitably would have connected it to Manicheanism. Augustine was a hearer of Manicheanism (though not one of the elect) for nine years before he converted to Christianity. He wrote many treatises against the Manicheans, which were influential for the subsequent history of the church. He turned against the Manicheans as only a former believer could, and he especially focused on their dietary beliefs as an object of ridicule. He knew that he was vulnerable to the charge of still being under their influence, and so he chose to belittle their vegetarianism in order to defend his theological orthodoxy. "Christ himself shows that to refrain from the killing of animals and the destroying of plants is the height of superstition, for, judging that there are no common rights between us and the beasts and trees, he sent the devil into a herd of swine and with a curse withered the tree on which he found no fruit" (1986, p.102). I have heard other people make this reference to the story of the Gerasene demoniac as a refutation of vegetarianism without realizing that Augustine was the first to use this argument.

The story is found in Matthew 8:28–34, Mark 5:1–20, and Luke 8:26–39. Jesus meets a man possessed by many demons, and the man falls down and begs Jesus for help. Jesus questions the demons and begins to command them to leave. The problem is that the demons cannot exist apart from a host body to prey upon, so they beg Jesus for permission to enter a herd of swine. The choice for Jesus was between a greater and a lesser evil. He could have let the demons stay in the man, or he could have banished them unconditionally. If he did the latter they would have returned to the man as soon as he left, for in the ancient world it was thought that demons always return to their first home if they cannot find another.

So Jesus permits the demons to enter the swine, the lesser of two evils. This does not mean that Jesus had no regard for the swine, and Jesus certainly did not cause the swine to then rush over a cliff and into the lake, where they drowned. The demons, with their chaotic and violent energy, were responsible for their own fate once they entered into the swine. Jesus was trying to make the best of a bad situation, but Augustine set a precedent that is followed to this day of using this story to justify human cruelty to animals.

If the Manicheans ruined the idea of vegetarianism for Christians in the ancient world, the Cathars placed a final obstacle to vegetarianism in the Middle Ages. The Cathars (also sometimes called Albigensians) appeared in the eleventh century, and their contemporaries often connected them to the Manicheans of the ancient world, although there is no direct evidence for that. As documented by historians Janet and Bernard Hamilton, they were probably influenced by the Bogomils, a dualistic group that began in Bulgaria in the ninth century and spread throughout the Byzantine world. The Bogomils believed that they inherited authentic Christianity, which went back to the apostles, and that the established church was corrupt. The Bogomils practiced vegetarianism, although an earlier group that influenced them, the Paulicians, did not. The Bogomils were few in number, and as wandering holy men, they did not create a crisis for the Eastern church. The movement gradually died out.

The Cathars, however, quickly grew to be an influential and powerful group in the West, especially in parts of southern France but also in parts of Italy and elsewhere. They were very critical of the established clergy. They rejected baptism by water because they believed that matter is evil, so that the sacraments of the church should be purely spiritual. They wanted to break from (rather than to reform) ecclesiastical authority, and they wanted to model their lives on the pattern of the apostles and the early church. More than that, they thought the established Catholic church was evil and that only the strictest acts of self-denial could prepare the way for salvation from this world. Catharism thus represents an expansion of monastic or ascetic ideals into everyday life. Cathars wanted the ideals of renunciation to be practiced by all good Christians, not just an elite few. They thus combined a stringent moralism with a populist critique of the church.

The Catholic church reacted by persecuting them, going so far as to burn them for the crime of heresy. Since the church provided political as well as social stability for medieval society, heretics were treated as a threat to the very foundation of public order. Like many dualistic groups, the Cathars divided their members into two groups, the perfect and their supporters. The perfect were celibate, and they did not eat meat. This made it easy for the inquisitors to find out if somebody was a leader of the Cathars—all they had to do was to ask them to eat meat or to kill an animal. "At Goslar in 1051, after a hearing in the presence of the emperor Henry III, heretics were hanged after refusing to kill a chicken" (Lambert, p. 9). The Dominican inquisitor Bernard Gui, in his handbook for inquisitors, treated vegetarianism as a "veritable criterion for their identification" (Bazell, p. 90). Consequently, eating meat and taking a husband were the quickest and easiest ways for a female perfect to escape execution for heresy. Many people could thus draw a simple conclusion: Heretics did not eat meat; Christians did. As a result, meat-eating became, for all practical purposes, an article of faith for orthodox Christians (Stoyanov, p. 184).

One reason the Cathars rejected meat is that they did not want to eat anything that was born from coition, since they blamed sex for the perpetuation of material existence. The Cathars ate fish (the Cathar scholar Malcom Lambert describes them as fish-eating vegans) because it was commonly believed that fish were born without sexual intercourse, and thus they were not polluted food. They also thought that fish were not endowed with a soul, because they thought that fish lack blood. The Cathars follow a long tradition in both heretical and orthodox Christian groups of not including fish as a subcategory of meat.

The Cathars avoided meat because of its association with sexuality, but they also based their compassion toward animals on the belief in metempsychosis, or reincarnation. One Cathar manuscript gives some practical advice about how to deal with an animal caught in a trap: "A perfect should normally release an animal, which contained an imprisoned soul, but must always leave a recompense for the hunter deprived of his prey—if that is not available, the perfect must not interfere" (Lambert, p. 143). They believed in the grim picture of souls wandering through a series of unhappy bodies before salvation becomes possible through a perfect life of self-denial. So great was their condemnation of the earth that when they got old and sick, they preferred to die through self-starvation (a controversial practice that they called the *endura*), because "they could not be sure that some well-meaning relative would not comfort the consoled with chicken broth" (Lambert, p. 241). As they were dying, they could drink cold but not hot water, because the latter might be heated in pots in which meat had been cooked.

St. Francis lived during the rise of the Cathars, and much of his teaching can be seen as a powerful corrective to this heresy. His songs in praise of creation are majestic affirmations of the world as a fundamentally good place. Lambert tells one story about St. Francis that was designed to expose him as a meat-eater and thus as inferior to the Cathars. As a guest in a house where capon (a castrated male chicken) was served, Francis joined in the dinner and, when a beggar stopped by, gave him a piece of capon. The beggar later displayed the capon while Francis was preaching in an effort to ridicule him, only to find a miracle had occurred. The capon had turned into fish! (Lambert, p. 173).

Another way the church combatted the Cathars was to reemphasize the importance of the doctrine of the resurrection of the flesh. The Cathars were required to accepted this belief as official church dogma at the Council of Lyons (1180/1). Indeed, that Council declared that the flesh that is resurrected is the same flesh in which Christ truly ate and drank. Thereafter, it became important to the church to affirm meat-eating as a way of illustrating the importance of the material world in accounts of the afterlife. To eat meat was to acknowledge the reality and the blessings of the physical world. It was also to make a statement about the importance of the human body. Heaven is for the human body as a whole. Consequently, the human body should be respected. Denying the human body meat became a sign, to the medieval mind, of denying the value of the human body in this life, and thus of denying the orthodox dogma of the resurrection of the flesh.

■ The Impact of the Protestant Reformation

If the Cathars made vegetarianism suspect in the Middle Ages, the Protestant Reformation pushed vegetarianism out of the modern world altogether. The Reformers, in their zeal to obliterate special pious practices and their rejection of the monastic orders, were very suspicious of fasting. Estimates are that in some parts of Europe meat-eating was forbidden on nearly one hundred and eighty days a year (Toussaint-Samat, p. 101). In one Roman Catholic pamphlet published during the Reformation, the Protestants were criticized for their lack of respect for tradition: "You do not go to confession, fast, pray, attend church, give alms, or make pilgrimages. You also eat meat [whenever you wish] . . ." (Ozment, p. 84). The Protestant reformers thought that honoring holy days by restricting one's diet was superstitious and frivolous. They also argued that battling gluttony through strenuous works of self-denial could only lead to the sin of pride. They wanted to simplify and purify humanity's relationship to God by circumventing the mediation of customs, traditions, and spiritual practices.

The attack on meatless fast days was at the heart of Ulrich Zwingli's acceptance of the Reformation. In Zurich, the civil authorities enforced the laws regulating the eating of meat. When Zwingli became interested in the relationship between Christian freedom and diet, he was set on a course that would lead inevitably to a break with Rome. The publication of a sermon he preached on this topic in 1522 was the first evidence of his interest in the Reformation. Zwingli thought fasting was a human custom not supported by the Bible. He was also concerned, however, with the common people, especially those who had to work hard every day. "You who are an idler should fast often, should often abstain from foods that make you lustful. But the labourers' lusts pass away at the hoe and plough in the field" (p. 87). Manual labor burnt up the heat and energy absorbed from meat, saving the workers from the sexual desire that meat was thought to enhance. Zwingli also wondered why meat should be prohibited when fish and eggs were permitted. Clearly, fasting had become, by Zwingli's day, a custom stripped of any theological foundation and thus imposed only by the force of law. It is not going too far to say that for Zwingli, Christian freedom began with the recognition that nobody can tell you when you can or cannot eat meat.

Today, Protestants are rediscovering the liturgical season of Lent, when fasting is recommended for the forty weekdays before Easter. But many Reformers, with the notable exception of Luther,

wanted to eliminate Lent as an emblem of Roman Catholic superstition. The decline of Lent meant the end of the primary tradition
that reminded Christians of their vegetarian ideal. Although not
mentioned in the Bible, Lent was a time when Christians remembered the concrete spiritual practices of Jesus. Jesus, at the beginning of his ministry, went into the wilderness to fast for forty
days, a symbolic acknowledgment of the forty years the Hebrews
wandered through the desert before entering Israel. The fourth-
century *Apostolic Constitution* explicitly forbade the consumption
of meat during Holy Week. A Frankish handbook of penance
assigned the penalty of death for eating meat during Lent (McNeill,
p. 384). In the Middle Ages, innkeepers faced fines and imprison-
ment if they served meat during this period. In France, police were
allowed to search houses during Lent in order to confiscate forbidden meat, which was then donated to hospitals. Today, Lent is
once again growing in popularity, but, unfortunately, many Protestants do not seem to be aware that fasting in Lent has traditionally
meant going without meat, not going without food altogether.

The Protestant Reformers did not like ascetic practices for two
reasons. First, they did not like the idea that some Christians could
set themselves apart from other Christians by performing special
acts. They thought such practices smacked of works righteousness, an attempt by the pious to prove their worthiness before God
rather than relying on God's unmerited grace. For the Reformers,
the idea of the priesthood of all believers meant that there should
not be a two-tiered structure of Christian morality. What God
expects of us should be required of all people. Moreover, Christians should be fully involved in this world, so that they should
find their spiritual vocation in their family life and their jobs, not
in some otherworldly calling.

Second, they were afraid that ascetic practices would lead to
the sin of pride. Christians who trained like spiritual athletes in
order to achieve physical acts of renunciation that took years of
practice and discipline were inevitably tempted to see themselves
as superior to ordinary Christians. They thus could be led to think
that their physical prowess was a means of meriting special grace
from God. The ability to go without food, to live in poverty, and to
renounce marriage could easily be taken as a sign of spirituality
that only a few could achieve. The Reformers, who emphasized the

absolute sinfulness of all human action and the inability of anyone to merit God's grace through good works, could not condone such spiritual virtuosity.

What the Reformers missed was the unique Christian framework for ascetic practices in the ancient world. The argument can be made that they went too far with their suspicions of Roman Catholic piety. By focusing on the drama of the human soul as the site of our encounter with God, they turned religion into a subjective and private affair of the heart, which has little to do with public matters of culture and intellect. Moreover, without the aid of church practices and traditions, believers had to measure their faith by emphasizing either their emotional response to God or their moral conduct. In either case, Protestantism left Christians with precious few outward means (what the church traditionally calls sacraments) for expressing and shaping their response to God's grace.

Inevitably, the Protestant suppression of diet as a means of religious devotion could not last. The nineteenth century saw a revival of interest in diet as one part of the general temperance movement that was so popular at the time. Nonetheless, those who advocated vegetarianism were usually seen as eccentrics and cranks, and thus they were not accepted by mainstream Christian churches. There was a Bible Christian Church founded by William Cowherd in England in 1809 that made vegetarianism a part of its beliefs. And there were influential vegetarians like Sylvester Graham and John Harvey Kellogg, who changed the way Americans eat. However, with the rise of modern technology, the memory of these vegetarian Christians faded away as Americans began to take advantage of the availability of cheap and plentiful meat. Vegetarianism was seen as just another health fad, and the only religious voices left to defend it came from those interested in Eastern religions, not Christianity. Christians continued to debate the merits of consuming alcohol (and, increasingly, smoking) into the twentieth century, but an overindulgence in meat-eating was complacently taken for granted until the revival of the animal rights movement in the 1970s forced the churches to consider once again its ramifications.

The Protestant Reformation served to silence the long tradition within the church of using diet as a spiritual exercise. The result is one of the most bitter ironies in church history. Without any theological support and with no knowledge of the role diet has long played in Christian history, vegetarians who wanted to ground their diet in a moral vision increasingly turned, for lack of a better alternative, to the very heretical and pagan traditions that Christianity spent so many centuries combatting. By moving food outside of the circle of theological discourse, Protestantism opened the door for the New Age vegetarians who so dominate discussions of the topic today.

■ Eating as a Way of Remembering

The church suffers from ecclesial amnesia. Given Christianity's teachings on the power of original sin, selective memory is to be expected. We remember those aspects of Jesus' teachings that are convenient for us, and we forget those that do not fit with our presuppositions and prejudices. This is natural, because Jesus preached a powerful message of peace and forgiveness that requires a total and constant state of radical conversion. Thinking about Jesus is dangerous business, and so our unquestioned assumptions protect us from uncomfortable demands.

Evidence that the church often has difficulty in grasping the full truth of Jesus' ministry begins with the earliest Christians. Rowan Williams has noted how those who encountered Jesus as the Risen One—often in the setting of a meal—were stirred with feeling of remorse and failure. In the postbreakfast conversation between the risen Jesus and Peter by the Lake of Galilee, for example, Jesus asks Peter three times if he loves him, and Peter felt hurt (John 21:17). The Emmaus story, too, is about the foolishness and embarrassment two disciples feel who do not recognize Jesus as he walks along the road with them until Jesus breaks bread with them (Luke 24:25). The Gospels are telling us not only that it is in meals that we are most likely to recognize who Jesus is, but also that such graceful meals can cause us to remember painful things that we wished we had not forgotten. These resurrection meals remind us that even the closest followers of Jesus rejected and misunderstood him. Indeed, the most important meal of all, the Lord's Supper, was a meal of crisis and disaster, when Jesus not only defined his ministry but also acknowledged that one of his disciples was going to betray him. Christian meals today—and not just the Eucharist—should not only celebrate the abundance of God's grace but also reflect on the many ways in which we still resist recognizing Jesus in the sorrows and sufferings of this world.

There are two things that the church today conveniently tends to forget about early Christianity. First, the church often forgets that Jesus was a Jew—indeed, that Christianity is in debt to God's continuing covenant with Judaism. Second, the church forgets all those debates about diet that played such a crucial role in early church history. The two are interrelated. Too often theologians have defined Christian freedom to mean the abolition of all social restrictions. The Christian lives in two kingdoms simultaneously, Luther argued, the spiritual world of God and the political world of humanity. Christian freedom thus means that the Christian is free from all religious superstitions and customs, while the Christian is still obedient to the political and economic order. Luther's emphasis on spiritual freedom resulted in a great destruction of many of the ancient practices that were meant to build Christian character and deepen Christian commitment.

By arguing that we are absolutely free in the spiritual realm even while we are subjected to earthly constraints and obligations, Luther evacuated the very physical act of eating of any spiritual significance. When Christian freedom is defined as the negation of all social restrictions, Judaism then comes to represent an arid and lifeless legalism, and any arguments about diet seem like a return to the irrational dietary rules of the Old Testament, and thus an unacceptable imposition on the freedom of the faithful.

What Luther could not see is that being a Christian vegetarian is a project of hopeful remembrance, not a numbing obligation to a dead past. John Wesley, the founder of Methodism, could practice vegetarianism for a time because he knew that although our justification was in the hands of God, sanctification is a long process—a matter of developing the right habits of mind and action that can move us closer to God (pp. 344–45). The Christian vegetarian remembers the dietary restrictions of the Jews and the early church fathers not out of a slavish attempt to imitate the past but out of a joyous expectation for the future that God has planned for us. We eat a vegetarian diet not out of Gnostic fear that meat will pollute us but out of a confidence in the triumph of God's ultimate intentions. Christians are those whose every meal, after all, should be shaped by memory. Whatever we eat, we should eat in a eucharistic state of mind, expressing gratitude not only to God the creator, who has given us an abundance of material blessings, but also to God the redeemer, whose Son put an end to animal sacrifices, as well as God the Holy Spirit, who empowers us to imagine the world anew.

10

The Diet of Christian Vegetarianism

■ No religion has a monopoly on vegetarianism. Vegetarianism is not a uniquely Christian practice. It is a social practice that people adopt for a variety of reasons. When Christians practice vegetarianism, however, that diet inevitably will be presented in ways that are distinct from other social and religious contexts for it. Vegetarianism as a quest for moral perfection, or as an attempt to save the world from ecological disaster, or as a symbolic statement about the equal worth of humans and animals will look very different from a vegetarianism based on the eschatological hope in the promises and the providential work of God.

Christians have been hesitant to adopt vegetarianism because they do not want to be identified with all that it represents. Taking a social practice that originates outside of Christianity and turning it into a part of the Christian tradition is a slow and complex process, but it happens all the time in Christian history. Most Christian practices, from baptism to almsgiving, have their correlates in other religions and their antecedents in ancient history. Perhaps the most significant example of such borrowing is the communion service, which began as the Jewish Passover meal and was also influenced by various pagan and Jewish ritual meals. The point is that Christianity did not invent its many rituals and practices from scratch. Instead, Christianity brought together a coherent set of beliefs and actions based on the announcement of the kingdom of God by Jesus Christ, who embodied that kingdom in his life and death.

When vegetarianism becomes a Christian practice, Christian ideas about diet will inevitably overlap with non-Christian thought. Christianity does not have a monopoly on the virtue of compassion and the idea that animals should be treated with respect and care, but Christian vegetarianism will also look like something new. As theologian Kathryn Tanner has argued, even when Christians do the same thing that others do, they do it with a different attitude and for a different purpose. To expressive, healthy-minded, Gnostic, New Age, and political vegetarians, Christian vegetarianism will look a bit odd. It will say something different because it will be a part of a different set of assumptions. It will be one more witness to the gospel, one more way of proclaiming faith in Jesus Christ.

Not all secular practices can be Christianized, of course. Some secular practices, like pornography or the celebration of wealth for its own sake, lie outside the boundaries of Christian faith. Christians cannot do everything that non-Christians do, but being a Christian does not mean doing the opposite of what the world does just for the sake of being different. Christians who detect the secular or New Age assumptions behind much modern vegetarianism often argue that there should be no restrictions on how farm animals are raised, slaughtered, and consumed. As a result, they end up playing into the hands of the secular capitalist economy, which does not want to impede the profit to be made from treating animals like meat machines. Some Christians affirm a meat-oriented diet today as a way of proclaiming their faith in the goodness of creation as a gift from God, but they thereby risk affirming the hedonistic values of our consumeristic and gluttonous society, where meat-eating is a symbol not of the Christian doctrine of creation but of the right of humans to satisfy all of their desires at the cheapest possible price.

Even the most secular vegetarians hold many of the same values and virtues as Christians—indeed, they are influenced by Christianity in ways that they themselves frequently do not understand—so it will be wise for Christians to try to learn from these groups before they too lightly dismiss them. The point is to figure out how to transform secular social practices when they are adopted by the church in order to affirm the values held in common by all people interested in treating animals compassionately, as well as to specify what distinctive virtues Christianity brings to the table.

■ Vegetarianism Without Schism

The most important point that Christianity can contribute to our society's current debates about diet is to help us to move away from thinking of vegetarianism as an all-or-nothing affair. Many people, when confronted with a zealous vegetarian, think that they could never live up to such high ideals, even if they share the vegetarian's compassion for animals. Perhaps as a defensive reaction, skeptics look for ways in which vegetarians act inconsistently or hypocritically. They see a vegetarian wearing a leather belt or leather shoes, and they immediately claim that since nobody can be completely free of using animal products, then it is okay to eat animals whenever you want. Conversely, vegetarians sometimes irritate and alienate carnivores with their self-righteous and purist attitudes.

Christians have an advantage in these debates because of their belief in original sin, which gives them a morally realistic picture of the world. Christian vegetarians know that no diet is pure and innocent of tragic consequences. Vegetarians often highlight the impact of cattle grazing on the land, noting that the enormous amount of land needed for cattle has led to deforestation at home and abroad. However, grazing is not the only culprit; a plant-based diet can also have negative consequences. Rachel Carson's *Silent Spring* (1962), which revealed the hidden impact of using pesticides in agriculture, helped spark the environmental movement, and the American Dust Bowl of the 1930s is a memorable example of how agriculture can cause an ecological disaster. Even though we think of the family farm as the paradigm of a healthy relationship to the earth, ecologist Paul B. Thompson has shown how raising crops can be a matter of exploitation when farming takes more out of the soil than it returns.

The fact that nature pays a heavy price for all human relationship to the land leads some environmentalists to argue that the land has intrinsic value, regardless of human benefit, so that we should set aside as much land as possible from human use and abuse. Others defend a wise use of the land, suggesting that sustainable practices benefit humans while maintaining the delicate balance of ecosystems. The biblical position defended here leads more toward the "sustainability" argument than the "intrinsic value" argument. Land can be intrinsically valuable only if it is viewed as sacred, that is, as being an object of ultimate concern and thus being an aspect of the divine. The Bible teaches that the land is good because it is a blessing from God for humans and animals alike, but not that it is part of God. The point of Christian ethics is not to protect as much land as possible by separating it from human contact. The point is to learn how to live in harmony with the land by exercising proper authority and humble stewardship, using the land in ways that will also respect the needs of animals.

Such goals, admittedly, are more idealistic than realistic. The world is fallen, and the food chain is an inescapable aspect of that fallenness. The very metaphor of the food chain implies links that connect species together in unbreakable and tragic ways. Christians can work toward a more charitable world, but Christianity is not a utopian belief system that makes unrealistic promises about what humans can accomplish. Christians cannot save the world. Only God can do that. Nevertheless, Christians can take a stand by working to alleviate unnecessary suffering. Christians can stand up for peace even as they recognize that conflict and suffering are inevitable. It is just that willingness to work toward an impossible goal, no matter the cost, that characterizes the christological element of self-sacrifice in Christian ethics.

Although vegetarians can be arrogant about their diet, the reverse situation is just as likely to be true. When I talk about this issue, people seem overly eager to point to my leather shoes, as if that were enough to convict me of hypocrisy and thus discredit my case for compassion for animals. These carnivores thus portray vegetarianism as an all-or-nothing proposition, and since I am wearing leather shoes, then it is permissible for them to eat all the meat they want. Moral decisions are rarely so simple. My leather shoes say to me that vegetarianism is an ideal that I can never live up to, and that even if I were to live an absolutely cruelty-free life, it is still acceptable to depend on the labor and products of animals. However, my shoes also tell me that I need to work harder at finding alternatives to the use of animal products that only add more profit to the exploitation of animals.

To what extent is it acceptable to rely on animals for human benefit? Animals are here in part to serve us, just as we are here to serve God. There is nothing inherently wrong with, say, drinking milk from dairy cows. However, that service is not the only purpose of animals. They also bring joy to God by their very existence and thus remind us that creation is greater than our own narrow circle of concern. The question is whether animals are treated merely as a means to a human end or are also given the respect due to creatures valued by God. If dairy cows were treated well and allowed a natural death, there would be nothing wrong with turning their skin into leather. The crucial point is that the goal of a Christian vegetarian is not to foreswear all use of animal products. It is to be good stewards of animals, raising them in conditions that affirm their dignity and thus entering into a reciprocal relationship of mutual respect. Being kind to animals does not mean that we have to recognize that we are of the same exact kind as the animals, but that every kind of creature is created by the very same God.

■ Christian Vegetarianisms

Christian vegetarianism should be one part of a wide range of dietary options that express a confidence in God's plan for the world. Some Christians will want just to cut down on their meat by buying free-range meat as a way of protesting factory farms. Free-range meat comes from animals that are allowed to live in ways that support rather than deny their God-given natures. These animals are not kept locked up in cages where they cannot smell the earth and feel the sun and bond with each other. These Christians will also work for legislation to make farming more humane and to support the independent, small farm owners who raise their animals in more traditional ways. Christians too will work for better slaughterhouse practices and better legislation concerning how animals are transported, in order to minimize their suffering.

Most Christian vegetarians will be ovo-lacto, which means they will continue to consume animal byproducts like eggs and milk, even when they do not eat meat. This is an important distinction because it testifies to the Christian belief that it is not wrong for humans to domesticate and benefit from animal labor. The conflict between using animals for our benefit and celebrating animal life as an inherently good part of creation may be inevitable, but it need not be necessary, because God intends for the world to be a structured whole, where all work together for God's glory. The proliferation and variety of life is pleasing to God, and that requires the human management of animal lives. If animal rights activists had their way, there would be very few animals on the earth, because no humans could benefit from them. Indeed, there would be little human-animal interaction, because animals would live on land removed from all human control. The perspective I have defended here acknowledges that humans and animals live in one world, where humans will benefit from animals, but it also argues that the relationship should be one of mutual aid and advancement, so that animals too gain something (food, shelter, protection from predators) from the relationship.

There is a difference, then, between taking the life of an animal and using the milk or eggs of an animal while feeding and treating the animal with respect. There is nothing wrong with acknowledging human authority over animals and treating animals as subordinate to humanity. If this is done in ways that do not exploit or abuse the animal, then it can be a way of working with and not against the order that God has built into the world.

However, Christians will also keep in mind that dairy cows and egg-laying hens are often treated poorly, kept in terrible conditions, pumped full of hormones, overworked, and killed long before the natural end of their lives. Dairy cows are given little rest between pregnancies, live about five years rather than the cow's normal life span of twenty to twenty-five years, and often suffer from painful udder infections caused by milking machines. Hens are squeezed into cages, their beaks sliced off to keep them from pecking at each other, and often forced to molt by being denied food, so that their molting cycle is speeded up and they can lay eggs again—a practice that has been banned in Great Britain. By the time weary hens are sent to the slaughter, many have broken bones, abscesses, and hemorrhaging, and their meat is used only for foods that hide the quality of their flesh, like chicken soup and pet food. Given this treatment of cows and hens, Christians should consider buying free-range eggs and cutting down on their milk consumption by drinking soy or rice milk instead.

Some Christians, a small but significant and growing minority, will want to eschew all animal products whatsoever. They will become vegans, avoiding any animal flesh or byproduct in their meals. In a way, they are to be admired for setting the standards to which the rest of us should aspire, but they are also treading on spiritually risky ground. The pursuit of a perfect diet, absolutely pure of animal products, is illusory. Every diet encroaches on the population of wild animals. Eating fruit, vegetables, and grains means relying on cultivated fields that were at one time wild, so that even the most compassionate diet competes with animals for land and resources. This is why all Christians should work to minimize suburban sprawl and to protect the wilderness so that wild animals will be able to pursue the lives that God has given them.

The very act of eating should remind us not only of our dependence on God—the bounty of God's generous provisions, which are the blessing of the goodness of creation—but also of the complex web of relations that bind together all forms of life. To eat is to grind, crush, and destroy, which makes eating the most singular sign that life is a constant struggle. Natural resources are scarce and human need is constantly expanding and multiplying, thus testing the very limits of the earth's ability to replenish itself. Given the scarcity of resources, to eat is to deny resources to others, whether other humans or animals. A vegetarian diet certainly uses the earth's resources in a more frugal manner, thus freeing up more food for others, but every diet is a part of the basic struggle for survival that is the lot of life on earth.

Vegans thus must be careful not to gloat over their diets. They can be fooled into thinking that they have crossed the line from evil to good and that their diet is an indication of moral purity and spiritual advancement. It is true that their diet is more morally sensitive, but claiming moral purity can be a spiritual setback. Taking pride in moral achievements and looking down on the ignorance of others can lead to spiritual disaster. The tragedy of all moral reformers is the consequence of the blindness that always comes with defending a just cause.

If veganism were held up as the only moral diet for Christians, it could easily lead to schism for the church. The result might be a scapegoating of all those who depend on the meat industry for their livelihood. There are also those who feel like they cannot change dietary habits that were formed and shaped in their childhood, habits that are so deeply ingrained that they feel as if they have no control over them. When I talk about vegetarianism to Christian groups, one source of the skeptical response I often receive is that people find it inconceivable that otherwise morally upright Christians could be thought to be so morally wrong for something so seemingly trivial as diet. The point that vegans must realize is that carnivores should not be condemned. They are eating a diet that is natural to the fallen world, a diet that has been reinforced by rhetoric about the American way of life and the myth that only meat can make you strong. Although a carnivorous diet is the norm in our fallen world, vegetarianism is the exception that points to possibilities that can be glimpsed even now as God prepares a new reality for us.

■ The Slippery Problem of Fish

Many Christians will continue to eat fish in their diets because Jesus probably ate fish. As Isidore of Seville wrote in the late sixth- or early seventh century, "We can eat fish because the Lord accepted it after the resurrection. Neither the Savior nor the apostles forbade it" (Grant, p. 112). Moreover, fish are taken directly from their habitat without being inhumanely raised in artificial environments. Arguably, they do not have the same complex nervous systems and brain stems as mammals, so their suffering is probably on a lower order than the killing of farm animals.

In the history of Christian fasting, fish were frequently exempted from restrictions on meat (McNeill, p. 208), so there is a long tradition of permitting the eating of fish as an abundant gift from God that is not on the same level as killing mammals. The reasons for this are numerous. Ancient thinkers like Philo of Alexandria argued that fish are at the bottom of creation (both literally and figuratively), since they were created first among the animals on the fifth day and thus have the simplest and most corporeal soul. Basil the Great, bishop of Caesarea who died in 379, demonstrated this line of thinking in his homilies on the six days of creation: "Aquatic animals not only are mute but savage and unteachable, incapable of sharing life with men. 'The ox knows its owner and the ass its feeder' (Isaiah 1:3), but the fish would not recognize its feeder" (Grant, pp. 88–89). He seems to have forgotten that one fish rescued Jonah and another provided a coin to Jesus for the temple tax. In a similar fashion, one of Plutarch's dinner companions, Lamprias, describes a general attitude toward fish that sounds remarkably contemporary:

> But we shall say that of all delicacies the most legitimate kind is that from the sea. As far as the land animals whose meat is here before us is concerned, we must admit at least this if nothing else, that they consume the same food and breathe the same air as we do, and drink and bathe in water no different from ours. This has in times past made people ashamed when they butchered them in spite of their pitiful cries and in spite of having made companions of most of them and shared their store of food with them. Sea animals, on the other hand, are a species entirely alien and remote from us, as if they had sprung up and were living in some different world. Neither look nor voice nor service rendered pleads with us not to eat them, for no animal can employ these pleas that has no life at all among us; nor need we feel any affection for them (pp. 349–51).

Fish cannot be taught or domesticated, so they are the furthest removed from human concern. We owe them no justice because we do not share their world.

Fish could also be looked at in a more positive light. Their fecundity and swift regeneration made them a natural symbol for prosperity and fertility (Jensen, pp. 46–59). For Jews and Christians, fish were thought to be in such great abundance that they were a potent symbol of God's blessings. Indeed, many people in the ancient world thought that fish were not born from sexual intercourse, so they were not tainted by original sin. This purity, to the ancient mind, implied that eating them would not pollute your soul or cause you to partake of fallen nature. As one food historian explains, "Meat and fat were regarded as red, rich, hot food. They were therefore likely to induce euphoria or even excitement. Fish, by association with water, was cold, and was white, lean fare, sober and soothing, and in any case pure" (Toussaint-Samat, p. 313). The innocence of fish was reinforced by the belief that fish were the only animal to survive the flood without Noah's help (Genesis 7:21–22). They were not punished by the divine wrath. Fish were good, and thus they were good to eat.

Finally, fish do not bleed like mammals when they are killed, so they do not seem to suffer in the same way as other animals. The Bible is most concerned about the spilling of blood when animals are killed because blood is the ultimate symbol of life and thus belongs to God, which is why animals had to be killed, if at all, according to the strict rules of sacrificial rituals. If ancient vegetarianism emerged as a protest against ritual animal sacrifices, then it makes sense that fish could still be eaten by these groups because fish were never associated with ritual sacrifices. Only domesticated animals, a product of human labor, were sacrificed, and fish were never a part of this religious cuisine.

Nevertheless, fish do suffer when they die, and they are becoming a scarce resource as we overfish our lakes, rivers, and oceans. The increasing need for water also has led to more dams being built on rivers, which also negatively affects the fish population. So even fish-eating Christians who will reduce or eliminate other meat from their diet will want to eat fish in moderation, only as a way to help balance their diets and not as their primary source of protein.

■ Animal Rites

As this discussion demonstrates, establishing the specificities of a vegetarian diet can be complicated. It is easy to get lost in the details of what constitutes the perfect diet. For Christians, however, vegetarianism is only part of the answer. What the church needs is not animal rights but animal rites—ways of incorporating animal compassion into the rituals, prayers, and practices of the worshiping community. Our society wants us to think of most animals only as food or entertainment, but not as real beings with their own needs and cares. To pray for the animals would be a radical way of fighting their absence from our daily concerns. Indeed, we need to go even further by literally bringing animals back into the church so that their presence can remind us of the breadth of God's family. One important movement that is aiding the churches to recover a theology of animals is the increasingly popular practice of setting aside a worship service to bless the animals, which is usually done in honor of St. Francis, whose feast day is October 4.

In fact, animals used to be taken to church quite regularly, as seen in a commission report prepared for the Council of Trent that complained about people frequently bringing their dogs to mass (Martos, p. 249). The office of the dog-whipper was established in England in the eighteenth century to keep dogs out of church because so many people brought their dogs that they became a disruption. In the ancient world, where worship usually involved the slaughter of animals and the distribution of meat, dogs were even more prevalent in temples. One of the Dead Sea Scrolls bans dogs from the Jerusalem temple because "they may eat some of the bones from the sanctuary and the meat which is still on them" (Wise, p. 362)! To let dogs into our homes but not into our churches makes our places of worship seem less real because we have to leave behind one of the relationships that matters most to us. Where I teach, a small, private, liberal arts college, the students bring their dogs to classes all the time, and the result is that the students feel at home in their classes. They know that they do not have to leave behind their passions when they come to talk about the great books; school is for the whole person, not just a disembodied intellect. Animals in the church would at the very least remind us that the church is more than the people of God, just as the body of Christ encompasses all bodies that suffer.

■ Dietary Pacifism

Christianity does not mandate vegetarianism. However, it does suggest vegetarianism as an ideal. As Richard Alan Young has wisely written, "We must be cautious about turning the eschatological hope into an absolute rule" (p. 149). Vegetarianism is not to be legislated, but it is to be commended. It is, to use medieval terminology, a supererogatory act, an act whose commission is morally praiseworthy even though its omission is not necessarily morally culpable or blameworthy. There are many such acts. Forgiving one's enemy is an ideal that all Christians are called to strive for, yet we do not condemn those who have trouble forgiving someone who has directly harmed them. Giving your life for someone is the highest Christian ideal, patterned on the sacrifice of Jesus Christ, yet we do not require all bystanders to jump into a raging river in order to try to save the person who has just tried to commit suicide by jumping off a bridge. Not everyone can be a hero, though we hope that there are a lot of heroes in the world, and we hope that, if tested, we can live up to such high standards and expectations. What we can do is support those institutions, rituals, and beliefs that provide the context for the moral formation that makes heroic action possible. Heroes and saints lead the way and beckon us to follow by setting an example that is beyond our ordinary practices but not outside our moral reach. Vegetarianism should be seen in the same light.

Vegetarians are like pacifists who refuse to inflict violence on others no matter what the personal cost. It is not surprising that the Christian groups that kept vegetarianism alive in the modern world were also groups that were committed to pacifism. Quakers like Thomas Tyron (1634–1703) and Joshua Evans (1731–1798) took that religious group's commitment to nonviolence to its logical conclusion by trying to persuade their fellow Quakers to abstain from killing animals (Brock, p. 64). That they failed should not keep us from admiring the prophetic force of their mission. Pacifists are looked upon by most Christians with both skepticism and admiration. Most Christians think that pacifism is a noble ideal and that it is probably more in tune with the teachings of Jesus than moral traditions that justify and rationalize warfare, they just are not sure if pacifism is practical. Thus many Christians follow a realistic middle course by making a distinction between individual and national pacifism, arguing that ideals that can be required of individuals cannot always also be required for nation-states. Furthermore, they worry about the temptation of self-righteousness and pride that befalls pacifists. Pacifism points to the peaceable kingdom of God, but here and now, in the fallen world, self-defense is justifiable. Wars that are fought on the basis of just-war criteria are permissible.

Even those who reject pacifism will agree, however, that the burden is on the nonpacifist to specify what situations permit the use of force and violence to achieve justice and social order. For the Christian, pacifism should be the rule, and exceptions to it need to be carefully scrutinized. Otherwise, the church can put its stamp of approval on the craven interests of nation-states, turning wars of national pride and greed into holy wars by claiming God's blessing for sinful conflict.

Nonvegetarians too will have the burden of justifying the killing of animals and their use in scientific and industrial research. They will want to eat meat as a last resort, just as the use of force to settle personal or international disputes should always be a last resort. Christians will legitimately differ on the criteria for when meat-eating is acceptable, just as Christians disagree on when and on what basis to support war. But in all of these discussions, vegetarianism should be treated as a biblical ideal, just as pacifism is. The Bible is full of wars and battles, just as the Bible is full of meat-eating, but that is because the Bible is a realistic book, written about and to a fallen humanity. We should not take the biblical description of human behavior as our norm and goal. Instead, we should look to the biblical prescriptions found in the accounts of what God originally intended and what God promises for the world. Vegetarianism is not a prerequisite for Christian faith, but it is a consequence of the Christian hope for a peaceable kingdom, where God will be all in all and all violence will come to an end.

Appendix

How to Think About Animals Ethically

■ There is no single Christian model of how to treat animals. Indeed, it can be argued that there is no single biblical model of ethics on any topic or issue. The many different books that comprise the Bible are full of prescriptions, injunctions, commandments, warnings, recommendations, counsel, parables, opinions, admonishments, advice—in sum, a plethora of do's and don'ts that appeal to a variety of ethical principles, rules, and insights. Moreover, the general ethical principle expressed in a specific biblical commandment is frequently hard to extract and turn into an absolute rule.

Take, for example, the issue of "family values." Many scholars argue that there is no single blueprint for the family in the Bible. The Old Testament allows for a variety of forms of marriage, including polygamy, obligatory marriage of a rapist and his victim (Deuteronomy 22:28–29), and levirate marriage (where the next of kin must marry the wife of his dead, childless relative). Furthermore, the Old Testament presupposes the right to divorce, even though there are many biblical passages that suggest that the marriage bond is sacred and should not be broken. Jesus dismissed the Mosaic divorce law as a concession to human sinfulness by vigorously arguing that divorce is a violation of God's original intentions for couples, as demonstrated with Adam and Eve (Mark

10:3–5), thus setting a precedent for vegetarians who argue that the permission to eat meat is likewise an accommodation of human sin, not an absolute right.

However, in Matthew, Jesus allows for divorce in the case of unchastity (19:9). This has led to many debates about what constitutes unchastity and whether one is allowed to remarry after a divorce. Paul quotes Jesus' teaching against divorce but also says that a Christian may grant his or her partner a divorce if the partner demands it (1 Corinthians 7:15). Paul also had a bias against marriage, advising young Christians to remain single if they can. How do we draw all of these verses together into a coherent whole?

The issue of animals in the Bible is equally complicated. For example, take the passage from the Old Testament, where the book of Proverbs says, "The righteous know the needs of their animals, but the mercy of the wicked is cruel" (12:10). What does that mean? What are the needs of animals, and how do we best meet them? Even if we eat them, are we meeting their needs if we raise them in factory-like conditions? Does treating animals like meat machines, depriving them of their social groupings, not letting them see the light of day or smell the earth's rich soil, pumping them full of hormones, genetically manipulating them so that they will grow fat quicker, raising them in overcrowded conditions in order to cut costs, and shipping them off to slaughterhouses where they are killed under less than ideal conditions—does all of this constitute meeting their needs?

Now listen to what Jesus says about animals: "Are not five sparrows sold for two pennies? Yet not one of them is forgotten in God's sight" (Luke 12:6). True, Jesus goes on to say that we humans are of more value than many sparrows, but are we more valuable than all the sparrows put together? Does our greater value completely negate the value of any individual sparrow? Do we have to choose between the value of humans and the value of birds? The argument that we are more valuable than the sparrows runs from the lesser to the greater, but it does not presuppose that the lesser, the sparrows, are equal to nothing. In point of fact, Jesus makes it clear that birds are valued by God as individuals. If God does not forget the sparrows, then will they too be restored when God redeems the whole world? How should we treat animals today if God remembers each and every one of them and provides for them just as God provides for us?

How do we make sense of these passages? The Bible is not philosophical prose, so systematic completeness, consistency, and comprehensiveness are not its guiding concerns. There is no single philosophical norm to which the Bible appeals in order to validate its many ethical judgments. Instead, the Bible is full of stories, letters, poetry, prayer, lament, history, arguments, predictions, and on and on. Any and every kind of literature can be found in the Bible. It is encyclopedic. In fact, it is its own entire world, a vast castle that can be entered and exited in so many places that you can visit it many times (or even move in!) without knowing exactly where you are or ever repeating your steps.

The image of a vast fortress, however, is misleading. Each book of the Bible was written for a different purpose and for a specific audience, and the writings of the Bible as a whole span many centuries. The Bible is thus more like a city than a single building, a series of castles that have been connected together with many pathways and improvised constructions. It should be no surprise, then, that sometimes it is hard to move from one book of the Bible to the next and find the overarching continuity that ties them all together. And yet Christians are people who, through the church, do precisely that: they find the pattern of God's grace throughout the Bible, and they read it as one long narrative that develops a single plot focused on the unfolding revelation of God's love.

To use a more modern image, Christians treat the Bible as if it were a cybertext—clicking on any particular passage will lead from one hypertext link to another. This format invites users to participate in a text that has no single entry point. There is also no easy exit because each passage has an endless number of interpretations. In fact, each passage only makes sense as a gateway to other passages, and the reader must make a dizzying journey through theological commentary, church practices, and personal experience in order to grasp it all. Only the theme of God's love holds the text together—a love so complex and rich that it takes a kaleidoscopic book like the Bible to express it.

Nevertheless, such a simple statement—the Bible is the story of God's love—does not do justice to sacred scripture. The complexity of the Bible makes the equally complex judgments of theology necessary. Theology gives Christians a map of the Bible so that they can know their way around it and feel at home. Church doctrines and their implications about creation, providence, human nature, Christology (the identity and salvific significance of Jesus Christ), ecclesiology (the structure and purpose of the church), and eschatology (the study of the end times) have to be inferred from the biblical materials and developed into a systematic account of Christian belief. Theologians serve the church by showing how church doctrines provide the necessary guideposts for organizing and understanding the vast variety of the books of the Bible. Any map, however, no matter how fascinating, should not be mistaken for the real thing; its purpose is to help you get from one place to another. Good theology, likewise, should conduct people from one place to another—from a state of sin to the gift of salvation—by showing how the Bible can give us direction and guide our decisions.

One way to organize the many insights of the Bible is to try to tell the biblical story all the way through, in the hope that by retelling it an ethical pattern will emerge. When the whole story is heard in all of its richness, the value of animals—their origin and destiny, as well as our responsibility for them—will become clear. Yet Christians have told the biblical story in many different ways over the centuries, and some of those ways have been used to justify practices like slavery, racism, nationalism, and wars of all kinds. The Bible is not like a magical formula that can change the world just by pronouncing its words. The Word of God speaks the truth only to those who are ready to hear it, and since even those who read it remain mired in sin, the Bible often struggles to rise above the prejudices of those who most closely guard it from attacks and criticism. It should be no cause for wonder, then, that the Bible frequently has not led to great concern for animals. Retelling the biblical story must be done thoughtfully and carefully, with an openness to the many ways that the Bible can surprise us with the unlimited power of God's grace.

Another way to consolidate the many ethical teachings of the Bible is to say that they point to the singular power of God's love as that is made known in Jesus Christ. Thus there is one principle that can serve as the foundation for all interpretations of the Bible. Even that principle, however, leaves open a lot of questions. What about the relationship between love and justice or love and judgment? Are there limits to love, and how do we know when love goes too far or is irresponsible? More fundamentally, what exactly is love? Are there different kinds of love? And how can we learn to love? These questions demonstrate the need for a theological model that would pull together biblical insights into a constructive and systematic account of our ethical obligations and responsibilities.

My goal in this book has been to retell key portions of the biblical story in order to highlight God's concern for the animals, and the integrity of my project can be judged only by my ability to persuade Christians to rethink their diets. I want to insist, however, that my retelling of the biblical narrative has not been a random product of my own imagination. Any attempt to preach the gospel (for that is what I have been doing) is guided by an overarching principle, and the principle that has guided me is the good news of God's unlimited love. When we interpret the Bible by telling its stories, we need to follow the commandment to love God above all else and to practice a life of love toward others. The ethical model that I have followed combines a reliance on an absolute principle, the love of God, with an emphasis on the importance of storytelling as a way of capturing the essence of the many stories that comprise the one Biblical narrative. The love of God would remain an abstract and easily manipulable idea if it were not for the specific stories that portray God's character and the variety of ways humans respond to God in the Bible.

In this appendix I will explain and examine several ethical models as they pertain to the issue of animals. I will evaluate them on how clearly they express the biblical theology of animals that I briefly stated in chapter two. I will also judge them on how well they express the Christian gospel to a world that is steeped in the kind of culture that I described in chapter two. I want to suggest that such models must be an accurate witness to the biblical emphasis on our responsibility for the animal world, a responsibility that is grounded in the doctrine of creation and exemplified in the self-sacrificial life of Jesus Christ. Ethical models must also be an adequate response to our cultural situation, able to inspire us in a time of great moral confusion and anxiety.

The first three models I will evaluate, environmentalism, ecofeminism, and process theology, follow the theology of animal rights and its pantheistic tendencies that I discussed in chapter two. The next model, Roman Catholic natural law theory, is an attempt to keep humanity at the center of the cosmos while still respecting the animal world, so that many Christians today, both Protestant and Catholic, are returning to natural law ethics as a basis for thinking about nature. However, I will argue that we should not draw our ethics from nature and that Catholic teaching is inconsistent about what moral duties we have toward animals. Finally, I will discuss two ethical theories that, when combined, can provide a helpful way for Christians to articulate a biblical theology of animals: narrative ethics and Reinhold Niebuhr's Christian realism.

■ Environmental Theology

Environmental theology is an attempt to bring together the best insights of the environmental movement with Christianity. Environmentalism, in turn, is the attempt to take the best insights of the scientific study of ecology and turn them into a workable worldview and political platform. Ecologists endorse a holistic approach to nature. That is, they see nature as a self-correcting system that is good in and of itself. Implicit in this view is the idea that, when there are problems in nature, they must be caused by human intervention. Pollution is a well-known problem, and over-development and suburban sprawl are increasingly becoming worries as well. Whatever we do to nature, it seems, is bad, because our interests conflict with the stability and harmony of natural ecosystems. Simplistically put, nature is good and humans are bad, so we should get out of nature as much as possible and try to protect a lot of it from human use and abuse.

Taken to extremes, this movement is sometimes called "deep ecology," which means that we should derive our moral principles from the ecological interconnections of species and plants in a specific natural environment. Aldo Leopold is the father of this movement, and in his *Sand County Almanac* he presents its basic moral rule: "A thing is right when it tends to preserve the integrity, stability, and beauty of the biotic community. It is wrong when it tends otherwise" (pp. 224–5). In other words, species and plants live off of each other and interact in ways that benefit the natural community as a whole. This fragile web of relationships can be easily broken. Environmentalists insist that when humans do intervene in nature, which is, of course, inevitable, they should do so in a way that respects this delicate network of relationships.

At first, such advice can seem perfectly reasonable and commendable. Any approach to nature needs to learn from ecologists about how ecosystems work. Too often theologians talk about nature without taking the sciences into account, and this is short-sighted and uninformed. Certainly, animals do interact in complex ways, and plants can only grow in certain types of soil and under certain weather conditions. To take one plant or animal species out of an ecosystem, or to alter the natural conditions of that ecosystem through pollution, can throw the whole system off balance. Speaking theologically, to disturb these conditions is fundamentally to alter God's design for the world, which is still evident even in spite of the fall. As Christians, we should work with nature as much as possible and not against nature, in order to be good stewards of the world that gives us shelter and provides us with the food and resources we need to survive and flourish.

However, environmental theologians often take this view much further than that. Theologians like Sallie McFague argue that we need to reconceive of God in order to encourage a better treatment of nature. Traditional metaphors of God depict the divine as a male ruler who acts without any sense of democratic cooperation with his subjects. Such images are metaphors because we know that God transcends all human imagination and that God is not literally a man or a king sitting on a throne. For McFague, metaphorical images of God need to be tested for their relevance to modern problems and perspectives. Metaphors that might have spoken to people in the ancient world do not necessarily speak to us, so we should start creating our own metaphorical language to capture the essence of God's grace.

McFague argues that a distant God who rules over the world like an autocratic king is not a good role model for how we should exercise our own authority over the world. Indeed, the portrait of God as an almighty ruler gives us a false sense of God's ability to intervene in the world and do with the world what God wants. This keeps us from worrying about the many adverse consequences of our exploitation of nature, since we assume that God can always step in to set things right. Moreover, if God rules the world like a king, then so can we. If God is distant from the world and treats the world as a mere backdrop to human history, then so can humans. Why should we be any kinder to nature than God is?

Thus McFague and others trace the problem of the Western attitude toward nature to its roots in the traditional portrait of God. As a solution, they argue that we need to think of God in terms of new metaphors that will emphasize God's closeness to the world. McFague suggests that we think of God as a mother, lover, and friend, not a father, ruler, and king. These metaphors would suggest that God is intimately connected to the world rather than a master of the universe. The world, McFague further argues, can even be construed as the *body* of God. We should thus give it the utmost respect because when we harm the world we are also harming God. We know God through nature, and God feels the pain and suffering that we inflict on nature. Nature, then, is where we can best encounter God. Nature is, in a way, divine. It is the place where God is most present to us, and in turn it is the place where we can worship that divine presence.

Much of McFague's criticism of the traditional model of God does not seem fair, given the Bible's overwhelming emphasis on God's steadfast love. Nevertheless, the religious rhetoric of environmental theology is gaining in popularity, so it is important to be very clear about its limitations from the perspective of traditional Christian belief. Let me suggest five basic criticisms. First and most fundamentally, environmental theology comes dangerously close to collapsing the differences between God and the world. The problem is that making the world a part of God leads to thinking about God as a part of the world. If God is a part of the world, then God can hardly stand over the world in order to direct it toward a more peaceful and harmonious destiny. The traditional Christian doctrine of God does not suggest that God must be either transcendent or immanent, but that God is intimately involved in every aspect of the world *precisely because* God is totally different than anything to be found in the world. In other words, God is present in the world without being a part of the world, and only a God who is wholly other can be this kind of God.

The revolutionary insight of monotheism leads not to a dismissal of the value of nature but a transformation in how we tend to invest finite things with too much value. While polytheism grants the things of this world absolute meaning, identifying natural phenomena with distinct divinities, monotheism renders all of these worldly values relative. The God of monotheism transcends the world and thus asks us likewise to gain some perspective on our environment so that we can put things into a wider framework. By loving God above all else, monotheists order their other loves so that nothing is idolized and thus given a distorted sense of importance. Things can be loved for what they are, not for what we want them to be. We are freed from the fantasies and illusions that shape much of the modern world's quest for meaning. Monotheists see the world as it actually is, without being romantic and thus less than honest about the violence in nature. At the same time, monotheists see the world as a gift from God, a gift to be cherished and respected.

If God were a part of the world, then the world as it is, in its fallen state, would be divine and thus unconditionally good. This position leads to the ecological argument that animal pain and suffering is good and should be complacently accepted. In fact, if God feels the world as God's body, then all parts of the world are equally good and it becomes difficult to make comparative decisions about animals having more value than plants or higher animals having more value than lower ones. The traditional Christian notion that the world is fallen better corresponds to most people's reaction to even the most natural of animal suffering. Even inevitable and environmentally useful suffering is still suffering, hard to watch, and troubling to fathom, and thus nature in its present form is not the best of all possible worlds.

Second, as a consequence of the tendency to divinize the world, environmental theology totally rejects the doctrine of the fall. Christians believe that all of nature is fallen, not just human nature, so that the world is not now what God originally meant it to be. Anyone who turns on the television to watch a nature show will be convinced that the traditional Christian understanding of nature is more realistic than the doctrines of environmentalism. Animals eating animals is necessary, but that does not make it morally good. Ecology presents animal strife and aggression as essential to the maintenance of an ecosystem, but theology teaches that what now appears to be essential is really an accident of history. Violence is a product of the fall. Though one must tolerate violence in nature as the way things are, such violence is not the way things were meant to be. Peace is more fundamental than violence when nature is seen from the long view of the biblical perspective.

Although humans have polluted the earth and destroyed sensitive ecological systems, not all of the violence in nature is a product of human actions. Nature is not in perfect balance today—think of floods, hurricanes, draughts—because, mysteriously, God allows evil in the world even as God works toward a greater good in the world that is yet to come. The result is disequilibrium and flux on a scale that is hard for us to imagine. True, many "natural disasters" need not be seen as evil in themselves; they are only crises when we get in their way. And we add to nature's problems with unwise decisions, overpopulation, and economic greed. Nevertheless, nature can be the object of sublime appreciation precisely because it is a power that frequently overwhelms, disrupts, and destroys human prospects for survival. Just as humans cannot be blamed for all of nature's problems, nature cannot be romanticized as a perfect, self-correcting organism. We cannot improve nature in any grand or dramatic way, but Christians do not accept the fall as permanent, nor do they accept it as evidence of what God wills and wants. Christians know there is another way, and they hope for and work toward those impossible possibilities that Jesus revealed as the kingdom of God.

Third, as a consequence of the denial of the fall of nature, environmentalists suggest that nature is good in and of itself—indeed, that nature can and should stand alone without human intervention. Political conservatives reject this view because they do not want to put limits on the growth and prosperity of human society. They put the economy and human interests ahead of the interests of the natural world. Christianity comes down in between these two groups. Christianity teaches that nature is good because God created the world, but nature was not meant to exist without and outside of its relationship to humanity. The drama of the creation account in Genesis reaches its climax with the creation of humanity precisely because God chose to make of humanity—through the incarnation—the ground of the divine revelation and presence. History has a direction and nature has meaning through God's relationship to Jesus Christ. True, the world was created for the glory of God, so that it has meaning beyond our relationship to it, but the world was also given to humanity as the necessary precondition for the unfolding of salvation history. The world does not stand alone any more than humanity or even God, does. Relationships, then, are fundamental to the Christian vision of nature. Even God's own being is essentially relational, given God's trinitarian nature. God chooses to be a creator, to have a world, and to be with us in Jesus Christ and the Holy Spirit. The world, then, is not an independent entity that stands apart from humans or the divine. The fundamental question for Christians concerns the nature of those relationships. We are here to tend to the world and to benefit from it, but how do we benefit from it while still treating it as a gift from God?

Fourth, as a matter of clarification, environmentalism should not be confused with the animal rights movement. Indeed, the two movements are often at odds with each other. Environmentalists insist that nature itself shows us how it wants to be treated, which means that we should not go out of our way to save animals from each other. All of nature is involved in killing, in the giving and taking of life, and that is natural according to the environmentalists. Nature does not waste life wantonly, but it also is not sentimental about the value of life. Animals must kill each other; that is just the way it is.

Environmentalists are not primarily concerned with individual animal life. Instead, they are dedicated to making sure that the animals and plants that are a part of an ecosystem continue to be a part of that system. They are most concerned with species that are on the verge of becoming extinct or with changes wrought by human beings that affect a certain plant or resource and thus could change the ecosystem as a whole. Individual animals do not count (although species do).

Environmentalists are right that it is impossible to draw the moral principle that individual life should be valued from nature alone. Nature is red in tooth and claw, as the poet said long ago. Individual animals must be sacrificed for the good of the whole ecosystem. Christianity, however, believes in a different kind of sacrifice. Christians do not infer their ethics from observations of nature. Christianity is about love, and love responds to any being who suffers. Jesus came not to ask for more animal sacrifices but to be the final sacrifice so that we might experience God's grace through him, not the killing of others. Christians know they cannot save the world from pain and suffering. That utopian dream must be left up to God. But Christians also know that it is important to act to help all of God's creatures if they are in trouble. Christians will thus act in ways contrary to environmentalists.

For example, an environmentalist would argue that feeding birds during the winter months merely enables the weaker ones to survive, contributing to an imbalance in the bird population relative to other animal groups. Christians, however, know that acting compassionately for others has a value regardless of the consequences. Certainly ethical action requires astute moral perception so that we can discern the morally relevant features of a situation and respond accordingly. A compassion that is uninformed can be reckless and even dangerous, yet love does not count the cost; compassion is not a cost-benefit calculation but an act of solidarity with those who suffer. Christians will work to alleviate suffering because God has acted in this way, becoming one with us by willingly suffering on our behalf. Those animal welfare groups that save beached whales or help cats and dogs during floods or hurricanes are acting more closely to Christian principles than ecologists who insist that animal pain is a necessary part of what makes the world go around.

Fifth and finally, the order of the world must ultimately be read from a biblical view of God, not from nature alone. According to Genesis, the world was created as a structured whole that manifests a God-given order. That order places humans in a unique position of authority and responsibility. Environmental theologians argue that humans should get their morality from nature; but according to Christianity, nature should get its purpose and direction from humans, who are created in God's image. Environmentalists therefore have the relationship between humans and nature exactly backwards. As a result, they forfeit possibilities for the creative exercise of human authority. By defining nature as good and human authority as bad, they condemn nature to exist without any human involvement, which is not only bad theology but also totally unrealistic public policy. The world is shrinking and humans are in charge of all of it, for better or worse. We cannot shirk our responsibility for nature. Nature is largely under our control. The only question is how we will exercise that control.

■ Ecofeminism

Ecofeminism is a unique blend of feminism and ecological or environmental thought. McFague could be placed in either the environmentalist or ecofeminist camp, except that those in the latter argue that sexism, not images of God, is at the root of how we think about and treat nature. They argue that all oppressions are interconnected, so that feminism has relevance for more than just relations between the genders. Ecofeminism is a form of liberation theology that wants to seek out and uproot all forms of oppression. Oppression is defined as any kind of hierarchy based on a prejudice that one group deserves something that another group does not. All oppressions follow the same brutal logic of making a human prejudice seem natural and inevitable. For ecofeminists, the root form of oppression is the masculine domination of nature (see Adams and Gaard).

Ecofeminists often blame the male domination of nature on the first book of the Bible. Their rejection of male domination is actually indicative of their rejection of any kind of authority, hierarchy, or natural order altogether. They often contrast what they call masculine thinking, which divides the world into opposing positions and thus is dualistic, with feminine thinking, which looks for connections and relationships rather than contrasts and oppositions. They do not argue that all men think in masculine ways or that all women think in feminine ways, but they do insist that there are basic differences between the two genders in how they approach the world. Women know the world differently from men, and this is the key to an ecofeminist ethics of nature and animals.

Men define themselves over and against nature, ecofeminists argue, and as a result they also place themselves over any group that is put on the side of nature. Traditionally, Western culture has treated women as more a part of nature than men. The male urge for domination leads them to portray women as beings who are not quite fully human and yet are higher than the animals. Women, after all, frequently have been denied basic rights, just like the animals. Moreover, the grounds for this deprivation are the same for both women and animals. Both are thought to be biologically closer to nature, and thus they are not as superior as men, who measure themselves by how far they transcend nature. Women are closer to animals because they maintain the animal functions of reproduction and childrearing. Women are also thought to be more emotional and thus more subjected to their bodies than men, who better use rationality to keep their emotions in check. Female skills are also often thought to be instinctual, so women need less education and deserve fewer rewards than men. Women are thus in between men and animals, sharing some of the privileges of the former but often suffering some of the degradations of the latter.

Since women are traditionally defined as a part of nature, men think that they have the right to dominate women along with nature. The root problem of all oppressions has to do with false notions of masculinity, so feminism, with its critique of masculinity, not only liberates women from men but also frees nature from its long travail. Some feminists, ecofeminists would argue, want women to become just like men, to have their same freedom and rights so that women too can exploit nature and benefit from the privileges of domination. Erasing gender differences leads to the spread of masculine, not feminine, values. Ecofeminists take a different route. They argue that women embody virtues and skills that need to be more highly valued as essential contributions to society. For example, some ecofeminists surprisingly argue that women really are closer to nature and can relate to nature and animals in better ways than men. Women experience nature through touching and holding, for example, gestures of intimacy that can be downplayed or shunned by men. Ironically, ecofeminism risks confirming the very stereotypes that it set out to critique.

This reevaluation of the emotions is certainly important. Young men too often are told that sentimentalism is a pathology and that strong displays of emotion are for women only. Men frequently suffer for this by being unable to express themselves fully later in life. Indeed, boys often turn to pets as the one attachment in their lives that can be deeply emotional and intimate. The Bible honors such emotions because it perceives all animals as God's pets. God loves them all, and all animals will one day be in a relationship with us that will be like the relationship of humans and pets. So ecofeminism can go a long way toward teaching Christians to take a more gentle and empathic approach to animals.

The problem arises when ecofeminists so emphasize the ways in which women connect to and participate in each other's lives and in nature that they end up wanting to wipe out the basic differences between humans and nature altogether. If oppression is identified with hierarchy, and if women are better able to experience nature because they do not stand apart from and over it, then it seems that the closer one gets to nature, the better. However, the exercise of responsible authority over nature requires a complex mix of virtues. Intimacy and compassion are important, but so are analysis and judgment, the very dispositions that ecofeminism ascribes to men. Surely we need not only an emotional bonding with nature but also a thoughtful and deliberate examination of what is best for nature. We should cultivate ethical reactions that are spontaneous and heartfelt, but we should not just trust our instincts. We need to adopt the broader perspective of what God desires, which entails becoming immersed in God's Word.

We need both traditionally masculine and feminine traits in dealing with nature, and that is what the Bible teaches about love. God's love for us does come from a hierarchical source, over and above us, but that does not mean that God's love is not intimate, emotional, and trustworthy. Too often ecofeminists define power in itself as evil, but there are different kinds of power, so that not all power is bad. Power that sustains us, guides us, and saves us is the power that God has over us and the power that Jesus models for us. God is able to love us precisely because God is transcendent, providentially guiding history and preparing the future for us. We are able to care for nature precisely because we have some distance from it.

Distance, when grounded in the difference that separates humans from animals, is not a bad thing, just as the basic gender differences that distinguish men from women are not necessarily bad. Philosopher Kathryn Paxton George has recently criticized ecofeminism for not paying attention to the differences in nutritional needs based on age, gender, race, and class. She argues that a strict vegetarian diet presupposes a "male physiological norm" that is incompatible with feminism's own emphasis on gender differences. Those gender differences, combined together, comprise precisely what Christians call love, an authority that is responsible and caring. We do not need to eliminate gender differences in order to save nature from men, just as we do not need to eliminate the differences between humans and animals in order to save animals from us. Instead, gender characteristics can complement each other for the good of nature. Men and women can love each other in their own unique ways, and they can work together for a better world as well. Gender differences, far from being the source of all the bad things we humans do to nature, can be, if both genders recognize the equal strengths of each other, the source of the proper authority needed for the management of nature, especially as the wilderness shrinks and more and more nature comes under our control.

In sum, while most Christians will agree with ecofeminists that there are basic trademarks that characterize the genders, they will disagree that these different inclinations are purely a byproduct of men's attempts to dominate women or that they always result in the advantage and promotion of men over women. Conservative Christians believe that a husband's authority over his wife is built into the natural order by God, while liberal Christians are often anxious to erase most gender differences based on our equality before God. These debates are complicated and extend beyond the scope of my concerns here. What is interesting is that ecofeminists argue that men dominate women because they dominate nature, and that therefore women can relate to nature and animals in a way that men cannot. The Christian view is that both men and women have special roles to play in the family, but that these diverse roles are not *in themselves* the source of our tendency to abuse each other or to exploit and pollute nature. Sin, more specifically greed, is the source of that problem. Both men and women have authority over nature and are responsible for exercising that authority in distinct but complementary ways. Both genders are tempted by sin to profit from nature in unhealthy and disrespectful ways, but by working together all people can learn to approach nature with the kind of gentle authority that acts out of a responsible compassion for the good of others, treating animals as the gift God intended them to be.

■ Process Theology

Process theology is a philosophical movement founded by Alfred North Whitehead that has become a theological school under the influence of Charles Hartshorne and others. Theologians like John Cobb, Daniel A. Dombrowski, and Jay McDaniel have applied process theology to the problems of nature and animals. Process theologians can sound a lot like environmentalists because they emphasize that all things are connected to each other, so that nothing exists as an isolated entity, alone and by itself. Not even God exists apart from everything else. In fact, the primary tenet of process theology is that God is essentially related to all things.

Process thinkers reject the traditional image of God as transcendent and self-sufficient. Classical theists argued that God existed before the world was created, so God does not need anything in order to be God. This is sometimes called God's aseity, a word which means that God is self-derived (*a se*) rather than derived from some external source (*ab alio*). God is totally and perfectly complete. God does not change, and God is not limited in any way. To say otherwise is to reduce God's power and to mar God's majesty. Only a limited God would need something outside of God in order to be complete.

Yet that is precisely what process theologians propose. They insist that the classical notion of God as unchanging and unmoved by any external forces does not do justice to the Bible's portrait of God as a loving being who is intimately involved in our lives. They want to correct such distortions, however, not by returning to the Bible so much as developing a metaphysical system that describes reality as a whole. All things, they argue, are essentially interconnected. Nothing stands alone. They agree with ecologists that everything is related to everything else, so that to change one part of the world is to change everything else.

Process theologians then argue that God too is connected to everything. In fact, they suggest that God is the most connected being of all. God is intimately involved with all things, which is why they argue that God is not all-powerful and transcendent. Classical theists emphasized God's transcendence because they believed that God is totally different from everything that we know and experience in the world. God does not exist in space and time, thus God is not an individual being like us, limited and vulnerable. If God created the world, then God stands apart from the world. And if God will some day judge and redeem the world, then God does not depend on the world for anything at all. But process theologians insist that God is not unmoved and unchanging. Instead, God's power is limited by the power of all other entities in the world, and God is dependent on the cooperation of these entities as God valiantly tries to pursue God's plan for the world.

Two implications of this theology are especially important for thinking about animals. First, God influences the world by providing all entities with initial aims and ultimate goals. God, then, cannot intervene unilaterally to save anybody. God has the power of persuasion, but God is not all-powerful. Process theologians say that it does not make sense to argue that God is all-powerful in light of the evil in the world that God apparently permits. They suggest that God too is a victim of the world's evils and that God cannot do whatever God wants. God, then, is vulnerable, relative, and contingent. God suffers with us as the most powerful being but not an all-powerful being. God, like everyone else, is in a process of becoming, that is, growing and changing as God influences and is influenced by other entities.

Second, all entities influence all other entities, which means that humans do not have a unique role in the universe. Process thinkers defend a notion of panpsychism—the idea that feeling is continuous throughout the cosmos. There are certainly differences of degree between humans, animals, and inanimate objects, but the mental and the material are not absolutely separated from each other. Everything has the power and capacity to affect something else positively, so process thinkers say that all things feel and experience each other on some level. Obviously more mentally developed entities, like the higher animals and human beings, can articulate those feelings with a great deal of sophistication that is denied to entities that are more completely material. Nevertheless, the process vision of reality is that of a continuous flow of entities and events that does not allow us to dismiss all nonhuman reality as mere passive matter.

This theological position is very popular for Christians trying to rethink their relation to nature, reimagine God, and engage in dialogue with Eastern religions about the value of nature. Nonetheless, some of the problems with process theology especially come to light when examined through the lens of God's relationship with animals. The first problem is that the process God is limited, so God is not able to redeem the world and restore it to its original harmony.

Process theologians, who usually reject the concept of heaven or any notion of an afterlife, counter this criticism by arguing that God remembers all things. God feels everything, and even though God cannot change everything, God can preserve each life in the divine memory. This kind of afterlife does not continue my objective existence, but it does preserve me subjectively in the mind of God. The notion of a subjective afterlife, however, will hardly do animals—or humans, for that matter—any good. If an animal has lived a life of pain and suffering, why would that animal want that life preserved in those terms? Pain demands healing and suffering cries out for justice. The brief lives of countless animals, as well as many unfortunate humans, beg for continuation and completion, not to be frozen in the memory banks of an infinite video recorder. Only a transcendent God, who is wholly other than us, has the power to heal all pain, redeem all suffering, and answer every prayer, even the voiceless prayers of those who cannot speak and must suffer in silence. Only such a God can both forgive and forget our sins and our suffering so that a new world without fear, resentment, or anger can become possible. Only a God who is the creator of the world, who stands outside the world and providentially guides it to completion, can be the source of trust and hope in the midst of a world so full of apparently meaningless pain and suffering.

The second problem concerns the process emphasis on God as a being who feels all things, equally and immediately. This does make God appear to be more intimate and loving than some of the traditional images of God as a ruler or king. Most countries do not even have kings anymore, so that language can appear to belong to the distant past and thus render God distant as well. Yet Christianity does not believe that God is only a ruler and king. Christianity teaches that this ruler gave up the royal privileges and became the one who suffers on our behalf. God, then, does suffer for us, but this is different from process theology's claim that God immediately feels and is affected by everything. The process God would feel not only the pain of the victims of violence but also the satisfaction of the aggressors. A God who feels all things equally would feel the full belly of the beast who kills as well as the torture of the creature who is torn apart. By making God radically dependent on the world, process theology is unable to distinguish between the kinds of suffering that God identifies with and the kinds of violence that God repudiates.

The third problem is that God is seen here as a being who lures all creatures to a higher good through acts of persuasion and solicitation. Process thinkers insist that God lures every entity toward the good by setting aims that are consistent with what that entity is. Thus there is no absolute good, no universal goal that transcends the world. Instead, there are only many different goods, because each entity, from a rock to an animal to a human being, has a particular good that fits what that entity can and cannot do. The problem is that this portrait of God omits the traditional doctrine of the fall. Many animals, as we all know, are pitted against each other, involved in relationships of aggression, violence, and parasitism. If God is luring each animal to fulfill its own nature, then God is luring animals against each other. Consequently, God is depicted as condoning and even encouraging violence.

This view makes much less sense than does the traditional view that God permits the world to be disordered as a result of the fall. If animals are fallen, then God does not rejoice in their behavior or contribute to it. Instead, the violence of the natural world is its own judgment, as even nature, as Paul wrote (Romans 8:19–22), groans with frustration as it awaits God's final redemption.

What makes process theology even more problematic is that it portrays God as a being who grows and changes, so that God's memory of and interaction with animals must be profitable to God. The process God cherishes all animal experience, and God is able to harmonize the carnivore and the herbivore through God's own private mental gymnastics. It is not enough that some animals are sacrificed to others in this world. On top of that, process thinkers ask us to imagine that these same animals also serve as food for God's own inner life, so that God can maximize God's own inner experience and get the most out of lives that are otherwise wasted. God must be seen as enjoying the strife of the animals and in taking delight when carnivorous animals fulfill themselves by attacking and eating other animals. The process God sounds more like the ancient pagan deities who demanded to be fed by bloody sacrifices than the Christian God who put an end to all animal sacrifices by the substitution of God's Son.

The fourth and final problem is that, when all is said and done, process theology, like environmentalism, does not lead to the protection of individual animals or compassion for the welfare of all animals. Although process thinkers claim that there is never anything material that is not also to some degree mental, they also argue that the more complex an entity is, the more it is able to feel other entities and contribute to them. Humans, therefore, have more complex relations with others than animals or rocks do. This is obvious and makes sense. But then process thinkers go on to develop a moral position that is little different from utilitarianism. They argue that we should act to maximize our relationships with others, and we should protect those entities that have the deepest and richest relationships with us. We should not regret or lament the fact that some entities seem placed here merely to serve our needs or to fulfill some basic function. In fact, as the very term *process* suggests, all entities are used (or processed) by others and in turn use others, so that we can never escape using entities that are less complex than we are.

If no entity stands alone, then it is foolish to try to protect less fortunate and more vulnerable entities from predators and aggressors. No entity has intrinsic value; nothing is an end in itself. In a world without absolutes, the moral criteria for process theology becomes the pursuit of intense experiences and rich relationships. Novelty and creativity within the limitations of interdependence are the goal. This inevitably involves influencing other entities in ways that might not be good for them. Rather than advocating an absolute ethic of love and compassion, process thinkers risk rationalizing the ways in which humans exploit nature and contribute to animal suffering. The process God turns the natural processes of nature into God, so that the ways in which animals live off of each other is seen as natural and right, rather than fallen and disordered. It is almost as if, in their zeal to make God more humanlike by limiting God's powers and magnifying God's vulnerabilities, they also end up reducing the moral demands of God, so that God becomes more like us even as we are not expected to become more like God. Process theology leaves us with no absolute standard by which we can take the measure of the world in order to find it wanting and to hope for something else.

■ Roman Catholic Natural Law Theory

Anybody who has spent much time with the animal rights literature soon finds that Roman Catholicism is often blamed for the plight of animals in the West today. I do not know how many times I have read about how Pope Pius IX refused permission for the establishment of a Society for the Prevention of Cruelty to Animals in Rome on the grounds that it would mistakenly suggest that humans have duties to animals. Much of this polemic should be taken very carefully. There is a bias against Catholicism in animal rights circles because the Catholic church defends strong notions of authority and hierarchy, which cut against the radically egalitarian ideology of environmentalism. Moreover, the Catholic moral tradition is very rich and complex. Few figures have matched the exuberant love for creation preached by St. Francis of Assisi, who nevertheless was no vegetarian. Francis, however, is overshadowed by the more dominant authority of St. Thomas Aquinas, and it is his unfriendly view of animals that has determined the official teachings of the Catholic Church.

St. Thomas is the "Common Doctor of the Church," and it is no exaggeration to say that all of Catholic morality is shaped by him. He was very influenced by Aristotle and develops his ethics not only from the Bible and the church fathers, especially Augustine, but also from what has come to be called the natural law tradition. For St. Thomas and Aristotle alike, it seemed natural that the less perfect were made for the more perfect. Aristotle notoriously believed that some people were just born inferior, so that slavery was an aspect of nature. Thomas believed the same thing about animals. They were born to be used by humans.

Nor did St. Thomas think that we should do much to help or befriend animals. We can only love, he argued, that which is rational. God's love for us, then, extends only as far as our neighbors, not to animals. Since animals do not share in our rational life, they cannot share in our charity. To most modern ears, this will sound like an artificially imposed limitation on compassion and love. For St. Thomas, love creates a fellowship, a community, and only those who are able to respond to love by loving in return can enter into that fellowship. To so respond, one must be capable of making rational decisions, and this, he thought, animals could not do. What he would say about the love of pets for their owners or the kinds of decisions well-trained dogs have made to save someone or to return our devotion with a heroic deed, I do not know. For St. Thomas, rationality was a property that belonged, in this world, to humans alone. There were no degrees of rationality for St. Thomas: either you are rational and thus human, or you are not.

The most that St. Thomas will say about our relationship to animals is that we have an indirect duty to them. This is a well-established argument in the philosophical literature, and it is repeated by philosophers like Immanuel Kant. The first-century Jewish philosopher Philo might have invented this argument when he suggested that Moses wanted the Israelites to treat animals fairly as a means of practicing the virtuous life toward each other (Winston, p. 291). The indirect duties argument goes like this: We do not have direct duties toward animals, but we do have indirect duties, because those who are kind to animals are more disposed to be kind to their fellow human beings. This is no doubt true. When we are kind to animals, we are developing habits of kindness that will help us to be kind to people. The opposite is also true, as psychologists tell us that many lives of crime begin with animal abuse. Nevertheless, the indirect duties argument portrays animal compassion as not a good thing in itself but a warm-up for the real thing, compassion toward humans. What might look like a duty to an animal is actually a duty toward humans; and in fact, we only have duties toward animals when those duties potentially benefit humans.

Treating an animal well is, therefore, a kind of dress rehearsal for the real performance. But, as this way of putting it suggests, it is hard to imagine that a rehearsal has absolutely no value for the opening night show. Indeed, everything in the life of a Christian is a rehearsal for the culmination of our vision of God in the afterlife. If being kind to animals does help us in being kind toward each other, then the kindness we display to animals must be a real kindness. It must be an act that God values and rewards just as God values and rewards our kindness to each other. Otherwise, how could it be a rehearsal or warm-up for the real thing?

There is, then, some merit to the indirect duties argument. Our duties for each other *are* more important that our duties toward animals, and the former should take precedence over the latter if and when they come into conflict. But is compassion for animals something we do not need to practice once we have learned to be kind to each other? Does the duty to animals have *no* merit for its own sake? If we can express kindness toward animals, and St.

Thomas says that we can, then that kindness originates in our love for God and God's love for us—and that kindness has real value as an expression of God's grace. True, our kindness toward animals does prepare us to be kind in even more complex and demanding situations. It is, in a way, easier to be kind toward a stray cat than toward the homeless person I see on the street on my way to work. When I take in the stray cat, I should also think about how to help the homeless humans who also wander our streets. But I see no reason why we should accept St. Thomas's conclusion that kindness toward cats is not really real, and that its only value lies in how it prepares us for greater and more difficult tasks.

Some recent Catholic theologians have looked to other Thomistic ethical principles in order to develop a more positive Catholic theology of animals. Andrew Tardiff, for example, begins a discussion of animals by noting that the just war tradition holds that killing is right only if it is done in self-defense. Such killing must be done with the right intention and in the right proportion for the desired end. You would not, to take an obvious case, wipe out an entire city if someone in that city were trying to kill you. Instead, you would use the minimal force necessary to protect yourself.

Applied to animals, it can be argued that if one were without suitable alternative sources of protein, the killing of animals would be justified to preserve one's life. But even then, the killing should be done in ways that are proportionate to the desired result. There is no reason that animals need to be raised or slaughtered in inhumane conditions in order for us to consume meat. Certainly, saving a few pennies at the grocery store is no justification for cruelty. If, however, one has access to plenty of sources of nonanimal protein, and if the treatment of animals is out of proportion to the need for protein, then the argument can be made on good Thomistic grounds that vegetarianism is an ethical requirement.

While this is a creative use of St. Thomas, it does nothing to uncover the root problem of the Thomistic position, which is its appeal to nature for ethical justification. In this respect, Thomism is much like the environmental movement in its attempt to ground human morality in the patterns and rhythms of nature. It is important to point out, though, that nature for St. Thomas is not necessarily a description of the world we see through our eyes, although he frequently does appeal to such empirical descriptions to back up his claims about human superiority. Instead, we should think of nature as a concept of what God intends for the world. Natural law, after all, is our rational participation in the eternal law, and our reason is a gift from God. We know the order of the world not just through observation but from being grateful to God for God's gift of order. God's order is not identical to the world as it is now. The only true order is the eternal intention of God the Creator, who is working even now to restore the world to what God originally intended. That is the nature that we need to keep in mind and the order that we need to promote. That order does place humans in a special role, but it does not allow us to do with nature whatever we want.

The recently published *Catechism of the Catholic Church* actually has some very interesting things to say about how we should treat animals. It says:

> 2416 Animals are God's creatures. He surrounds them with his providential care. By their mere existence they bless him and give him glory. Thus men owe them kindness. We should recall the gentleness with which saints like St. Francis of Assisi or St. Philip Neri treated animals.

This passage seems to go further than St. Thomas by advocating compassion for animals because God loves them and guides them and rejoices in them. The catechism also states:

> 2417 God entrusted animals to the stewardship of those whom he created in his own image. Hence it is legitimate to use animals for food and clothing. They may be domesticated to help man in his work and leisure. Medical and scientific experimentation on animals, if it remains within reasonable limits, is a morally acceptable practice since it contributes to caring for or saving human life.

Here the catechism teaches that it is acceptable to use animals within reasonable limits, and I agree. But what are those limits? Presumably those limits are established in the earlier teaching. We should always be kind to animals. We owe them that kindness, so we should never use them in ways that violate kindness. These two teachings, which almost seem to contradict each other, are brought together in the final passage about animals from the catechism:

2418 It is contrary to human dignity to cause animals to suffer or die needlessly. It is likewise unworthy to spend money on them that should as a priority go to the relief of human misery. One can love animals; one should not direct to them the affection due only to persons.

So we should not make animals suffer unless we absolutely have to. I have already argued that we do not have to eat meat. Surely we also do not have to run cosmetic tests on animals. But what about researching on animals in order possibly to expand our life expectancy? Does the quest to keep lengthening our life expectancy through animal experimentation add to or impair human dignity? Should we, in other words, try to live forever? At what point do we take our finitude as a natural limitation, a gift from God and not something to forever struggle against and postpone with every possible resource? Isn't the mad quest for immortality, with its devil-be-damned attitude about anything that gets in the way, a consequence of a pagan hope for immortality and not a Christian faith in the resurrection of the dead and the restoration of the world?

The catechism goes on to criticize the keeping of pets, which will sound strange to most North American ears. I would agree that the catechism has the right priorities, that human needs should come before animal needs. However, the two sets of needs are not mutually exclusive. We spend a lot of money on a lot of consumer goods that we hardly need. Showing affection to animals is surely less wasteful than showing affection for sport teams or a favorite television show. Taking pleasure in God's creation by sharing one's life with a domesticated animal is surely a worthy activity in itself and not a waste of time.

Moreover, the catechism already argued that we should show kindness to animals, and such kindness inevitably involves inviting domesticated animals into our homes, sharing our lives with them, and treating them well. The domestication of animals and the keeping of pets is deeply embedded in human nature and present in every culture, ancient or modern. Keeping pets is one way in which humans exercise thoughtful and caring authority over animals, and it should not be looked upon as an unnatural extravagance or a perversion of the true authority humans have over animals.

In sum, the Catholic church offers some contradictory and unclear advice about how to treat animals, but in its most recent teachings it has gone further than St. Thomas in making kindness a duty to all Catholics. Catholics themselves can ask what needless suffering is in the animal world and what we can do to stop it.

■ Narrative Theology

The best way to get to know other people is to hear stories about them. In fact, when we introduce ourselves to others, it is hard to pick out a few abstract adjectives that describe us. What does it mean to say that I am thoughtful or rash, funny or depressed, energetic or slothful? It is much more revealing to tell a story about myself or for me to hear your story—where you were born, what kind of family you have, why you made the decisions that have brought you to this point in your life. Even very specific stories can tell a lot about who you are. How you handled a recent tragedy in your life, when you first decided that religious faith was important to you, or some silly event that made you stop and think twice about your life—all of these elements of your personal identity are best expressed in narrative form.

Even when we think of our friends and our closest loved ones, we often think of a story that captures their personalities perfectly. After we tell the story we do not feel obligated to add a lot of commentary. If the story is well told there is not much more to say. It is like a well-told joke; you only have to explain the joke if it does not work, that is, if nobody thinks it is very funny.

In the past two decades many theological ethicists have been increasingly turning to the idea of story to explain how virtues are developed, how ethical decisions are made, and how institutions like the church cultivate moral codes among their members. The category of narrative has become a catch-word that has been used by nearly every theologian and for a wide variety of purposes. It is a convenient term because hardly anyone would dispute the importance of narrative for the formation and practice of the Christian life.

Christianity is a religion rooted in narrative, and for too long ethicists have focused on rules, principles, or laws at the expense of the narrative basis of the Christian life. Nevertheless, it is easier to *talk* about the significance of stories than to show how they actually *work* in shaping our moral lives. From the stories in the Bible, through the history of Christianity and its many saints and theologians and leaders, to the many stories we tell about ourselves and the competing narratives that our culture tries to tell about us, narratives are multiple and contestable. Depending on who is telling the story and for what purpose, the story of anything will change from one telling to another. As William C. Placher, one of the foremost narrative theologians, has written about the Gospels, "Perhaps their very diversity and ambiguity represent part of the meaning of these texts, one of the ways in which they function for readers by raising questions about the varied voices within the world they narrate and the relation of that world to history and to the reality of their readers. One cannot judge their truth without first having understood their complex meanings" (p. 88). The complexity of the biblical narratives forces us to make them a part of our lives in order to touch their depths. A careful reading of the Bible would resist translating its stories into a superficial summary of abstract propositions and rules.

As Stanley Hauerwas, the most influential narrative theologian, has argued, we need to read the Bible from within a community and on a regular basis in order to develop the kind of character that the Bible recommends. The Bible is not a textbook that can be studied by an isolated individual in search of some magical formula that will make all of life's problems suddenly go away. The Bible is the Word of God given to the church. It draws Christians together in community, and it is only in a devotional setting that Christians can put the Bible into practice. Applying the message of the Bible to current events and social problems involves a lot of skill that can only be learned by being immersed in the rituals and traditions of the church.

Yet the problem with any theology that places religious authority in the communal interpretation of the Bible is that there are so many different Christian communities. Moreover, the church as a whole has changed so much over time. For most of its history, for example, the church thought that slavery was an institution that the Bible permitted. Many even thought that slavery did not contradict the biblical message of love, although Christians now perceive how slavery does not harmonize with the proclamation of the gospel. On some issues it takes a long time for Christians to discern what the Bible teaches as the Holy Spirit works through history to guide the church toward the truth.

Narrative ethicists reject the Enlightenment's attempt to defend a rational ethic that would be universally true. All ethical thinking, they argue, is based in a particular time and place. There is no one ethical principle or set of principles that can be rationally demonstrated as true for all people, regardless of local customs and traditions. Philosophical ethicists often try to connect ethics to individual freedom, but narrative theologians have a radically different portrait of what it means to be moral. Morality means that we are shaped by demands and obligations that are greater than we are, commitments that constitute our most personal identity. Morality for Christians begins in a gratitude for a relationship to something higher and better, something that we ourselves could not have produced or fashioned. Freedom comes from recognizing this higher power rather than from exercising some intrinsic ability to exist as individuals apart from all relationships.

These commitments are born in community, but this does not mean that their truth cannot be defended in front of others. Part of the narrative of Christianity, as Hauerwas insists, is to proclaim this particular story as the truth for all people, so that biblical narrative results in the missionary witness of the church. Moreover, this particular story should result in more truthful lives, sustained by the power of God's grace. God thus confirms the truth of the Christian story by changing the people who dare to try to tell it.

The problem with the modern age is that we live amid the fragments of the moral traditions that used to sustain us in the past. No religious tradition has survived the transition to the modern world without a lot of bumps, bruises, and worse. What we are left with is an emphasis on freedom, so that we are told that we must choose for ourselves what morality best fits our own needs and inclinations. Freedom is thus a second-best substitute for belonging to a community. If we spend all of our time trying to become free, then we will develop those habits of mind and character that will preclude us from ever experiencing what belonging to a community is all about.

The modern emphasis on freedom gives morality over to a consumer-oriented logic. Consumers try to maximize their desires given their limited resources. Such individualism now pervades the moral sphere. We increasingly talk about what is good for ourselves rather than what is good for others. To morally justify an act, we have to use the therapeutic language of self-fulfillment. We have no story that can encompass the goods we hold in common, and thus our impoverished culture cannot encourage and sustain moral commitment as anything other than a good investment or a healthy lifestyle.

Narrative theologians oppose this kind of moral relativism, but not with a commitment to moral absolutes. On the contrary, if ethics is about belonging to a community and hearing its stories, then morality will be fluid, open, and developmental. Ethical principles will change and evolve as religious communities themselves grow and mature. The rapid technological advances of the modern world alone make ethical reflection difficult and challenging. The Christian tradition is flexible enough to meet those challenges. The rich story of the Bible can be stretched to cover any situation, yet such stretching involves wisdom. It is an art, not a science, but this does not entail a relativism based purely on self-interest.

To be a Christian is to locate oneself within a story that has already been told but is still unfolding. The author of this story is God, so being a Christian means accepting the story of our lives as a gift that we ourselves have not written and are not writing. We want to think that we are writing our own stories, that we are in control of our own narrative. In fact, self-authorship comes so naturally to us that we only come to see it as sin when we begin to see the world as the product of God's authority, not our own.

To be truly free, we have to have a well-formed character; and to have character, we have to be part of a tradition that gives us the values and virtues that enable us to act well and to stand behind our actions. True freedom is not a matter of having the ability to choose this or that. Instead, it is the ability to describe what is happening to us in such a way that we make it a part of an ongoing narrative. We need the skills that will enable us to see our life as a coherent whole. Only by being part of a larger narrative can we imagine that our lives make sense and that we are, in the end, who we were meant to be.

In this book I have tried to retell the biblical story in ways that are both faithful to the Bible and relevant to the complex issue of how to treat animals in the modern world. I do not think, however, that a narrative theology, in and of itself, is sufficient for a biblical ethic of animal compassion. The Bible is just too complex, too full of too many different stories (as well as hymns, prayers, and other literary genres), to base ethics on narrative alone.

I think narrative ethics must be supplemented with a recognition that there is a biblical theme, the love of God, that serves as a kind of logic or grammar to the Bible as a whole. This theme can be used to think through our moral responsibilities for animals. The love of God, for Christians, is found in its fullest form in the teachings of Jesus concerning the coming kingdom of God. That kingdom contradicts all worldly values because it is based on mercy and forgiveness, not coercion and force. Christians can be nonviolent because God has promised a new world, thus giving us an eschatological confidence that the powers of this world will be overcome. Christians also can be nonviolent because we are a forgiven people who have been surprised by God's grace and granted a new life of love and peace. Growing into God's story, Christians can become a people of peace.

A recognition of the love of God as the basic theme of the Bible is also needed in order to protect the Bible from distortions and misreadings, from Christians as well as others. In order to witness to the world, Christians need to be reminded of their own sinful limitations. Too often narrative theologians collapse ethical principles into current Christian practices, so that ethics becomes a description of how the church presently reads the Bible. This ethical strategy can be dangerous when applied to diet because most Christians accept meat-eating as an inherent part of the biblical narrative, even as a basic human right guaranteed by God. But which should have priority, current dietary practices or the biblical story? That is, most Christians eat meat, and thus they read into the Bible the justification for their dietary preferences, just as slaveholders eagerly found the justification they were looking for in the Bible. The Bible, however, should be read against not only the world but also the church. Christians must be open to new readings of the Bible that challenge their customary habits and ingrained prejudices. The love of God works in surprising and disorienting ways, for Christians and non-Christians alike. In the next section I will examine more closely how Christians can practice the love of God by a hopeful expectation for the coming kingdom of God.

◼ Reinhold Niebuhr and Christian Realism

Reinhold Niebuhr developed a school of theological ethics called Christian Realism. For Niebuhr, the New Testament is about the absolute love of God, which is displayed in the ethical teachings of Jesus. Jesus preached an uncompromising submission to the kingdom of God. He required his followers to be perfect. Most ethicists allow prudential considerations for the protection of the ego and the satisfaction of individual desires. Jesus rejects the wisdom of moderation and instead embraces the extravagance of an absolute love ethic.

The result is a rigorous ethic that is difficult to apply to everyday life decisions. Niebuhr talks about the love of God as the vertical dimension of life, an absolute demand that penetrates every moment of our lives with a standard that we cannot live up to. The horizontal aspect of our lives includes the ways in which we have to compromise with others by learning to adjust our own interests accordingly. The horizontal also includes the ways that we have to provide for ourselves and our families, collecting material possessions and becoming more and more attached to worldly goods. For Niebuhr, the verticality of God's love can never be translated fully into the horizontal concerns of our worldly existence. In a way, then, the love ethic of Jesus is a demand that risks being irrelevant to our lives. How can we possibly hope to live in the kingdom of God when we live in a world that falls so far short of that?

Jesus tells us to love our enemy, care not for tomorrow, and love not the world. These claims are justified not on the basis of their social utility but because they express an absolute trust in God. In this world, however, these claims cannot easily be put into practice. Indeed, Niebuhr calls them impossible commandments. No judicial system can be based on the idea of loving your enemy. Neither can a nation-state care nothing for tomorrow. Nobody with a family to support can turn their back completely to the world. We all must try to provide for ourselves, and yet once we do so we become ensnared in the world and all of its vanities.

The impossibly extreme commandments of the love ethic are, nevertheless, relevant in this life because they add a depth to our existence that gives life meaning and direction. If we cannot fully comply with the love ethic, we can at least respond to God's love with an awareness of our own pride and selfishness. Moreover, we can try to improve our judicial systems. If the courts cannot let criminals go free, Christians can at least forgive those who hurt them and ask that punishment be for the criminal's own good and not for revenge. If nations cannot completely avoid war, Christians can at least work for peace and urge that war be used as a last resort. If parents must do everything to support their children, they can at least teach them that consumerism is not the best path to happiness and that families should welcome those who are victims of poverty and neglect. Thus the love ethic works to pressure society, through the witness of Christians, toward a more peaceable world.

Yet Niebuhr is quick to argue that we must be realistic about how far the kingdom of God can be accomplished here and now. His method is called Christian Realism precisely because he is critical of liberal Christians for thinking that hard work can usher in a perfect society. Liberals too often translate the love ethic into political reforms, forgetting that political legislation can just as easily betray as implement Christian ideals. Liberals ignore the fundamental reality of human sin, especially pride. Too often we are tempted to think that we have already achieved the gospel ideals, and thus we prematurely identify the gospel with our own political preferences and goals. This does not do justice to the transformative demands of grace. It also results in self-righteousness rather than true selflessness. Indeed, one reason the vertical demands of love cannot be directly applied to the horizontal dimension of the everyday is that pride always gets in the way. As soon as we think we have done a loving deed, then we have nullified that act by our very attitude of arrogance and self-congratulations.

Liberals compromise the gospel by identifying it with social and political goals that promise more than they can deliver. Conservatives, Niebuhr argues, make the opposite mistake. They identify the love ethic with the social and political practices and customs of the past. They do not let the gospel speak to the problems of today. Moreover, they apply the love ethic to the personal realm, but they tend not to apply it to the social realm. They emphasize repentance and forgiveness but they do not advocate pacifism or the better treatment of prisoners. By making love a subjective, personal, and emotional state, they drain it of its radical power to criticize and transform society as a whole.

There is a healthy, even an essential, tension between the love ethic and our everyday life. Without that ethic we would not have an absolute standard by which to measure our lives. We would be tempted to be satisfied with what we have already done, rather than continuously working for a better world. Yet that love ethic is also a form of judgment because we always fall short of the will of God. We must try to obey the commandments of Jesus even as we must be aware that we will also pervert those commandments with our pride and vanity. We must, then, be realistic about the love of God. We have to realize that the world is fallen and that we cannot turn it into the kingdom of God. Yet we should also respond to God's grace wherever we find it, being grateful for all the ways God has given us to learn how to love and to experience God's love.

This interpretation of the love of God does have some limitations. Niebuhr downplays the role of personal decisions and practical testimonies in the advancement of the gospel message. He also does not sufficiently emphasize the role that hope plays in directing moral action. Moreover, his thematic reading of the Bible can miss the subtle nuances that narrative theology highlights and develops. Nevertheless, Niebuhr's emphasis on the absoluteness of divine love combined with a realistic view of politics can provide guiding principles for Christians who want to apply the biblical narrative to the problem of animals and diet. The Bible is about not rights but generosity, self-sacrifice, giving, and grace. The Bible is about God's love, but that love unfolds over the course of the biblical story and is still unfolding today. We have to look at the biblical narrative and try to ascertain what God's original intentions for the world were. We also have to try to see how God does not expect those intentions to be completely attained all at once. Patience is one important aspect of God's mercy, and I have argued that God allows meat-eating as a concession to human sin, just as God allows divorce but still upholds the sanctity of marriage. Meat-eating is something that goes against the grain of the biblical story, yet God tolerates it as a symptom of our gluttony and stubbornness. What God reluctantly permits today must be put in the perspective of what God will do in the end. The prophets often speak of a day that is coming when all animals will lie down in peace with each other and with us. This is the full scope of the biblical narrative that I have tried to unfold.

Although the Bible does temporarily permit meat-eating, I have argued that, given the principle of God's abundant love, we can see today how meat-eating is no longer in harmony with God's ultimate purposes. But we can also see, as we learned from Niebuhr, that we cannot expect to save the world from all animal suffering. There is no getting around the fact that we must compete with animals for the earth's scarce resources, and this competition will only worsen as the human population continues to increase. Vegetarianism, then, is an impossible ideal for Christians. We can begin to live it today, but we should not take any pride in it. We cannot congratulate ourselves while making our meat-eating friends feel guilty and unworthy. Vegetarianism is not a pure diet. Every diet utilizes land and resources that could have been used by animals. Even the strictest vegetarian diet takes something away from the animal world or infringes on animals indirectly.

Vegetarianism, understood theologically, is a response to God's grace, an attempt to see animals as a gift from God and to treat them appropriately. It is not a blueprint to save the world by creating a utopia for animals here and now. It is not a program to wipe out all pain, precisely because that is the job of God alone. Christian vegetarianism is a diet of hope. It is a witness to what the world should be and will be some day. Christian vegetarianism is good eating that can taste good, but more importantly, Christian vegetarians have the good taste to eat only what their Host has set before them.

Bibliography

Adams, Carol J., ed. *Ecofeminism and the Sacred.* New York: Continuum, 1993.

Akers, Keith. *The Lost Religion of Jesus.* New York: Lantern Books, 2000.

Althaus, Paul. *The Theology of Martin Luther.* Philadelphia: Fortress Press, 1966.

Amidon, Philip R., trans. *The Panarion of St. Epiphanius, Bishop of Salamis.* New York: Oxford University Press, 1990.

Aquinas, Saint Thomas. *Summa Contra Gentiles, Book Four: Salvation.* Trans. Charles J. O'Neil. Notre Dame: University of Notre Dame Press, 1975.

Arbesmann, Rudolph. "Fasting and Prophecy in Pagan and Christian Antiquity." *Traditio* 7 (1966): 1–71.

Ashby, Godfrey. *Sacrifice: Its Nature and Purpose.* London: SCM Press, 1988.

Auster, Paul. *Timbuktu.* New York: Henry Holt and Company, 1999.

Augustine. *The Catholic and Manichean Ways of Life.* Trans. Donald A. Gallagher and Idella J. Gallagher. Washington, D.C.: University of America Press, 1986.

———. *City of God.* Trans. Henry Bettenson. New York: Penguin Books, 1984.

Barth, Karl. *Church Dogmatics,* III/1. Ed. G. W. Bromiley and T. F. Torrance. Edinburgh: T. & T. Clark, 1958.

———. *Church Dogmatics,* III/4. Ed. G. W. Bromiley and T. F. Torrance. Edinburgh: T. & T. Clark, 1961.

Bazell, Dianne M. "Strife among the Table-Fellows: Conflicting Attitudes of Early and Medieval Christians Toward the Eating of Meat." *Journal of the American Academy of Religion* 65 (Spring 1997): 73–99.

BeDuhn, Jason David. *The Manichaean Body in Discipline and Ritual.* Baltimore: Johns Hopkins University Press, 2000.

Bellesiles, Michael A. *Arming America: The Origins of a National Gun Culture.* New York: Knopf, 2000.

Berman, Louis A. *Vegetarianism and the Jewish Tradition.* New York: Ktav, 1982.

Berry, Rynn. *Food for the Gods: Vegetarianism and the World Religions.* New York: Pythagorean Publishers, 1998.

Bokser, Ben Zion, trans. *The Talmud: Selected Writings.* New York: Paulist Press, 1989.

Bibliography

Borowski, Oded. *Every Living Thing: Daily Use of Animals in Ancient Israel*. London: Alta Mira Press, 1998.

Boyle, T. Coraghessan. *The Road to Wellville*. New York: Viking, 1993.

Brakke, David. *Athanasius and Asceticism*. Baltimore: Johns Hopkins University Press, 1995.

Brock, Peter. *Pioneers of the Peaceable Kingdom*. Princeton: Princeton University Press, 1968.

Brooks, David. *Bobos in Paradise: The New Upper Class and How They Got There*. New York: Simon & Schuster, 2000.

Brown, Peter. *The Body and Society: Men, Women, and Sexual Renunciation in Early Christianity*. New York: Columbia University Press, 1988.

Budde, Michael. *The (Magic) Kingdom of God: Christianity and Global Culture Industries*. Boulder: Westview Press, 1997.

Burkert, Walter. *Homo Necans: The Anthropology of Ancient Greek Sacrificial Ritual and Myth*. Trans. Peter Bing. Berkeley: University of California Press, 1983.

Burton-Christie, Douglas. *The Word in the Desert: Scripture and the Quest for Holiness in Early Christian Monasticism*. New York: Oxford University Press, 1993.

Bynum, Caroline Walker. *The Resurrection of the Body in Western Christianity, 200–1336*. New York: Columbia University Press, 1995.

——. *Holy Feast and Holy Fast, The Religious Significance of Food to Medieval Women*. Berkeley: University of California Press, 1987.

Catechism of the Catholic Church. Liguori, Mo.: Liguori Publications, 1994.

Carson, Gerald. *The Cornflake Crusade*. New York: Rinehart & Co., 1957.

Cherry, Reginald. *The Bible Cure*. Orlando: Creation House, 1998.

Chilton, Bruce. *The Temple of Jesus: His Sacrificial Program within a Cultural History of Sacrifice*. University Park: Pennsylvania State University Press, 1992.

——. *A Feast of Meanings: Eucharistic Theologies from Jesus through Johanine Circles*. Leiden: E. J. Brill, 1994.

Clapp, Rodney. *A Peculiar People: The Church as Culture in a Post-Christian Society*. Downers Grove, Ill.: InterVarsity Press, 1996.

Clark, Stephen R. L. "Good Dogs and Other Animals." *In Defense of Animals*. Ed. Peter Singer. New York: Harper & Row, 1985.

Cobb, John, "Economics for Animals as well as People." *Good News for Animals?* Ed. Charles Pinches and Jay B. McDaniel. Maryknoll, N.Y.: Orbis Books, 1993.

Couliano, Ioan P. *The Tree of Gnosis*. San Francisco: Harper, 1992.

Crossan, John Dominic. *The Historical Jesus: The Life of a Mediterranean Jewish Peasant*. San Francisco: Harper, 1992.

Danielou, Jean. *The Theology of Jewish Christianity*. Trans. John A. Baker. London: Darton, Longman & Todd, 1964.

Davidson, James. *Courtesans and Fishcakes: The Consuming Passions of Classical Athens*. New York: HarperCollins, 1997.

Dombrowski, Daniel A. *Hartshorne and the Metaphysics of Animal Rights*. Albany: SUNY Press, 1988.

Douglas, Mary. "The Eucharist: Its Continuity with the Bread Sacrifice of Leviticus." *Modern Theology* 15 (1999): 209–24.

Duchesne, Louis. *Early History of the Christian Church: From Its Foundation to the End of the Fifth Century.* Vol. II. London: John Murray, 1957.

Eisenman, Robert. *James the Brother of Jesus.* New York: Penguin Books, 1997.

Eliade, Mircea. *The Myth of the Eternal Return: Or, Cosmos and History.* Princeton: Princeton University Press, 1974.

Elliott, J. K. *The Apocryphal New Testament.* Oxford: Clarendon Press, 1993.

Evans, Craig A. "Jesus and James, Martyrs of the Temple." *James the Just and Christian Origins.* Ed. Bruce Chilton and Craig A. Evans. Leiden: E. J. Brill, 1999.

Ferry, Luc. *The New Ecological Order.* Trans. Carol Volk. Chicago: University of Chicago Press, 1992.

Fideler, David, ed. *The Pythagorean Sourcebook and Library.* Trans. Kenneth Sylvan Guthrie. Grand Rapids: Phanes Press, 1987.

Fuller, Robert C. *Religion and Wine: A Cultural History of Wine Drinking in the United States.* Knoxville: The University of Tennessee Press, 1996.

Gaard, Greta, ed. *Ecofeminism: Women, Animals, Nature.* Philadelphia: Temple University Press, 1993.

Gabler, Neal. *Life the Movie: How Entertainment Conquered Reality.* New York: Knopf, 1998.

George, Kathryn Paxton. *Animal, Vegetable, or Woman? A Feminist Critique of Ethical Vegetarianism.* Albany: SUNY Press, 2000.

Ginzberg, Louis. *The Legends of the Jews.* Vol. 1 and 2. Baltimore: Johns Hopkins University Press, 1998.

Girard, René. *The Scapegoat.* Trans. Yvonne Freccero. Baltimore: Johns Hopkins University Press, 1986.

Grant, Robert M. *Early Christians and Animals.* New York: Routledge, 1999.

Griffith, R. Marie. *God's Daughters: Evangelical Women and the Power of Submission.* Berkeley: University of California Press, 1997.

Grimm, Veronika E. *From Feasting to Fasting: The Evolution of a Sin.* New York: Routledge, 1996.

Hamerton-Kelly, Robert G. *The Gospel and the Sacred: Poetics of Violence in Mark.* Minneapolis: Fortress Press, 1994.

Hamilton, Janet, and Bernard Hamilton, *Christian Dualist Heresies in the Byzantine World, c. 650–1405.* Manchester: Manchester University Press, 1998.

Harrod, Howard L. *The Animals Came Dancing: Native American Sacred Ecology and Animal Kinship.* Tucson: The University of Arizona Press, 2000.

Hauerwas, Stanley. *A Community of Character.* Notre Dame, Ind.: University of Notre Dame Press, 1981.

Hick, John. *The Metaphor of God Incarnate: Christology in a Pluralistic Age.* Louisville: Westminster/John Knox Press, 1993.

Hiers, Richard H. and Charles A. Kennedy. "Bread and Fish Eucharist in the Gospels and Early Christian Art." *Perspectives in Religious Studies* 3 (1976): 20–47.

Hoffman, Lawrence. "A Symbol of Salvation in the Passover Haggadah." *Worship* 53 (1979): 519–37.

Horsley, Richard A. *Jesus and the Spiral of Violence.* San Francisco: Harper & Row, 1987.

Hultgren, Arland J. and Steven A. Haggmark. *The Earliest Christian Heretics.* Minneapolis: Fortress Press, 1996.

Hyland, J. R. "After the Fall." *Humane Religion* 3 (May/June 1998): 12–14.

———. *God's Covenant with Animals: A Biblical Basis for the Humane Treatment of All Creatures*. New York: Lantern Books, 2000.

James, Montague Rhodes. *The Apocryphal New Testament*. Oxford: Clarendon Press, 1975.

James, William. *The Varieties of Religious Belief*. New York: Vintage Books, 1990.

Jay, Nancy. *Throughout Your Generations Forever: Sacrifice, Religion, and Paternity*. Chicago: University of Chicago Press, 1992.

Jensen, Robin Margaret. *Understanding Early Christian Art*. New York: Routledge, 2000.

Jones, F. Stanley. *An Ancient Jewish Christian Source on the History of Christianity: Pseudo-Clementine Recognitions 1.27–71*. Atlanta: Scholars Press, 1995.

Kelly, J. N. D. *Jerome*. Peabody, Mass.: Hendrickson Publishers, 1975.

Koenig, John. *The Feast of the World's Redemption: Eucharistic Origins and Christian Mission*. Harrisburg, Penn.: Trinity Press International, 2000.

Krech, Shepard. *The Ecological Indian: Myth and History*. New York: Norton, 1999.

Leopold, Aldo. *A Sand County Almanac*. New York: Oxford University Press, 1949.

Lewis, C. S. *The Problem of Pain*. New York: Macmillan, 1962.

Leyerle, Blake. "Clement of Alexandria on the Importance of Table Etiquette." *Journal of Early Christian Studies* 3/2 (Summer 1995): 125–141.

Lorenz, Konrad. *Man Meets Dog*. New York: Penguin Books, 1964.

Lowery, Richard H. *Sabbath and Jubilee*. St. Louis: Chalice Press, 2000.

Martos, Joseph. *Doors to the Sacred: A Historical Introduction to Sacraments in the Catholic Church*. Ligouri, Mo.: Triumph Books, 1991.

McCormick, Patrick T. "How Could We Break the Lord's Bread in a Foreign Land? The Eucharist in 'Diet America'." *Horizons* 25/1 (1998): 43–57.

McDaniel, Jay B. *Of God and Pelicans: A Theology of Reverence for Life*. Louisville: Westminster/John Knox Press, 1989.

McDannell, Colleen and Bernhard Lang. *Heaven: A History*. New York: Vintage Books, 1990.

McElroy, Susan Chernak. *Animals as Teachers and Healers*. New York: Random House, 1997.

McFague, Sallie. *Models of God: Theology for an Ecological, Nuclear Age*. Philadelphia: Fortress Press, 1987.

McGowan, Andrew. *Ascetic Eucharist, Food and Drink in Early Christian Ritual Meals*. Oxford: Clarendon Press, 1999.

McNeill, John T., and Helena M. Gamer. *Medieval Handbooks of Penance*. New York: Columbia University Press, 1990.

Mead, Rebecca. "Slim for Hm." *The New Yorker* (January 15, 2001): 48–55.

Milbank, John, and Catherine Pickstock. *Truth in Aquinas*. New York: Routledge, 2001.

Money, John. *The Destroying Angel: Sex, Fitness, and Food in the Legacy of Degeneracy Theory*. Buffalo: Prometheus Books, 1985.

Musurillo, Herbert. "The Problem of Ascetical Fasting in the Greek Patristic Writers." *Traditio* 12 (1956): 1–64.

Neusner, Jacob, and Bruce Chilton. *Jewish-Christian Debates: God, Kingdom, Messiah*. Minneapolis: Fortress Press, 1998.

Newman, John Henry. "The Crucifixion." *Parochial and Plain Sermons*. Vol. 7. London: Rivingtons, 1868.

Niebuhr, Reinhold. *An Interpretation of Christian Ethics*. New York: Harper & Brothers, 1963.

Norwich, John Julius. *Byzantium, Decline and Fall*. New York: Alfred A. Knopf, 1996.

Ozment, Steve. *Protestants, The Birth of a Revolution*. New York: Doubleday, 1992.

Bibliography

Painter, John. *Just James, the Brother of Jesus in History and Tradition.* Columbia: University of South Carolina Press, 1997.

Passmore, John. "The Treatment of Animals." *Journal of the History of Ideas* 36 (1975): 195–218.

Pearl, Chaim. *Theology in Rabbinic Stories.* Peabody, Mass.: Hendrickson Publishers, 1997.

Percival, Henry R., ed. *The Seven Ecumenical Councils of the Undivided Church.* Vol. 14 of *The Nicene and Post-Nicene Fathers of the Christian Church.* Second series. Grand Rapids: Wm. B. Eerdmans, 1977.

Placher, William C. *Narratives of a Vulnerable God.* Louisville: Westminster/John Knox, 1984.

Plutarch, *Moralia.* Trans. Paul A. Clement and Herbert B. Hoffleit. Vol. 8. Cambridge: Harvard University Press, 1969.

Ramsey, Boniface, O.P., trans. *John Cassian: The Conferences.* New York: Paulist Press, 1997.

Reasoner, Mark. *The Strong and the Weak: Romans 14.1–15.13 in Context.* Cambridge: Cambridge University Press, 1999.

Roberts, Alexander, and James Donaldson, eds. *The Ante-Nicene Fathers.* 10 vols. Grand Rapids: Wm. B. Eerdmans, 1950–1969.

Roof, Wade Clark, "Blood in the Barbecue? Food and Faith in the American South." *God in the Details: American Religion in Popular Culture.* Ed. Eric Michael Mazur and Kate McCarthy. New York: Routledge, 2001.

Russell, Jeffrey Burton. *A History of Heaven: The Singing Silence.* Princeton: Princeton University Press, 1997.

Sack, Daniel. *Whitebread Protestants: Food and Religion in American Culture.* New York: St. Martin's Press, 2000.

Sanders, E. P. *The Historical Figure of Jesus.* New York: Penguin, 1993.

Sax, Boria. *Animals in the Third Reich: Pets, Scapegoats, and the Holocaust.* New York: Continuum, 2000.

Schaff, Philip, and Henry Wace, eds. *The Church History of Eusebius.* Vol. I of *The Nicene and Post-Nicene Fathers.* Second series. Grand Rapids: Wm. B. Eerdmans, 1961.

Schlosser, Eric. "Why McDonald's Fries Taste so Good." *Atlantic Monthly* (January 2001): 50–56.

Schoeps, Hans-Joachim. *Jewish Christianity.* Trans. Douglas R. A. Hare. Philadelphia: Fortress Press, 1969.

Shaw, Teresa M. *The Burden of the Flesh.* Minneapolis: Fortress Press, 1998.

Simkins, Ronald A. *Creator & Creation: Nature in the Worldview of Ancient Israel.* Peabody, Mass.: Hendrickson Publishers, 1994.

Singer, Peter, ed. *In Defense of Animals.* New York: Harper & Row, 1985.

Spang, Rebecca L. *The Invention of the Restaurant: Paris and Modern Gastronomic Culture.* Cambridge: Harvard University Press, 2000.

Stowers, Stanley K. "Greeks Who Sacrifice and Those Who Do Not: Toward an Anthropology of Greek Religion." *The Social World of the First Christians: Essays in Honor of Wayne A. Meeks.* Ed. L. Michael White and O. Larry Yarbrough. Minneapolis: Augsburg Fortress, 1995.

Stoyanov, Yuri. *The Other God: Dualist Religions from Antiquity to the Cathar Heresy.* New Haven: Yale University Press, 2000.

Tanner, Kathryn. *Theories of Culture: A New Agenda for Theology.* Minneapolis: Fortress Press, 1997.

Tardiff, Andrew. "A Catholic Case for Vegetarianism." *Faith and Philosophy* 15 (1998): 210–22.

Taylor, Joan E. *The Immerser: John the Baptist Within Second Temple Judaism.* Grand Rapids: Wm. B. Eerdmans, 1997.

Theissen, Gerd. "The Strong and the Weak in Corinth: A Sociological Analysis of a Theological Quarrel." *The Social Setting of Pauline Christianity: Essays on Corinth.* John H. Schütz, ed. Philadelphia: Fortress Press, 1982.

Theroux, Paul. *Millroy the Magician.* New York: Random House, 1994.

Thompson, Paul B. *The Spirit of the Soil: Agriculture and Environmental Ethics.* New York: Routledge, 1995.

Toussaint-Samat, Maguelonne. *History of Food.* Trans. Anthea Bell. Oxford: Blackwell Publishers, 1992.

Updike, John. *Of the Farm.* New York: Fawcett Books, 1987.

Vaclavik, Charles P. *The Vegetarianism of Jesus Christ: The Pacifism, Communalism, and Vegetarianism of Primitive Christianity.* Three Rivers, Cal.: Kaweah Publishing Company, 1986.

Visser, Margaret. *The Rituals of Dinner: The Origins, Evolution, Eccentricities, and Meaning of Table Manners.* New York: Penguin Books, 1991.

Waddell, Helen. *Beasts and Saints.* Grand Rapids: Wm. B. Eerdmans, 1995.

Walters, Kerry S., and Lisa Portmess, eds. *Ethical Vegetarianism: From Pythagoras to Peter Singer.* Albany: SUNY Press, 1999.

Webb, Stephen H. "Putting Animals on the Theological Agenda." *Reviews in Religion and Theology* 6/1 (February 1999): 5–10. A revised version of this essay appeared as "Do All Good Dogs Go To Heaven?" *Books & Culture* (January/February 1999): 40–1.

———. *On God and Dogs: A Christian Theology of Compassion for Animals.* New York: Oxford University Press, 1998.

———. "Should We Love All of Nature? A Critique of Sallie McFague's *Super, Natural Christians.*" *Encounter* 59 (Summer 1998): 409–19.

———. "Whatever Happened to the Sin of Gluttony? Or, Why Christians Do Not Serve Meat with the Eucharist." *Encounter* 58/3 (Summer 1997): 243–50.

———. "Ecology vs. the Peaceable Kingdom: Toward a Better Theology of Nature." *Soundings* 79 (Spring/Summer 1996): 239–252.

———. "Pet Theories: A Theology for the Dogs." *Soundings* 78 (Summer 1995): 213–237.

Wesley, John. *Works.* Vol. 11. Nashville: Abingdon Press, 1989.

Williams, Rowan. *Resurrection: Interpreting the Easter Gospel.* New York: Pilgrim Press, 1984.

Wilson, A. N. *Jesus, A Life.* New York: W. W. Norton, 1992.

Winston, David, trans. *Philo of Alexandria, The Contemplative Life, Giants, and Selections.* New York: Paulist Press, 1981.

Wise, Michael, Martin Abegg Jr., and Edward Cook. *The Dead Sea Scrolls: A New Translation.* San Francisco: HarperCollins, 1999.

Wortley, John, trans. *The Spiritual Meadows of John Moschos.* Kalamazoo: Cistercian Publications, 1992.

Wright, N. T. *Jesus and the Victory of God.* Minneapolis: Fortress Press, 1996.

Young, Richard Alan. *Is God a Vegetarian?* Chicago: Open Court, 1999.

Zwingli, Ulrich. *Early Writings.* Ed. Samuel Macauley Jackson. Durham, N.C.: The Labyrinth Press, 1987.

Scripture Index